# Personal Best

**B2** Upper Intermediate

**Student's Book and Workbook** combined edition **A**

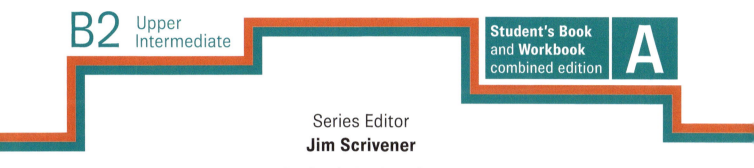

Series Editor
**Jim Scrivener**

Student's Book Author
**Luiz Otávio Barros**

Workbook Authors
**Elizabeth Walters and Kate Woodford**

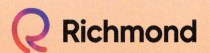

# STUDENT'S BOOK CONTENTS

| | | | LANGUAGE | | | SKILLS | |
|---|---|---|---|---|---|---|---|
| | | | GRAMMAR | PRONUNCIATION | VOCABULARY | | |
| **1** | **Your unique style** | | • present forms; *like*, *as if*, and *as though*<br>• narrative tenses | • *as*<br>• stress in narrative tenses | • body language and communication<br>• compound adjectives<br>• expectations | **LISTENING**<br>• identifying attitude<br>• consonant-consonant reduction | **WRITING**<br>• making a narrative interesting<br>• time linkers<br>**PERSONAL BEST**<br>• a blog post about an unexpected event |
| 1A | Communication and you | p4 | | | | | |
| 1B | The cool factor | p6 | | | | | |
| 1C | Great expectations | p8 | | | | | |
| 1D | My bad purchase! | p10 | | | | | |
| **2** | **Culture vultures** | | • question patterns<br>• using linkers (1) | • intonation in tag questions<br>• sentence stress | • adjective suffixes<br>• phrasal verbs (1) | **READING**<br>• skimming and scanning<br>• clauses with *what* | **SPEAKING**<br>• making recommendations<br>• describing a movie<br>**PERSONAL BEST**<br>• recommending and deciding what to see |
| 2A | But is it art? | p12 | | | | | |
| 2B | Dear Juliet … | p14 | | | | | |
| 2C | It's music to my ears! | p16 | | | | | |
| 2D | It's definitely worth seeing | p18 | | | | | |
| **1 and 2** | **REVIEW and PRACTICE** | p20 | | | | | |
| **3** | **A sense of place** | | • advice, expectation, and obligation<br>• phrasal verbs | • *supposed*, *ought*, and *allowed*<br>• linking in phrasal verbs | • urban places and problems<br>• easily confused words | **LISTENING**<br>• identifying advice<br>• intonation in negative questions | **WRITING**<br>• writing a persuasive article<br>• contrasting expectations with reality<br>**PERSONAL BEST**<br>• a text persuading someone to move to a new city |
| 3A | You're not supposed to do that here! | p22 | | | | | |
| 3B | My special place | p24 | | | | | |
| 3C | To go, or not to go | p26 | | | | | |
| 3D | A fantastic place to live | p28 | | | | | |
| **4** | **Mind and behavior** | | • subject-verb agreement<br>• perfect and past forms | • *of*<br>• sentence stress in perfect forms | • personality and behavior<br>• word families | **READING**<br>• identifying attitude<br>• conditionals for advice and suggestions | **SPEAKING**<br>• responding to arguments<br>• describing memorable experiences<br>**PERSONAL BEST**<br>• talking about a memorable experience |
| 4A | It really annoys me … | p30 | | | | | |
| 4B | How to get along | p32 | | | | | |
| 4C | I see you've been busy! | p34 | | | | | |
| 4D | Road rage | p36 | | | | | |
| **3 and 4** | **REVIEW and PRACTICE** | p38 | | | | | |
| **5** | **Our planet** | | • *so* and *such*; *so much/many*, *so little/few*<br>• future predictions | • sentence stress with *so* and *such*<br>• *will have* | • the environment<br>• moods<br>• adjective prefixes | **LISTENING**<br>• identifying cause and effect<br>• linking consonants and vowels | **WRITING**<br>• writing an opinion essay<br>• formal linkers<br>**PERSONAL BEST**<br>• an essay using topic sentences and formal linkers |
| 5A | Going green | p40 | | | | | |
| 5B | Weather effects | p42 | | | | | |
| 5C | In the year 2100 … | p44 | | | | | |
| 5D | Let me persuade you … | p46 | | | | | |
| **6** | **Habits and change** | | • the habitual past<br>• *be used to* and *get used to* | • *use* and *used*<br>• sentence stress with *be used to* and *get used to* | • expressions with *time*<br>• expressions with prepositions | **READING**<br>• understanding non-literal meaning<br>• contradicting | **SPEAKING**<br>• challenging assumptions<br>• solving problems<br>**PERSONAL BEST**<br>• solving a family problem |
| 6A | My best decade | p48 | | | | | |
| 6B | Healthy living: myths and facts | p50 | | | | | |
| 6C | My generation and me | p52 | | | | | |
| 6D | A suitable roommate | p54 | | | | | |
| **5 and 6** | **REVIEW and PRACTICE** | p56 | | | | | |

Grammar practice p112   Vocabulary practice p136   Communication practice p158   Phrasal verbs p174   Irregular verbs p175

Language App with unit-by-unit grammar and vocabulary games

# WORKBOOK CONTENTS

| | | LANGUAGE | | | SKILLS | |
|---|---|---|---|---|---|---|
| | | GRAMMAR | PRONUNCIATION | VOCABULARY | | |
| **1** Your unique style<br>1A p2<br>1B p3<br>1C p4<br>1D p5 | | • present forms; *like*, *as if*, and *as though*<br>• narrative tenses | • *as*<br>• stress in narrative tenses | • body language and communication<br>• compound adjectives<br>• expectations | LISTENING<br>• identifying attitude | WRITING<br>• making a narrative interesting |

**1 — REVIEW and PRACTICE   p6**

| **2** Culture vultures<br>2A p8<br>2B p9<br>2C p10<br>2D p11 | | • question patterns<br>• using linkers (1) | • intonation in tag questions<br>• sentence stress | • adjective suffixes<br>• phrasal verbs (1) | READING<br>• skimming and scanning | SPEAKING<br>• making recommendations |

**2 — REVIEW and PRACTICE   p12**

| **3** A sense of place<br>3A p14<br>3B p15<br>3C p16<br>3D p17 | | • advice, expectation, and obligation<br>• phrasal verbs | • *supposed*, *ought*, and *allowed*<br>• linking in phrasal verbs | • urban places and problems<br>• easily confused words | LISTENING<br>• identifying advice | WRITING<br>• writing a persuasive article |

**3 — REVIEW and PRACTICE   p18**

| **4** Mind and behavior<br>4A p20<br>4B p21<br>4C p22<br>4D p23 | | • subject-verb agreement<br>• perfect and past forms | • *of*<br>• sentence stress in perfect forms | • personality and behavior<br>• word families | READING<br>• identifying attitude | SPEAKING<br>• responding to arguments |

**4 — REVIEW and PRACTICE   p24**

| **5** Our planet<br>5A p26<br>5B p27<br>5C p28<br>5D p29 | | • *so* and *such*; *so much/many*, *so little/few*<br>• future predictions | • sentence stress with *so* and *such*<br>• *will have* | • the environment<br>• moods<br>• adjective prefixes | LISTENING<br>• identifying cause and effect | WRITING<br>• writing an opinion essay |

**5 — REVIEW and PRACTICE   p30**

| **6** Habits and change<br>6A p32<br>6B p33<br>6C p34<br>6D p35 | | • the habitual past<br>• *be used to* and *get used to* | • *use* and *used*<br>• sentence stress with *be used to* and *get used to* | • expressions with *time*<br>• expressions with prepositions | READING<br>• understanding non-literal meaning | SPEAKING<br>• challenging assumptions |

**6 — REVIEW and PRACTICE   p36**

Writing practice **p74**

# UNIT 1 Your unique style

**LANGUAGE** present forms; *like*, *as if*, and *as though* ■ body language and communication

## 1A Communication and you

**1 A** Complete the quiz. Choose a, b, or c for each question.

### What's your communication style?

**1** If you try to hide something from someone, …
a your voice changes.
b you don't make eye contact.
c your body language changes.

**2** When you're angry, you tend to …
a raise your voice.
b imagine a response in your head.
c physically show you're angry, e.g., slam the door.

**3** If you want to get someone's attention, you …
a say his/her name.
b look at the person.
c tap him/her on the shoulder.

**B** Discuss your answers in pairs. Did you choose mostly *a*, *b*, or *c* answers?

**Go to Vocabulary practice:** body language and communication, page 136

**2** Check your answers to the quiz in exercise 1A. What type of communicator are you?

**a answers: audio communicators**
Audio communicators mainly interact with the world using their ears, and enjoy listening to people. They often notice small changes in people's voices, so they can tell immediately if someone sounds sad or worried. They often say things like, "I hear what you're saying," "How does that sound?," or "Sounds good!"

**b answers: visual communicators**
Visual communicators primarily interact with the world using their eyes. They understand ideas through images, and when they try to remember information, they feel as if a little movie is running in their heads. They often nod and say things like, "I see what you mean," "As I see it … ," or "It looks (like rain)." They can lose focus if other speakers talk too much.

**c answers: kinesthetic communicators**
Kinesthetic communicators interact with the world mostly using their body and intuition. They're attracted to people and situations that feel familiar. They like to learn by using their hands and moving as though they're acting in a play. They often need more words to communicate their message than visual and audio communicators. They say things like, "I know how you feel."

**3 A** Choose the correct options and check your answers in exercise 2. Which sentence refers to right now?
1 Audio communicators *interact / are interacting* with the world using their ears.
2 Visual communicators *understand / are understanding* ideas through images.
3 When they try to remember information, they feel as if a little movie *runs / is running* in their heads.
4 Kinesthetic communicators *need / are needing* more words to communicate their message.

**B** Underline *sound*, *look*, and *feel* in exercise 2. Complete the rules with *noun*, *adjective*, or *clause*. Then read the Grammar box.

1 Use *sound/look/feel* + _____ .
2 Use *sound/look/feel like* + _____ .
3 Use *sound/look/feel as if/though* + _____ .

4

present forms; *like*, *as if*, and *as though* ■ body language and communication

**LANGUAGE 1A**

## Grammar — present forms; *like*, *as if*, and *as though*

**Simple present with action or state verbs:**
The sun (always) **sets** in the west.
I **think** / **know** the answer.
It definitely **sounds**/**looks**/**feels** weird.

**Present continuous with action verbs:**
Look outside. The sun**'s setting** (right now).
I**'m thinking** of going to London
She**'s** always **criticizing** me!

**Sense verbs with adjectives, nouns, and clauses:**
It **looks** strange. (adjective)
It **sounds like** a nightmare! (noun)
It **feels as if** I've been here before. (clause)
It **sounds as though** you need help. (clause)

**Look!** We can also use *like* before a clause, but only in informal speech:
It looks **like** Mary's not coming to the party. (= informal conversation)
**As though** is a little more formal than **as if**:
It sounds **as if**/**as though** John's health is improving. (= neutral/formal speech and writing)

Go to Grammar practice: present forms; *like*, *as if*, and *as though*, page 112

**4 A** ▶1.3 **Pronunciation:** *as* Listen to the sentences. Notice how *as* is pronounced.
1 It sounds as if you're working really hard.
2 This coat looks as if it's never been cleaned!
3 It feels as though we've lived here for ages.
4 It looks as though he'll be late.

**B** ▶1.3 Listen again and repeat. Then practice saying the sentences in pairs.

**5 A** Fill in the blanks with the correct form of *sound*, *look*, or *feel*, adding *like*, *as if*, or *as though* where necessary. Then choose the correct verb forms.

### Six things a good listener might say

Good listeners are authentic in their desire to hear what the other person has to say. Before rushing to give advice, they often say things like:

1 You l_____ worried. What's on your mind? *Do you need / Are you needing* some help?

2 It s_____ you've had an exhausting day. *You work / You're working* too hard these days!

3 Wow! Your class s_____ a nightmare. *Do you want / Are you wanting* to talk about it?

4 You l_____ you could use a friend. *Does something bother / Is something bothering* you?

5 Hmm … You l_____ you're not sure what to do. *Do you think / Are you thinking* of dropping out of college?

6 Your boss s_____ awful! I mean, he *never listens / is never listening* to you.

**B** Choose two sentences in exercise 5A to start conversations. Your partner will give his/her own response.

Go to Communication practice: Both students, page 170

**6 A** Complete the sentences below about prompts 1–4 on the right.
1 I just received an e-mail telling me _____ .
2 Tomorrow's weather _____ .
3 Did you hear the news about _____ ?
4 You won't believe it, but Lucy _____ .

**B** Discuss the sentences in exercise 6A in pairs. Respond using sense verbs and ask follow-up questions.
A *I just received an e-mail telling me I won some money.*
B *It sounds like a trick to me. Are you planning to reply?*

1 E-mail to: Lucky winners
Subject: Cash prize!

2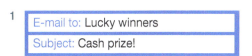

3

4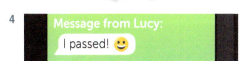

**Personal Best** Think of a good communicator you know. List five things he/she does or says.

# 1 SKILLS LISTENING identifying attitude ■ consonant-consonant reduction ■ compound adjectives

## 1B The cool factor

**1 A** Have you ever thought about what makes someone "cool"? Discuss the question in pairs.

**B** In pairs, discuss which words in the box you would use to describe the people in the pictures. In your opinion, are any of these people cool?

> open-minded   world-famous   good-looking   forward-thinking

**Go to Vocabulary practice:** compound adjectives, page 137

### 🔧 Skill   identifying attitude

You can often identify a speaker's attitude by listening to how certain or fixed his/her opinions are. Some clues include:

- words or expressions showing more or less certainty:
  *Definitely not! I have no doubt that ... , I tend to think ... , In a way, I think ...*
- modal verbs or adverbs expressing probability:
  *It might be ... , This is probably the most important ...*
- tone of voice and style:
  A rising, louder tone may show the speaker feels strongly. A moderate tone and "filler" words like *uh*, *I mean* or *you know* may show uncertainty.

**2** ▶ 1.5   Read the Skill box. Then watch or listen to the first part of a webshow called *Talking Zone*. What is Albany's attitude toward being cool? Choose the correct answer.

  a   She tries very hard to be cool all the time.
  b   She sometimes tries to be cool.
  c   She never thinks about being cool and doesn't try.

6

identifying attitude ■ consonant-consonant reduction ■ compound adjectives   LISTENING   SKILLS   1B

**3 A** ▶ 1.5   Watch or listen again. Check (✓) the things the speakers say about being cool.

1 Cool people are just people who act very naturally. ☐
2 It's easy to act cool. ☐
3 It's important to care about being cool. ☐
4 You should tell people when you think they're cool. ☐
5 You can't plan to be cool since the definition keeps changing. ☐

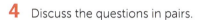

Cathy

Tom

Sara

**B** What do you remember from the video so far? Use the Skill box to help you. Complete the blanks.

1 _____, I think cool is just being yourself.
2 _____, most people care about that kind of thing.
3 I have _____ that you're the ones who really deserve the award.
4 I _____ think it's because I'm 'warm'.

**4** Discuss the questions in pairs.

1 Which statements in exercise 3A do you agree with?
2 Has your own definition of "cool" changed since high school? In what way?

**5** Look at the pictures. Tell your partner which one best matches your personal definition of "cool."

a

b

c

**6** ▶ 1.6   Watch or listen to the second part of the show. What is Albany's most important advice?

**7** ▶ 1.6   Watch or listen again. Are the sentences true (T) or false (F)?

1 Albany isn't surprised that she has two million viewers.   _____
2 She acts as if she knows her viewers and talks directly to them.   _____
3 Albany only promotes products she identifies with.   _____
4 Albany thinks you can succeed quickly.   _____

---

**Listening builder**   consonant-consonant reduction

In fast speech, similar sounds can merge between words so that you only hear one sound. This can sometimes make the words harder to understand.
Same sound: *Do you expect to be home early?*
Different sounds: *Not in my wildest dreams!*

---

**8 A** ▶ 1.7   Read the Listening builder. Then listen to the sentences from the video. Cross out the sounds you don't hear in the underlined words.

1 She's <u>been nominated</u> for a "Cool Tube" award.
2 Did you <u>expect to</u> be so successful?
3 I <u>just create</u> videos about my everyday life.
4 I <u>hoped that</u> my friends and coworkers would watch them.
5 It <u>might be</u> that my videos are natural and unrehearsed.
6 Sounds like a dream job and leads me to my <u>next question</u>.

**B** ▶ 1.7   Listen again and repeat each sentence.

**9** In pairs, discuss these questions.

1 Do you follow any YouTubers? What do they talk about?
2 Would you ever start your own channel? What would it be about?

**Personal Best**   Describe someone you think is cool and explain why.

7

# 1 LANGUAGE — narrative tenses ■ expectations

## 1C Great expectations

**1 A** Match the two parts to make complete sentences.

1 If you don't succeed at first,
2 You never get a second chance
3 If you want to avoid disappointment,
4 It is impossible to live without

a lower your expectations.
b failing at something.
c try again until you do.
d to make a good first impression.

**B** In pairs, discuss whether or not you agree with the statements, and give a reason.

Go to Vocabulary practice: expectations, page 137

**2 A** Read the comments on a forum about people's disappointing experiences. Who feels more negative about his/her experience?

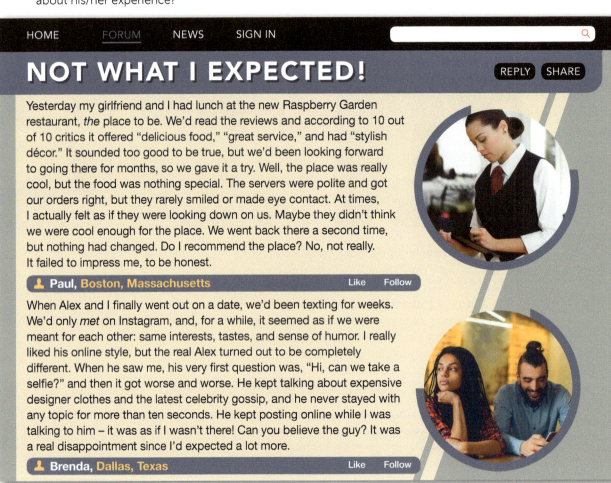

**NOT WHAT I EXPECTED!**

Yesterday my girlfriend and I had lunch at the new Raspberry Garden restaurant, *the* place to be. We'd read the reviews and according to 10 out of 10 critics it offered "delicious food," "great service," and had "stylish décor." It sounded too good to be true, but we'd been looking forward to going there for months, so we gave it a try. Well, the place was really cool, but the food was nothing special. The servers were polite and got our orders right, but they rarely smiled or made eye contact. At times, I actually felt as if they were looking down on us. Maybe they didn't think we were cool enough for the place. We went back there a second time, but nothing had changed. Do I recommend the place? No, not really. It failed to impress me, to be honest.

**Paul,** Boston, Massachusetts

When Alex and I finally went out on a date, we'd been texting for weeks. We'd only *met* on Instagram, and, for a while, it seemed as if we were meant for each other: same interests, tastes, and sense of humor. I really liked his online style, but the real Alex turned out to be completely different. When he saw me, his very first question was, "Hi, can we take a selfie?" and then it got worse and worse. He kept talking about expensive designer clothes and the latest celebrity gossip, and he never stayed with any topic for more than ten seconds. He kept posting online while I was talking to him – it was as if I wasn't there! Can you believe the guy? It was a real disappointment since I'd expected a lot more.

**Brenda,** Dallas, Texas

**B** Read the text again. Order the events for each story.

Story 1:
a ☐ Paul and his girlfriend went to the restaurant.
b ☐ They ate at the restaurant for a second time.
c ☐ They read the restaurant reviews.

Story 2:
a ☐ They met face to face.
b ☐ Brenda and Alex spent weeks texting each other.
c ☐ Brenda was surprised by Alex's behavior.

**3** Choose the correct options to complete the sentences. Check your answers in the text in exercise 2A.

1 We *looked / 'd been looking* forward to going there for months, so we gave it a try.
2 At times, I actually felt as if they *were looking / had looked* down on us.
3 We went back there a second time, but nothing *had changed / had been changing*.
4 When Alex and I finally went out on a date, we *texted / 'd been texting* for weeks.
5 He kept posting online while I *was talking / had talked* to him.

narrative tenses ■ expectations    LANGUAGE  **1C**

**4** In pairs, match sentences 1–5 in exercise 3 with timelines a–c below. What are the tenses in a–c called? Then read the Grammar box.

a A was in progress at the same time as B.
b A happened before B.
c A was in progress before B.

### Grammar — narrative tenses

**Simple past:**
I **parked** the car and **walked** into the restaurant.
I **wrote** to her every day for several months.
We **didn't enjoy** our vacation much.

**Past continuous:**
The phone rang while I **was taking** a shower.
She spent ages talking to her friend while we **were waiting** for our food.

**Past perfect:**
The place we went to looked familiar. It felt as if I**'d been** there before.
When I arrived, they **had** already **started**.

**Past perfect continuous:**
I was tired because I**'d been working** hard.
It **had been snowing** for days.

**Look!** The past continuous and past perfect continuous usually aren't used with state verbs:
I**'d had** my car for five years when I sold it. NOT ~~I'd been having~~

Go to Grammar practice: narrative tenses, page 113

**5** ▶1.11  **Pronunciation: stress in narrative tenses** Listen to the sentences. Circle the stressed word in each underlined phrase.
1 I was feeling a bit nervous before the interview.
2 I had never done anything like skiing before.
3 I'd been saving money for a trip for months.
4 I fell when I was walking home from work.
5 It felt as if we'd known each other for a long time.

**6** Read the second part of Brenda's story and complete the sentences with the correct tense of the verbs in parentheses. Have you ever changed your mind about someone you met online?

At the end of our disastrous date, I ¹_____ (not think) Alex and I would ever see each other again. I mean, clearly we didn't really know each other at all, although we ²_____ (spend) months texting each other. But he called me and said he ³_____ (think) a lot about me since that day and wanted to see me again, so I decided to give him a second chance. As it turns out, we ⁴_____ (have) much better chemistry when we met again. We ⁵_____ (talk) about lots of different things, and, surprisingly, he was a lot more interesting than he ⁶_____ (seem) on our first date. Lesson learned: everyone deserves a second chance.

Go to Communication practice: Student A page 158, Student B page 164

**7** Tell your partner about a person, place, or event that surprised you. Use the prompts to help you, and different narrative tenses.

- What was the situation?
- Had you been looking forward to it?
- What happened?
- Had you ever had a similar experience before?
- Did the person/place/event turn out to be better/worse than you thought?
- What did you learn from the experience?

**Personal Best** — Using narrative tenses, write a paragraph about something funny or embarrassing that happened to you.

9

# 1 SKILLS  WRITING  making a narrative interesting ■ time linkers

## 1D  My bad purchase!

**1** In pairs, talk about a bad purchase you made, for example, an item of clothing, a piece of furniture, or a gadget. Think about something:
1. you bought, but couldn't really afford.
2. you thought was cool, but didn't really need.
3. you paid a lot of money for and quickly got tired of.

**2** Read the blog post about Donald and his dog, Buster. In what ways was Buster a good purchase and a bad purchase? What do you think happened next?

---

Home | About | **Blog** | Contact

# What was I thinking?

*Posted 3.45pm*

1  I still remember my 30th birthday. It seems like only yesterday. I'd been invited to my sister's place for lunch, and I was walking by a pet shop, when I saw the cutest little dog watching me from the window. **In the beginning**, I wasn't sure as I was very busy at work. Then I looked at him and started to wonder if a pet might fit my lifestyle. After all, I often take a walk in the park after work. As soon as he saw me, he gave me a look that seemed to say, "Please take me home!" We should never have made eye contact.

2  After lunch, I walked back to the pet shop, and, **before long**, that little dog, which felt like a tiny black and white teddy bear, was in my arms. "He's affectionate and full of energy," the salesclerk assured me. I'd been thinking of giving myself a birthday gift for weeks, so one hour later, I was on my way home with a smile on my face, a six-month-old puppy, and a hole in my bank account. I had no idea what the next few months would be like.

3  For a while, it felt as if Buster – I named him after a cartoon character that I love – made my life complete. It was nice to come home to a friendly face after a long, stressful day and have some company. I didn't mind the torn sofa or the missing remote controls. [1]My apartment looked like a disaster area, but I kept telling myself, [2]"Don't worry! That's what puppies do." I hoped Buster would start to behave, and [3]I would soon find out if my hope was realistic.

4  Unfortunately, Buster seemed to get worse with every passing day. He ran around the apartment, jumping on and off the furniture, like a mad frog, and barking for no reason. I'd never seen anything like it! **As time went on**, Buster developed other strange habits, such as moving food from his bowl to the floor before eating it, or pulling off my socks and hiding them – every single day. I failed at every attempt to train him. **Eventually**, I told myself, "Enough is enough!" I knew what I had to do.

5  In despair, I Skyped my brother, Barry. He lives on a small farm with his wife, kids, and two dogs, so I asked him how he'd feel about having a third one. He finally agreed, and **in a matter of hours**, Buster was gone. I still miss him, but it looks as if he's adapted well to his new home. As for me, I swear I'll never buy another pet again. Well, maybe a goldfish.

*Donald F. Brattleboro, Vermont*

 Share    Like    Comment

making a narrative interesting ■ time linkers  **WRITING**  SKILLS  **1D**

**3** Read the story again. In which paragraph (1–5) does Donald:
- a  talk about the "honeymoon" phase?  ___
- b  give the background to the story?  ___
- c  solve the problem?  ___
- d  realize that he'd made a mistake?  ___
- e  talk about buying the dog?  ___

**4** Read the blog post again. Find examples of simple past, past continuous, past perfect, and past perfect continuous verbs.

**Skill  making a narrative interesting**

When writing a narrative, make your story more interesting by including:
- predictions or comments about the future: *I had no idea what the next few months would be like.*
- interesting comparisons: *... that little dog, which felt like a tiny black and white teddy bear ...*
- examples of direct speech: *"He's affectionate and full of energy," the salesclerk assured me.*
- a variety of narrative tenses, e.g., simple past, past continuous, past perfect, past perfect continuous.

**5 A** Read the Skill box. Match strategies 1–3 below with their purpose a–c. Which strategy is each underlined sentence in paragraph 3?

1  provide a comparison
2  make a prediction
3  use direct speech

a  to give someone a "voice"
b  to help the reader visualize your descriptions
c  to create suspense for the next paragraph

**B** Find one more example of a comparison and one of direct speech in paragraph 4.

**Text builder  time linkers**

We use time linkers like *at first*, *in no time*, and *after a while* to say how much time has passed between different past actions:

**1 at the start**
*At first*, Donald wasn't sure he should buy a dog.

**2 after a short time**
He held Buster in his arms and, *in no time*, changed his mind.

**3 some time later**
*After a while*, Donald regretted his decision.

**6** Read the Text builder. Which meaning (1, 2, or 3) do the **bold** linkers in the blog post have?

**7** Read Donald's brother's message to a friend a few weeks later. Choose the correct time linkers.

Last month, my brother Donald asked me if I could adopt his dog. I said yes, and ¹*before long / in the beginning*, he brought the dog over. ²*At first / After a while*, we were happy to welcome him, but ³*in the beginning / in no time*, Buster showed his true colors. He spent most of the day bullying the other dogs and destroying our living room, which Donald hadn't warned us about! ⁴*As time went on / At the start*, though, the dogs became best friends. Are we going to keep him? Yes! We've grown fond of him, I guess.

**8 A** PREPARE  Choose an experience below that didn't turn out as you had expected. Make notes about the main events.

| something you bought | a blind date | a new restaurant | a party | a vacation |

**B** PRACTICE  Write a blog post, using your notes to help you. Include different narrative tenses and time linkers. Use comparisons, predictions, and direct speech to make your story more interesting.

**C** PERSONAL BEST  Exchange your blog post with your partner. Do your stories have anything in common?

Personal Best  Write a one-paragraph summary of your partner's story in exercise 8. Give it a different ending.

# UNIT 2 Culture vultures

**LANGUAGE**  question patterns ■ adjective suffixes

## 2A But is it art?

**1** Discuss the questions in pairs.
1. What pictures or posters do you have on your walls at home?
2. Describe the pieces of art below. What do you think of them? Which is your favorite?

**2** Read the text. In pairs, share one interesting fact you learned about each piece of art.

### *Raccoon* (2015) by Artur Bordalo (Bordalo II)

Bordalo's *Trash Animals* series gives a whole new meaning to the word "garbage." Old tires, useless appliances, and discarded items combine to create larger-than-life colorful 3D murals like *Raccoon*. Born in Lisbon in 1987, Bordalo is helping the city's recycling effort and increasing social awareness. He is an environmentally conscious young artist.

### *The Kiss* (1908) by Gustav Klimt

Austrian painter Klimt rebelled against the traditional art of the time, and while his subject matter was controversial, his works created considerable excitement in the art world. *The Kiss*, one of Klimt's most famous and memorable paintings, is known for its highly decorative style. In his "golden phase," Klimt used the effective technique of gold leafing (applying very thin sheets of gold) to make his paintings shine.

### *Fearless Girl* (2017) by Kristen Visbal

Visbal's *Fearless Girl* strikes a confident pose in downtown New York. Placed in front of *Charging Bull* (sculpted by Arturo Di Modica), the girl seems to challenge the powerful bull, even though this was not Visbal's intention. Di Modica feels the new sculpture detracts from the bull as a symbol of prosperity and strength, instead making it look aggressive.

**3** Look at the highlighted words in the text. What do they have in common? How are they different?

Go to Vocabulary practice: adjective suffixes, page 138

**4** Find six more adjectives in the text with the suffixes *-al*, *-able*, *-ful*, *-ive*, *-less*, and *-ous*.

**5 A** ▶ 2.2  Listen to three conversations. Which piece of art in exercise 2 is each conversation about?
Conversation 1 _____   Conversation 2 _____   Conversation 3 _____

**B** ▶ 2.3  Choose the correct option to complete 1–6 below. Then listen and check.
1. You don't really like this painting, *do you / don't you*?
2. Do you know what *is the title / the title is*?
3. What a contrast! This is a bit surprising, *doesn't it / isn't it*?
4. *Isn't / Is not* the bull a symbol of strength?
5. Who *painted / did he paint* it?
6. Excuse me, could you tell me if a local artist *made / did make* this?

question patterns ■ adjective suffixes   LANGUAGE   2A

**6** Look at 1–6 in exercise 5B again and answer the questions below. Then read the Grammar box.
Which ones:
a ask about the subject of a sentence? ____
b include a tag question? ____ ____
c are negative questions? ____
d ask a question indirectly? ____ ____

### Grammar | question patterns

**wh- subject and object questions:**
Who **gave you** this present?
Who **did you give** the book to?

**Negative questions:**
**Doesn't** the bus **come** every 20 minutes?
Why **didn't** you **call** me?

**Tag questions:**
You haven't heard from James, **have you**?
Ann wants to go out tonight, **doesn't she**?

**Indirect questions:**
Do you have any idea **where Tom is**?
Could you tell me **if the museum is** open today?

**Look!** When forming questions, check the correct use (or not) of auxiliary verbs:
Could you tell me **where the bus stops**? NOT where does the bus stop?
You live upstairs, **don't you**?

Go to Grammar practice: question patterns, page 114

**7 A** ▶2.5  **Pronunciation:** intonation in tag questions  Listen to the questions. Does the intonation go up (↗) or down (↘) at the end of the questions?
1 The weather's awful today, isn't it?
2 This silk shirt's washable, isn't it?
3 These cheap umbrellas don't last long, do they?
4 John didn't call, did he?

**B** ▶2.5  Match the sentences in exercise 7A with functions a–b below. Listen again and repeat.
a real question ____ ____
b comment or conversation opener ____ ____

**8 A** ▶2.6  Complete the conversations with appropriate question forms. Use the verbs in parentheses. Then listen and check.
1 A **Street art**'s so cool, _____ it? (be) What kind of **art** _____ you _____? (like)
   B I prefer more conventional art, actually.
2 A Do you have any idea what time **the movie** _____ tonight? (start)
   B I think at eight. Why? Are you thinking of going?
3 A Your **leg's bleeding**! What _____? (happen)
   B I fell while I was crossing the street. It's OK. It's not painful.
4 A _____ we _____ before? (not met) _____ you at **Meg's party** last month? (not be)
   B No, but maybe my twin sister was there.
5 A You really _____ **dancing**, _____ you? (not enjoy)
   B No, I don't. You're right. I look ridiculous on the dance floor.

**B** In pairs, practice the conversations. Then ask your partner new questions, changing the parts in **bold**. Your partner will give an appropriate answer.

Go to Communication practice: Student A page 158, Student B page 164

**9** Ask which of these activities your partner enjoys. Then ask follow-up questions to comment on or ask about three of the activities, using the different question patterns.

| photography | going to the movies | reading novels | going to concerts | going to exhibits |

A *Do you like photography?*
B *Yeah, I love taking pictures of people on my cell phone.*
A *That's great, but shouldn't you be a little cautious? I mean, you need to ask permission, don't you?*

Personal Best  Think of a painting, sculpture, or mural you've seen. Write six questions about it.   13

# 2 SKILLS READING skimming and scanning ■ clauses with *what*

## 2B Dear Juliet …

**1** What do you know about the story of *Romeo and Juliet*? Compare your answers in pairs.

**2** Read the first paragraph of the article on page 15. Check (✓) the information you think the rest of the text will contain.

1 the story of *Romeo and Juliet* ☐
2 the history of the Juliet Club ☐
3 the history of Verona ☐
4 the life of Shakespeare ☐
5 who writes letters to Juliet ☐
6 who replies to the letters ☐

### Skill    skimming and scanning

**Skimming and scanning are reading techniques that help us find and understand information in a text quickly.**

- Skimming gives us a general understanding of the main ideas in the text. Read the introduction and first sentence of each paragraph carefully, and then move your eyes quickly over the rest of the text, skimming it to find key words and ideas.
- Scanning helps us find and understand specific information. Move your eyes quickly over the text, looking for key words or synonyms that correspond to the specific information that you are looking for. Read that part in detail to see if it contains the information. If not, continue scanning.

**3** Read the Skill box. Then skim the article and check your answers to exercise 2.

**4** Scan the article to answer the questions.
1 When was the first letter to Juliet received?
2 Who was the first person to reply to the letters?
3 When did the Juliet Club start replying to the letters?
4 Why was the Juliet Club created?
5 How many letters are received nowadays?
6 What is the nationality and age group of the people who write to Juliet most?
7 Are the messages to Juliet only written in English?
8 Do letter writers often use the Internet to write to Juliet?
9 How much are the people who reply to the letters paid?
10 Why do Giovanni Carabetta and Elena Marchi work for the Juliet Club?

**5** Read the underlined sentences 1–4 in the article. What does the word *what* mean in each sentence?

### Text builder    clauses with *what*

Clauses with *what* can be about the subject or the object of the sentence. *What* can refer to singular or plural things. Subject clauses with *what* are often at the start of a sentence. The verb is singular, not plural:
*What people say* is *very important.* (= the things people say)
*What they do* is *even more important, though.* (= the things they do)

Object clauses with *what* are often at the end of a sentence:
*I just finished reading* **what you wrote.** (= the thing/things you wrote)
*I like* **what you wrote in the last sentence.** (= the thing/things you wrote in the last sentence)

**6** Read the Text builder. Look at sentences 1–4 in the article again. In which sentences is the clause with *what* the subject?

**7** What does the word *what* refer to in the sentences below?
1 What I don't understand is why someone would write to a fictional character.
2 I don't think I'd enjoy reading what people write to Juliet. It's too personal!

**8** Would you like to be a secretary for the Juliet Club? Why/Why not?

14

skimming and scanning ■ clauses with *what* READING | SKILLS | 2B

# Lovesick? Broken heart?
## Write to Juliet

If you know the famous story of *Romeo and Juliet*, written by Shakespeare in the 16th century, you'll know that their home city is Verona, Italy. Verona is now also the home of the *Club di Giulietta* (the Juliet Club), a remarkable association that receives letters from all over the world addressed to Shakespeare's heroine. The writers, often in love, write to Juliet to seek advice or to unburden themselves. [1]And a group of committed volunteers, known as Juliet's secretaries, read what they write and reply to every single letter that arrives.

Probably as the result of George Cukor's 1936 film version of Shakespeare's tragedy, the first letter, addressed simply to "Juliet, Verona," arrived in the 1930s. The letter found its way to "Juliet's tomb," in a monastery just outside the city walls. The attendant there, a veteran who had picked up some English in the First World War, decided to reply. And he carried on replying as more letters arrived. After the Second World War, a local poet secretly took on the role of Juliet's secretary, but gave it up, apparently in embarrassment, when his identity became known. Finally, in the 1980s, the mayor of Verona decided to give the task to the *Club di Giulietta*, a group formed to promote initiatives linking their city to the famous play.

Sitting around a table strewn with handwritten letters, three of Juliet's "secretaries," Giovanna Tamassia, Elena Marchi, and Gioia Ambrosi, tell stories that are by turns touching and weird, thought-provoking, and heart-rending. "It's a great responsibility," says Tamassia, whose father Giulio is the club's president and a founder member. Ambrosi, a 25-year-old student, describes the correspondence as "a blog on humanity." "We get more than 5,000 letters a year," says Tamassia. "And then there are the thousands of notes that get left behind at Juliet's house and tomb."

She reckons about three-quarters of the messages are from women, and that the biggest single group is made up of American teenagers. On the wall of the arch leading to Juliet's house in the medieval centre of Verona, though, there are notes in every conceivable language. Some of the letters and professions of undying love are genuinely poetic: "For hope and love; for the one I loved most, my heart"; others less so: "I've got a stomach ache in the heart." When letters are serious, the secretaries can call on the services of a psychologist, and sometimes they need them.

Juliet's house also has a post box where letters can be left and four computer work stations where visitors may tap out a message to her. But surprisingly, perhaps, emails account for fewer than 10% of the messages that end up in her secretaries' offices. Of the letters, the vast majority are handwritten in pen and ink. And that is how they are always replied to. "[2]What people often write is: 'You are the only one who can understand me'," says Giovanni Carabetta, the club's archivist. Perhaps the most extraordinary aspect of this whole endeavor is that the secretaries do it for free. "Well, the council gives us the money for the stamps," explains Giulio Tamassia. "But it's not even enough to cover the postage. Right now, I'm having a battle with the council. [3]What we do brings all sorts of advantages for Verona, and I think it is time they stopped treating us like this. We're all working for nothing." Carabetta smiles. "Not for nothing, Giulio … for the pleasure of reading these wonderful letters."

And perhaps, in some cases, for other, more personal reasons. "It has helped me to believe again in feelings," says Marchi. "[4]But what counts is to have a heart that is alive, no? To be in touch with your feelings, however things go. It's not as if there is a guarantee as to the future." A sentiment with which the real – or rather, fictional – Juliet would have fervently agreed.

Adapted from theguardian.com

Personal Best — Write a paragraph to Juliet with an imagined problem.

## 2 LANGUAGE    using linkers (1) ■ phrasal verbs (1)

### 2C It's music to my ears!

**1 A** Read the questions. In pairs, explain the meaning of the phrasal verbs in **bold**.

1 Who's your favorite musician? Are there any musicians you really **look up to**?
2 Have you **come across** any new groups or albums lately that you really like?
3 Would you be able to **do without** music? How would you feel without it?
4 Have you ever tried to get tickets for a concert that had **sold out**? What was it?

**B** Discuss the questions with your partner.

Go to Vocabulary practice: phrasal verbs (1), page 139

**2 A** Read the text about Taylor Swift and Ed Sheeran. Complete the phrasal verbs 1–5.

# The secret of success

**Taylor Swift and Ed Sheeran have a very special friendship and often sing together. They may come from very different backgrounds, but both have had a similar path to success.**

Swift, who grew up on a family farm in Pennsylvania, had two passions: writing and music. In spite of the fact that her writing talent was noticed very early (she won a national poetry contest and even wrote an unpublished novel), Swift really wanted to be a singer. How did she achieve her goal to become the Taylor Swift we know today?

To put it simply, Swift had determination. In 2004, she ¹**talked** her family _____ moving to Nashville so she could be part of the country music scene. (Despite having a grandmother who was a well-known opera singer, Swift preferred country music.) She wrote and performed non-stop and, before long, her concerts started to ²**sell** _____ the minute tickets went on sale. Those who know her say her secret is an ability to visualize her lyrics before she writes a song. Maybe all that writing as a child ³**paid** _____ in the end!

Superficially, Ed Sheeran could not have been more different. He was a shy child who stuttered when he spoke, so he would repeat the lyrics of an old Eminem album hundreds of times. In spite of his shyness, Sheeran moved to London at 16 in order to become a professional musician. In the beginning, it was hard to ⁴**figure** _____ how to make a living, and even though he was playing over 300 live shows a year, he often had to sleep on the Underground, the London subway system. Sheeran never ⁵**gave** _____ , though, and he released his first album in 2011. Two years later, everything changed when he went on a world tour supporting Taylor Swift. So what was his secret? According to Sheeran, he played music instead of video games when he was growing up.

Incredible tales like Swift's or Sheeran's are an inspiration to us all!

**B** Read the text again. What do the two success stories have in common?

**3 A** Match the two parts to make sentences from the text.

1 **In spite of** the fact that her writing talent was noticed very early,
2 She talked her family into moving to Nashville **so**
3 **Despite** having a grandmother who was a well-known opera singer,
4 **In spite of** his shyness,
5 Sheeran moved to London at 16 **in order to**
6 **Even though** he was playing over 300 live shows a year,

a Sheeran moved to London at 16.
b she could be part of the country music scene.
c he often had to sleep on the Underground.
d Swift really wanted to be a singer.
e become a professional musician.
f Swift preferred country music.

using linkers (1)  ■  phrasal verbs (1)     **LANGUAGE  2C**

**B** Look at the sentences in exercise 3A again and answer the questions. Then read the Grammar box.
1 Which of the linking words in **bold** express contrast and which express purpose?
2 Which one means the same as *although*?
3 Which one can be replaced by *to*?
4 Which three grammatical forms can follow *despite* and *in spite of*?

### Grammar  using linkers (1)

Expressing contrast:
***Despite*** *taking lessons/all the lessons, I still can't play the guitar.*
***In spite of*** *the fact that I've taken lessons, I still can't play the guitar.*
***Even though/Although*** *I listen to a lot of jazz, I prefer rock music.*
*I listen to a lot of jazz.* ***However****, I prefer rock music.*

Expressing purpose:
*I listen to music* ***in order to*** *feel more relaxed.*
*I listen to music* ***to*** *feel more relaxed.*
*I upgraded my phone* ***so*** **(*that*)** *I could stream music.*

**Look!** We can also end a sentence with ***though***:
*I listen to a lot of jazz. I prefer rock music,* ***though****.*

Go to Grammar practice: using linkers (1), page 115

**4 A** ▶ 2.10 **Pronunciation:** sentence stress Listen to the sentences. Circle the stressed words in the underlined phrases.
1 I haven't eaten in spite of the fact that I'm hungry.
2 My best friend came in the end despite not feeling well.
3 Despite having had a bad day, I had a great evening.
4 I called my parents so that they wouldn't worry.
5 We left in a rush in order not to be late.
6 It ended up being a great day in spite of the weather.

**B** ▶ 2.10 Listen again and repeat.

**5 A** Rewrite the sentences so they have the same meaning, using the words in parentheses.
1 I love rock, pop, and dance music, but I never listen to classical music. (however)
2 I'd travel for a whole day so I could see my favorite singer perform live. (in order to)
3 Despite being a good dancer, I never go to clubs. (although)
4 I wear headphones to listen to music on the subway. (so)
5 I don't have any CDs any longer. However, I still have some records. (though)
6 I love foreign music, but I can't understand the lyrics. (even though)
7 In spite of having bought tickets to the concert, I didn't go in the end. (the fact that)
8 Even though I don't have a good voice, singing makes me happy. (despite not)

**B** Are the sentences true for you? If not, change them so that they are true.

Go to Communication practice: Both students, page 170

**6** Which different kinds of music do you prefer in the following situations? Why? Tell your partner.

on a road trip with friends
jogging in the park
studying    cleaning the house
getting ready to go out    commuting to work/college
relaxing at home    dancing at a party

**Personal Best**  Write two advantages and two disadvantages of streaming music online.

17

## 2 SKILLS  SPEAKING  making recommendations ■ describing a movie

### 2D It's definitely worth seeing

**1 A** Look at the posters. Which movie looks the most interesting?

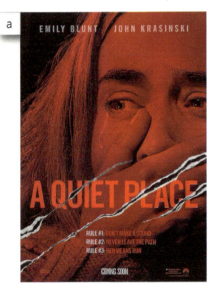
a

b

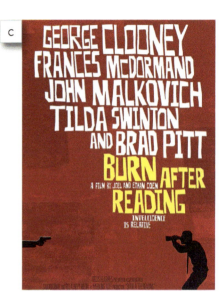
c

**B** In pairs, discuss which movie to see. Use some of the adjectives in the box.

> cheerful  controversial  conventional  harmless  impressive  memorable  painless  powerful

**A** *What do you think this one's about?*
**B** *Let's see. I think …*

**2 A** ▶ 2.11  Watch or listen to the first part of *Talking Zone*. Fill in Ben and Abigail's missing words.

| 1 | **Ben** | I'm not really big on _____ movies. |
|---|---|---|
| 2 | **Abigail** | Oh, if you like George Clooney, you're going to _____ it. |
| 3 | **Ben** | Good. I'm not in the mood for anything too _____ . |
| 4 | **Abigail** | It's both _____ and _____ at the same time. Oh and Brad Pitt is in it. |
| 5 | **Ben** | Look – here's one that's definitely worth _____ . |
| 6 | **Abigail** | I'm not really into _____ . |
| 7 | **Ben** | It's one of the _____ things I've seen in a long time. |

**B** ▶ 2.11  Watch or listen again. Match sentences 1–7 in exercise 2A with the correct movies a–d. One sentence refers to two movies.

a *A Quiet Place* ____
b *Paranormal Activity* ____
c *Burn After Reading* ____ ____ ____
d *Mamma Mia! Here We Go Again* ____ ____ ____

### Conversation builder  making recommendations

**Making recommendations:**
*If you like comedies, you're going to love this one.*
*It's both entertaining and serious at the same time.*
*This documentary is definitely worth seeing.*
*It's one of the best things I've seen in a long time.*

**Responding to recommendations:**
*I'm not big on romances.*
*I'm (not) in the mood for a comedy.*
*I'm (not) crazy about/really into documentaries.*
*I (don't) feel like watching that movie today.*

**3** Read the Conversation builder. In pairs, recommend three movies you've seen recently. Choose sentences from the box to make recommendations and give responses.

making recommendations ■ describing a movie  **SPEAKING**   **SKILLS**  **2D**

**4** Make a list of four movies you'd like to see soon. In pairs, practice short dialogues, beginning with the recommendations in 1–4 below.
1 Let's see … . They say it's one of the … movies that's showing.
2 If you like … , you're going to love … . It's definitely worth seeing.
3 How about seeing … ? It's both … and … at the same time.
4 I'm in the mood for a … . The movie … is …

**5 A** Look at the poster and the pictures from the movie. Predict what *Brooklyn* will be about. When do you think the movie takes place?

**B** ▶ 2.12 Watch or listen to the second part of the show. Choose the correct answer. Abigail tells us that *Brooklyn* is about a young woman who leaves Ireland …
a and moves permanently to Brooklyn.
b and moves to Brooklyn, but returns to Ireland to live.
c and moves to Brooklyn, but we don't really know what happens after that.

**Skill** describing a movie

When we describe a movie, we need to give enough information for someone to decide whether he/she would like to see it.
• Say when the movie takes place: *It's set in …*
• Briefly describe the plot: *It tells the story of …*
• Mention the cast and scriptwriter: *… is in it, it was written by …*
• Give your overall impressions: *I think what I loved was …*

**6** ▶ 2.12 Read the Skill box. Number the sentences in Abigail's description in the order you hear them. Then watch or listen again and check.
a ☐ But the whole cast is fantastic and the script is written by Nick Hornby.
b ☐ It got great reviews at the time, and was nominated for two or three Oscars.
c ☐ It's set in the 1950s.
d ☐ I don't want to spoil the ending, but I think what I loved was the message.
e ☐ I don't remember the actors' names, except for Saoirse Ronan, who plays the leading role.
f ☐ It tells the story of a young Irish woman who moves to New York, where she falls in love.

**7** Cover exercise 6. Looking only at the Skill box, take turns recommending *Brooklyn* to your partner. Did you forget any important details?

**8** Would you like to see *Brooklyn*? Why/Why not?

Go to Communication practice: Student A page 159, Student B page 165

**9 A** **PREPARE** Find a movie, concert, or show online that you'd really like to see or go to. Prepare a recommendation to convince your partner.

**B** **PRACTICE** Practice a conversation about the event. Were you able to decide whether to see or go to it together?

**C** **PERSONAL BEST** Choose a new activity and practice a similar conversation. Which time was your recommendation more convincing?

**Personal Best** Describe the last movie you saw. Give it 1–5 stars (1 = bad, 5 = great).

# 1 and 2 REVIEW and PRACTICE

## Grammar

**1** Cross (**X**) the sentence that is NOT correct.

1. a I know London quite well now.
   b I'm getting to know London quite well now.
   c I'm knowing London quite well now.
2. a I just went to bed when the phone rang.
   b I had just gone to bed when the phone rang.
   c I went to bed, and then the phone rang.
3. a Why did you laugh when she said her name?
   b Why you laughed when she said her name?
   c Why were you laughing when she said her name?
4. a Where can I get coffee?
   b Do you know where can I get coffee?
   c Do you know where I can get coffee?
5. a Even I've lived in Spain for a long time, I don't speak very good Spanish.
   b Despite living in Spain for a long time, I don't speak very good Spanish.
   c I've lived in Spain for a long time. I don't speak very good Spanish, though.
6. a I leave work early on Fridays so that I can pick up the kids from school.
   b I leave work early on Fridays to pick up the kids from school.
   c I leave work early on Fridays that I can pick up the kids from school.
7. a You've done this before, don't you?
   b Haven't you done this before?
   c You've done this before, haven't you?
8. a Hadn't you been pretty lonely before you met your boyfriend?
   b You'd been pretty lonely before you met your boyfriend, hadn't you?
   c You'd been being pretty lonely before you met your boyfriend, hadn't you?

**2** Use the words in parentheses to complete the sentences so they mean the same as the first sentence.

1. I've saved a lot of money, but I still can't afford it.
   _____ a lot of money, I still can't afford it. (spite)
2. Although we only just met, I have the sensation that we've known each other for ages.
   Although we only just met, _____ we've known each other for ages. (feels)
3. What time does the post office close?
   _____ the post office closes? (could)
4. I go running every day so that I get in shape.
   I go running every day _____ get in shape. (order)
5. From what you are saying, I think you've had a good day.
   _____ you've had a good day. (sounds)
6. Is Buenos Aires the capital of Argentina?
   Buenos Aires _____ ? (isn't)

**3** Choose the correct options to complete the interview.

Each week we talk to a graduate of our university ¹*in order to find / despite finding* out about his or her job and how he or she went from college into the world of work. This week we ²*spoke / had spoken* to Julia Gonzales, who graduated in 2016.

**Hi Julia. Could you tell me what ³*your job title is / is your job title*?**

I'm a junior fashion designer. I work for a company that ⁴*makes / is making* clothes for children.

**And what ⁵*are you doing / do you do* on a typical day? It sounds ⁶*as / like* an interesting job.**

It can be interesting. I travel a lot and I meet a lot of cool people. ⁷*Even though / However*, I ⁸*spend / spent* most of my day at my desk researching new ideas and reading and sending e-mails.

**And how did you get your job? The fashion industry is very difficult to get into, ⁹*doesn't / isn't* it?**

Yes, you're right. You have to work very hard to be successful in fashion. Most of my classmates from college didn't apply for jobs until after they ¹⁰*had graduated / were graduating*, but by then, I ¹¹*had been contacting / was contacting* companies for months. Luckily for me, ¹²*even though / despite* I didn't have much experience, one of those companies liked my designs and offered me a job.

## Vocabulary

**1** Circle the word or expression that is different. Explain why.

1. wink  nod  stare  gaze
2. open-minded  forward-thinking  well-educated  middle-aged
3. fail to impress  make a good impression  be a success  impress
4. shake hands  give someone a hug  kiss on the cheek  shrug your shoulders
5. accidental  cheerful  endless  breakable
6. dreadful  harmless  ridiculous  useless

20

## REVIEW and PRACTICE 1 and 2

**2** Match the words in the box with definitions 1–8.

> frown   wave   effective   reasonable   attractive
> far-reaching   highly-respected   record-breaking

1. have an influence on a lot of people or things  _____
2. move your hand as a greeting  _____
3. fair and sensible  _____
4. admired by many people  _____
5. beating the previous best performance  _____
6. nice to look at  _____
7. facial expression for disapproval  _____
8. producing the intended or expected result  _____

**3** Complete the sentences with the words in the box.

> time-consuming   raise your voice   pay off   impress
> get a second chance   controversial   turn down
> be a disappointment   forward-thinking   look up to

1. It's not because of the money that I want a good job. It's because I don't want to _____ to my parents.
2. As a teacher, you need to _____ sometimes or the children just won't listen!
3. I thought everyone would agree to my idea, but, actually, it seems to be quite _____ .
4. I spent two hours reorganizing my lecture notes yesterday. I know it's useful, but it's so _____ !
5. I'm really grateful to _____ because I thought my first interview went so badly!
6. It's important to have people in your life that you can _____ .
7. My girlfriend and I are very different. She's very _____ and is always planning ahead. I just think about today!
8. Christina spends a lot of money on her clothes because she likes to _____ people.
9. Don't _____ this job. It's perfect for you!
10. I know you're very tired, but I promise that all this exam preparation will _____ in the end!

**4** Complete the story with the correct form of the words and expressions in the box.

> show up   be a success   memorable
> lower your expectations   give   shake hands
> ridiculous   kiss   make a good first impression

I had a job interview yesterday. I was desperate for it to [1]_____ . However, it started badly. I knew how important it was to [2]_____ , but I did something very silly as soon as I [3]_____ . Instead of [4]_____ like you should in a formal interview, I [5]_____ the interviewer a hug and [6]_____ her on the cheek! I felt [7]_____ ! Anyway, because the interview started badly, I [8]_____ , but by the end, it had gone quite well. And at least I was a [9]_____ candidate. Who could forget that introduction?

## Personal Best

**Lesson 1A:** Name four things you do when greeting someone or saying good-bye.

**Lesson 2A:** Write four questions: a *wh-* question, a tag question, a negative question, and an indirect question.

**Lesson 1A:** Describe a situation using three different sense verbs.

**Lesson 2A:** Write four sentences that include an adjective with the suffix *-ous*, *-ful*, *-able*, or *-less*.

**Lesson 1B:** Describe someone you know using four different compound adjectives.

**Lesson 2B:** Write four sentences including a clause with *what* about things you believe very strongly.

**Lesson 1C:** Describe something that happened when you were a child. Use different narrative tenses.

**Lesson 2C:** Name four things you regularly do and explain why you do them.

**Lesson 1C:** Write two sentences describing a positive experience and two sentences about a negative one.

**Lesson 2C:** Describe three things that happened recently using phrasal verbs.

**Lesson 1D:** Describe a time you changed your mind about something using time linkers.

**Lesson 2D:** Recommend a movie, a book, and a TV program and explain why each one is good.

21

# UNIT 3

# A sense of place

**LANGUAGE** advice, expectation, and obligation ■ urban places and problems

## 3A You're not supposed to do that here!

**1** Read the dictionary definition. Which customs, rules, or behavior might visitors to your city find different from their own?

> *"When in Rome, do as the Romans do."* (saying)
> When you are in a different country or unfamiliar situation, follow the customs, rules, and behavior of the people around you.

**2** Read Ana and Piotr's stories about their trips to the U.S. Which local custom or rule didn't they know about? Are these the same or different where you are from?

### Ana's story:

My boyfriend Raúl and I were on vacation in New York last year, and the first evening we were there, we went out for dinner at a nice restaurant, down by the harbor. The meal was delicious, and I wanted to leave a generous tip. I left a tip in cash – about 10%, which is more than I would leave at home in Madrid. But I was shocked when the waiter told me it wasn't enough. [1]He explained that in New York the tip ought to be 20%. He even told us that it was an important part of his salary! Raúl said quietly, "[2]You'd better give him 20% – [3]it's what you're supposed to do here." So I left the tip he wanted, and we left in a hurry. We really hadn't expected dinner to cost that much, and when we got to the taxi stand, we realized we didn't have any money left for a taxi back. It was all kind of embarrassing, but I learned a lesson about New York for my next trip.

### Piotr's story:

I was on a business trip in the Washington D.C. area and was staying at a hotel in a fairly central business district. I arrived one rainy Monday morning. The sky was dark gray (I wondered if it was smog), and I was just about to cross the street to get to the hotel when a man in a suit said, "You can't cross here." I ignored him – it didn't seem dangerous. In fact, the traffic was moving slowly because of the congestion. But just as I stepped off the sidewalk he suddenly yelled, "Sir, stop! [4]You're not allowed to cross here." Imagine my surprise when he pulled out his police badge! I had no idea that the guy was a police officer, and I wasn't aware that in many U.S. cities [5]you have to cross the street at a crosswalk – jaywalking is forbidden. The officer gave me an $80 fine, which I was really annoyed about, as a colleague told me later that these rules are rarely enforced. Not a great start to my week!

**3** Find words in the stories that match definitions 1–5.

1 a place to keep boats and ships _____
2 a place where you can get a taxi _____
3 a commercial area in a city _____
4 a type of weather that affects cities _____
5 when roads are blocked by cars _____

**Go to Vocabulary practice:** urban places and problems, page 140

22

advice, expectation, and obligation ■ urban places and problems    LANGUAGE   3A

**4  A** Look at the underlined sentences 1–5 in the text on page 22. Which function does each sentence express? Write *A* (advice), *E* (expectation) or *O* (obligation).

1 ____   2 ____   3 ____   4 ____   5 ____

**B** Read the Grammar box and check.

> **Grammar** advice, expectation, and obligation
>
> **Advice:**
> You **should**/**ought to** take a pill for your headache.
> **I'd** take a pill (if I were you).
>
> **Strong advice/warning:**
> You**'d better** buy your plane ticket right away.
> You**'d better** not make noise!
>
> **Expectation:**
> You**'re supposed to** leave the waiter a tip.
>
> **Personal obligation:**
> I **should**/**ought to** visit my grandparents this weekend.
>
> **External obligation/rules:**
> You **can** park over there.
> You **can't** cross the street here.
> You **have to**/**must** cross at the crosswalk.
> You**'re allowed to** vote at the age of 18.
> You**'re not allowed to** turn left here.
>
> **Look!** We can use *prohibited* or *forbidden* to talk about rules in more formal or written English:
> *Driving while using your cell phone is strictly **prohibited**/**forbidden**.*

Go to Grammar practice: advice, expectation, and obligation, page 116

**5  A**  3.3  **Pronunciation:** *supposed*, *ought*, and *allowed* Listen to three sentences from the text. Notice how the sounds in **bold** are pronounced.

1 You're not all**ow**ed to cross here.
2 In New York, the tip **ou**ght to be 20%.
3 It's what you're supp**o**sed to do here.

**B**  3.4  Listen and repeat the sentences.

1 You're **supposed** to take off your shoes.
2 I think you **ought** to apologize for being late.
3 You're not **allowed** to use your cell phone here.
4 You **ought** to get your mom some flowers.
5 I'm not **supposed** to study today. It's Saturday.
6 Are you **allowed** to drive so fast on this street?

**6  A** Complete the sentences with the modals or expressions in the box.

| supposed    has    'd better    not allowed (x2)    have (x2) |

### In which countries might someone say these things?

1 You're _____ to buy chewing gum here. Selling or importing it is against the law.
2 You _____ to wear a bike helmet. The police will fine you for not wearing one.
3 At least 20% of music played on the radio _____ to be from this country. It's the law.
4 You _____ not give the waiter a tip. It can be considered bad manners.
5 By law, you _____ to have a license to watch TV.
6 I think we're _____ to get in line. Everyone else is lining up.
7 In this part of the country, the official language is French, so restaurants are _____ to have menus written only in English.

**B**  3.5  Guess the country for each sentence in exercise 6A. Listen and check.

Australia ____   Canada ____ ____   Japan ____   Singapore ____   the UK ____ ____

Go to Communication practice: Both students, page 171

**7** How would you improve life in your city? What new customs or laws would you introduce? Discuss in pairs, and write a list of ten customs or laws that you decide together.

**Personal Best**  Write ten real or imaginary rules or customs that the people living in your house should follow.

23

# 3 SKILLS LISTENING identifying advice ■ intonation in negative questions ■ easily confused words

## 3B My special place

**1 A** Choose the correct word. Then complete the questionnaire.

| When I'm alone and I want to think … | Yes | No |
|---|---|---|
| 1  I really *mind / matter* when the phone rings. | ☐ | ☐ |
| 2  I *discuss / argue* with people who try to talk to me. | ☐ | ☐ |
| 3  I *claim / pretend* not to be home. | ☐ | ☐ |
| 4  I *choose / elect* a quiet place to go to. | ☐ | ☐ |

**B** In pairs, compare your answers. If you answered "Yes" to item 4, where do you go?

**Go to Vocabulary practice:** easily confused words, page 141

**2 A** ▶ 3.8 Watch or listen to the first part of *Talking Zone*. What is a 'third place'? Why do we need one?

**B** ▶ 3.8 Listen to the three speakers. What are their 'special places'?

**3** ▶ 3.8 Watch or listen again. Fill in the missing words in Tasha and David's advice.
1  These hideaways are _____ . According to _____ , we're all supposed to have one.
2  _____ really ought to have somewhere like that.
3  Many workplaces can be … stressful. _____ advise that we're really not supposed to live like this.
4  You _____ tell someone what their safe place should be.
5  It can be _____ . It doesn't even have to be a particularly quiet or peaceful place.
6  You _____ come and go whenever you want.

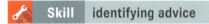

**Skill** identifying advice

When we give advice, it is often more polite to be indirect. It is easier to tell that someone is giving you advice if you listen for:
- a confident tone of voice showing the speaker is sure the advice is a good idea.
- words that mention people in authority: *Most doctors emphasize the need to exercise.*
- modal verbs and expressions: *You can't just expect to pass if you don't study.*
- sentences starting with general *you* that may also apply to you as an individual.
- other general statements: *Everyone should get eight hours' sleep a night.*

**4** Read the Skill box. Look at the sentences in exercise 3 again. In pairs, identify the words that tell you that these sentences are giving advice.

identifying advice ■ intonation in negative questions ■ easily confused words **LISTENING**  **SKILLS 3B**

**5** ▶ 3.9 Watch or listen to the second part of the show. Choose the correct answer.
David created the MyThirdPlace app when …
a he came back from a trip to London.
b he did some historical research.
c he moved to New York.

**6** ▶ 3.9 Watch or listen again. Number the reasons for having the app in the order David mentions them. There is one extra.
a ☐ An app can match you to places based on your personality.
b ☐ There are fewer quiet places than in the past because of technology.
c ☐ It's cheaper to use an app than to visit possible safe places.
d ☐ You might move to a new city and not know where the quiet places are.

**Listening builder | intonation in negative questions**

When we hear a negative question, the intonation is an important clue to its meaning.
When we want to check information we think we know, the intonation rises:

*Isn't Spruce Street the street after this one?* ↗

However, when we give an opinion or make a comment, the intonation falls:

*Wasn't that movie awful!* ↗↘

**7 A** ▶ 3.10 Read the Listening builder. Then listen to the negative questions from the video. Does the intonation rise (R) or fall (F)?
1 And don't we all want to keep our special places to ourselves? _____
2 Wouldn't you want to be free of your boss or even … your mother-in-law? _____
3 Isn't it hard for an app to get to know us as individuals? _____

**B** ▶ 3.10 Listen again and repeat each question.

**8** Fill in the blanks, and, in pairs, take turns asking the questions. Your partner will decide if you are checking something or giving an opinion, and will then respond.
1 Isn't learning _____ difficult?
2 Don't people around here ever _____ ?
3 Wouldn't you be mad if _____ ?

**9** Look at the pictures. In pairs, discuss which one you would choose as your third place and explain why.

a
b
c

**10** In pairs, discuss these questions.
1 Which aspects of your daily life are most stressful?
2 What good ways have you found to reduce stress?
3 What are the best 'third places' where you live?
4 Would you like to buy the MyThirdPlace app? Why/Why not?

**Personal Best** Describe the ideal third place for you.

# 3 LANGUAGE  phrasal verbs

## 3C To go, or not to go

**1** Discuss the questions in pairs.
1. Do you prefer to go to popular tourist destinations or to places where tourists don't usually go? Why?
2. What are the most and least touristy places you've ever visited? What were they like?
3. What do you understand by the expression "mass tourism"?

**2** Read the preview of a radio show about mass tourism. Is the situation similar or different in cities in your country? How?

## Tourism heaven, tourism hell?

Barcelona, Venice, Prague, Dubrovnik – four of the most beautiful cities in Europe, and very popular tourist destinations. The cities are eager to attract visitors, who bring cities to life and greatly benefit local economies. But recently, in cities all over Europe, more and more residents have begun to voice their concerns about the impact of mass tourism. They're worried about issues such as the environmental impact of tourism and the increase in the cost of living for local people.
Barbara Vitez, a tour guide from Dubrovnik, in the south of Croatia, gives her views on tourism in her city.

**3 A** ▶ 3.11  Listen to the interview with Barbara. Which points below does she think are the benefits (B) and problems (P) of tourism in Dubrovnik?

1. the economic impact        _____
2. the cultural life of the city   _____
3. the number of tourists     _____
4. the environmental impact   _____
5. the cost of a place to live   _____
6. the tourists in general    _____

**B** Discuss the questions in pairs.
1. Why do you think each point in exercise 3A is a benefit or a problem?
2. What two things could local authorities do to reduce the negative impact of mass tourism?
3. Would you like to visit Dubrovnik?

**4** ▶ 3.12  Complete the phrasal verbs in **bold** with the words in the box. Listen and check.

> come  look  grew  throw

1. I _____ **up** in Dubrovnik.
2. The mayor of Dubrovnik has _____ **up with** a good idea.
3. We really need to _____ **after** our city.
4. They _____ their garbage **out** in the cans in the old town.

**5** Look at the sentences in exercise 4 again and answer the questions below. Then read the Grammar box. Which sentences contain a phrasal verb with:

a  an object after the phrasal verb?                    _____ _____
b  an object between the two parts of the phrasal verb?  _____
c  no object?                                            _____
d  three parts?                                          _____

phrasal verbs  **LANGUAGE**  **3C**

📖 **Grammar** phrasal verbs

Without an object:
We're going to **come back** very early tomorrow morning.
The plane **took off** twenty minutes late.

With an object (separable):
You can **try** the dress **on**.
The music's loud. **Turn** it **down**.

With an object (non-separable):
I'm **looking for** my phone. NOT ~~looking my phone for~~
I can't **do without** coffee. NOT ~~do coffee without~~

With three words (non-separable):
We've **run out of** sugar. NOT ~~run sugar out of~~
I **look forward to** Fridays. NOT ~~look forward Fridays to~~

Go to Grammar practice: phrasal verbs, page 117

**6 A** ▶ 3.14 **Pronunciation:** linking in phrasal verbs Listen to the sentences. Notice how the words in the phrasal verbs link together.

1 Ben and Julia have broken‿up.
2 We've run‿out‿of juice.
3 Adam's taken‿up yoga!
4 He grew‿up in the United States.
5 Did you hear about the game? They called‿it‿off.
6 There's no more shampoo. Sue used‿it‿up.

**B** ▶ 3.14 Listen again and repeat.

**7 A** Choose the correct option to complete the sentences. In two of the sentences, both options are correct.

1 I *take after my father / take my father after*. We're both cheerful.
2 Please *turn the lights off / turn off the lights* when you leave.
3 We have to *get off the bus / get the bus off* at the next stop.
4 Those jeans are great. Do you want to *try them on / try on them*?
5 Are you *looking forward the party to / looking forward to the party*?
6 I'm going to *throw out my old coat / throw my old coat out*.
7 I won't *put up your behavior with / put up with your behavior* any longer!
8 You've dropped some trash. *Pick it up / Pick up it*!

**B** ▶ 3.15 Listen and repeat the sentences in exercise 7A. Pay attention to how the words in the phrasal verbs link together.

Go to Communication practice: Student A page 159, Student B page 165

**8 A** Complete the questionnaire with the best answers for you.

When you go on **vacation,** do you usually …

1 a ☐ look forward to going away?
   b ☐ look forward to getting back?
2 a ☐ look up information before you go?
   b ☐ figure it out when you get there?
3 a ☐ come up with a plan for each day?
   b ☐ figure it out when you're there?
4 a ☐ go back to work the day after you get home?
   b ☐ show up at work after a few days' rest?
5 a ☐ get up early every day?
   b ☐ wake up late and relax?
6 a ☐ eat out once or twice?
   b ☐ go back to the same restaurant every day?
7 a ☐ get around by car?
   b ☐ do without a car and use public transportation?
8 a ☐ talk your friends into doing what you want to do?
   b ☐ put up with doing things you don't want to do?

**B** In pairs, discuss and explain your answers.

**Personal Best** Write a paragraph about a friend. Use five phrasal verbs.

# 3 SKILLS WRITING — writing a persuasive article ■ contrasting expectations with reality

## 3D A fantastic place to live

1  Look at the pictures below. What do you know about the city of Reykjavik, in Iceland?

2  Read the article. In your opinion, does the author make Reykjavik sound like a good place to live?

**Why not move to …**
# REYKJAVIK?

I've been living in Reykjavik for several months now, and I can highly recommend it as a fantastic place to move to. One of my favorite things is the beautiful nature surrounding it and the clean and healthy life you can live here.

Because Reykjavik is the capital of Iceland, you might think it is a bit dirty and polluted like many other capital cities. However, it is, without doubt, one of the cleanest places you will ever visit. One of the most popular activities here is swimming or bathing in spas. In addition to the many heated swimming pools in Reykjavik, just outside the city is the "Blue Lagoon," a geothermal spa in the most incredible surroundings. Overlooking the city is Mount Esja, where locals go hiking among the beautiful mountain flowers and breathe in the fresh air. In just a few hours you can go skiing, caving, snorkeling, or even whale-watching. And because the air is so clean, you get some simply stunning views of the star-filled sky. Of course, the sky is even more spectacular when you can see the Aurora, a natural light display that can be seen this far north. This magical sight is something you just have to see at least once in your life.

With only 200,000 inhabitants, initially you get the impression that Reykjavik is a quiet city in a beautiful location, but, actually, there are a lot of really cool things going on. For music lovers, there are great venues like Paloma and Hurra where you can see some of Iceland's best bands perform. And we now have a world-class music festival in the city called Sónar, when some of the biggest names in dance music come and play. The nightlife in Reykjavik is not to be missed, with many of the nightclubs staying open till 4 a.m. on the weekends! There are also museums, including a fantastic modern art museum, concert halls, and theaters. And being fairly small, it's a great city to walk or bike around.

Another thing that makes Reykjavik a great place to live is the excellent food. At first glance, the city may seem to be all about fish (and the fish here is great, you have to try the salmon!), but, in fact, there are also plenty of places serving more international food. The most famous is Baejarins Betzu, which has the most delicious hot dogs in the world. And then there is the ice cream. You might think Reykjavik is too cold for ice cream. However, Icelanders can never get enough! You often see long lines of people waiting in the rain or snow to buy their favorite ice cream from Valdis, the best parlor in the city.

If you ask me, Reykjavik is truly unique, with all of the advantages of a city, like interesting cultural activities, delicious food, and a lively nightlife, but also the most beautiful countryside in the world. Come join me here. You won't regret it!

3  Read the article again and complete the notes in the chart about reasons for moving to Reykjavik.

| Reason | Facts and examples |
| --- | --- |
| *Healthy living* | *Clean air, hiking, bathing in spas…* |
|  |  |
|  |  |

writing a persuasive article ■ contrasting expectations with reality  **WRITING**  **SKILLS** **3D**

**4** Look at this sentence from the article. Why do you think the writer uses exaggerated language like this?
This _magical_ sight is something you just _have to see_ _at least once in your life_.

### Skill  writing a persuasive article

When you write a persuasive article, state your opinion about a subject and try to convince the reader to agree with you.
- Clearly state your point of view on the topic.
- Give reasons for your opinion, and support them with facts and examples.
- Use persuasive language to convince your reader, e.g., _fascinating_, _without a doubt_, etc.

**5** Read the Skill box. Choose the correct option to complete the sentences below. Check your answers in the article.
1 I can highly recommend it as _an interesting / a fantastic_ place to move to.
2 It is _without doubt / definitely_ one of the cleanest places you will ever visit.
3 You get some _simply stunning / pretty_ views of the star-filled sky.
4 And we now have a _very good / world-class_ music festival in the city, called Sónar ...
5 The nightlife in Reykjavik is _not to be missed / a lot of fun_.
6 The most famous is Baejarins Betzu which has _tasty / the most delicious_ hot dogs in the world.

**6** Complete the sentences with the words in the box. Then check your answers in the article.

| initially   first glance   might think   but, in fact   however   actually |

1 Because Reykjavik is the capital of Iceland, you _____ it is a bit dirty and polluted like many other capital cities. _____ , it is, without doubt, one of the cleanest places you will ever visit.
2 With only 200,000 inhabitants, _____ you get the impression that Reykjavik is a quiet city in a beautiful location, but, _____ , there are a lot of really cool things going on.
3 At _____ , the city may seem to be all about fish ... _____ , there are also plenty of places serving more international food.

### Text builder  contrasting expectations with reality

We use the following expressions to contrast expectations and first impressions with the reality of a situation:
... **initially you get the impression that** Reykjavik is a quiet city in a beautiful location, **but, actually,** there are a lot of really cool things going on.
**At first glance,** the city may seem to be all about fish, **but, in fact,** there are also plenty of places serving more international food.
**You might think** Reykjavik is too cold for ice cream. **However,** Icelanders can never get enough!

**7** Read the Text builder. Match the two parts to make complete sentences.
1 Initially you get the impression it's a busy place,
2 You might think it's too cold for a vacation destination.
3 At first glance, it seems a bit expensive,

a However, you can enjoy the various spas and hot springs most times of the year.
b but, actually, there are many budget hotels available.
c but, in fact, there are some lovely quiet back streets.

**8** **A** PREPARE  Think about a city you know well. Make a list of reasons why you think people should move there and make notes with examples and facts to support the reasons.
**B** PRACTICE  Using your notes, write an article encouraging someone to move to the city. Use persuasive language and include some expressions for contrasting expectations with reality.
**C** PERSONAL BEST  Exchange your article with a partner. Is the article persuasive? Why/Why not?

Personal Best  Write a paragraph explaining why you would/wouldn't want to live in Reykjavik.  29

# UNIT 4

# Mind and behavior

**LANGUAGE** subject-verb agreement ■ personality and behavior

## 4A It really annoys me …

**1 A** What do the words in **bold** mean in the questions below? Discuss them in pairs.

1 When you're out on the street, what kind of behavior really **gets on your nerves**?
2 What kind of behavior do you think is **unreasonable** from neighbors?
3 Do you assume that strangers are kind, or that they are **mean** and will **take advantage of** you?

**B** In pairs, answer the questions in exercise 1A and compare your opinions.

Go to Vocabulary practice: personality and behavior, page 141

**2** Read the blog post and answer the questions.

1 What three things does Jana get annoyed by in New York?
2 Is she still annoyed by these things in Tokyo? Why/Why not?
3 Do these three things annoy you? Why/Why not?

## Pet peeves

*Most of you reading this blog know that I moved from New York to Tokyo a few months ago. I usually post (or boast) about learning Japanese and discovering Japanese food, but today I want to tell you about something I never expected would happen: all my usual pet peeves have disappeared!*

So, for instance, "subway behavior" drives me absolutely crazy at home in New York, but do you know what happens here in Tokyo? Everyone waits patiently as the train arrives and then moves to the center of the car. Even when the train is very crowded, no one blocks the door. People are so thoughtful.

Another pet peeve I no longer have is bad-tempered salespeople. In pretty much every store I've been to here, the staff has always been polite and charming. Plus, anything you buy as a gift is beautifully wrapped: all the salespeople must have taken courses in gift-wrapping and are so enthusiastic about it.

Pet peeve number three is noise. At home, people are so noisy, but many of the neighborhoods in Tokyo are surprisingly quiet. That's because commercial activity is concentrated near the train station, and because people really value peace and quiet.

Of course, no place is perfect, and eventually I'll probably develop some new pet peeves. But if you hate noise and rude behavior, my advice to you is … come join me in Tokyo!

**3** Does a singular or plural verb form follow these words? Read the text again and check.

1 most of you _____
2 everyone _____
3 people _____
4 staff _____
5 anything _____
6 advice _____

subject-verb agreement ■ personality and behavior    LANGUAGE   4A

**4** ▶ 4.3  Listen to two friends from New York talking about Jana's blog post. What two pet peeves do they have?

**5** ▶ 4.4  Complete the sentences. Listen and check your answers. Then read the Grammar box.

In New York …
1 even the hairdresser is someone who _____ a tip for the holidays.
2 everyone in my building _____ to tip the postal worker.
3 more and more people _____ taxi apps these days.
4 have you ever been about to get into a taxi when a group of people _____ in front of you?
5 I can't believe anyone _____ that's OK!

### Grammar: subject-verb agreement

**Countable and uncountable nouns:**
A lot of **news articles are** depressing.
Some of my friends' **advice isn't** very helpful.

**Indefinite pronouns:**
**One** of them **is** a doctor.
**Everyone needs** help from other people.

**Collective nouns:**
That new import-export **company is** hiring workers.

**Asides:**
Many **people**, including myself, **don't save** enough money.

Go to Grammar practice: subject-verb agreement, page 118

**6 A** ▶ 4.6  **Pronunciation:** *of* Listen to the conversations. When is *of* pronounced /əv/? When is it pronounced /ə/?

1 A Some **of** the trains here are incredibly crowded.
  B Yes, a lot **of** them are so bad I sometimes have to let two or three go by!
2 A Most **of** us have many pet peeves, don't you think?
  B Yes, I think so. Maybe one person out **of** a thousand people isn't annoyed by anything!

**B** ▶ 4.6  Listen again and repeat. Practice the conversations in pairs.

**7 A** Read the newspaper story about a pet peeve. Choose the correct answers.

## Problem solved

In a small town in the UK, some families ¹*has / have* found a unique solution to their pet peeve. Everyone in the town ²*agree / agrees* that the speed of vehicles in residential areas ³*are / is* a danger, and what has made people so angry is that few drivers ⁴*pay / pays* any attention to the speed limit. Now, even children as young as ten ⁵*have / has* joined a unique speeding awareness campaign. People ⁶*have / has* been dressing in fluorescent jackets, and each of them ⁷*point / points* a hairdryer at the cars as they go by. This is a deterrent to drivers as the hairdryers look like police radar guns. The police ⁸*like / likes* the idea, but their advice to families ⁹*are / is* to be careful when standing by the side of the road. However, the local community still ¹⁰*feel / feels* that the solution to the problem is to install more speed cameras in built-up areas.

**B** ▶ 4.7  Listen and check. Then, in pairs, discuss possible solutions to one of your pet peeves.

Go to Communication practice: Student A page 159, Student B page 165

**8** Complete the sentences. Then discuss your ideas in pairs. Does your partner feel the same way?

1 It drives me crazy when people …
2 What makes me really annoyed is when someone …
3 I can't believe anyone thinks it's OK when …
4 In my family, my …, as well as my …, are always …
5 It used to get on my nerves when everyone at school …
6 I don't think it's OK that the government …

Personal Best  Write a paragraph about one of your ideas in exercise 8.

31

# 4 SKILLS READING identifying attitude ■ conditionals for advice and suggestions

## 4B How to get along

**1** Look at the title of the text on page 33. In pairs, make some suggestions for having good relationships with other people.

**2** Read the text and choose the correct answer from a–d.

All of the writers …
a tell their own story about friendship.
b make suggestions for readers.
c advise readers to listen and offer help.
d say how difficult it is to get along with people.

### Skill  identifying attitude

When reading a text, try to figure out the writer's attitude towards the topic. Attitude is not always explicitly stated, so try to understand the details of the text first, and then consider how the writer feels about the topic in general.
- Look for language that expresses opinions and feelings, which is often more explicitly stated than attitude.
- If there are questions with the text, look for key words in the questions and find synonyms for these in the text. Then read that part of the text in detail.

**3  A** Read the Skill box. Then match questions a–f below with paragraphs 1–5. There is one question that you don't need.

Which person:
a believes in seeing things from other people's perspectives? _____
b feels we need to avoid offending people? _____
c feels people don't take friendship seriously enough? _____
d thinks everyone appreciates a little assistance from time to time? _____
e recommends paying close attention to what people are saying? _____
f likes finding things in common with others? _____

**B** Underline the parts of each paragraph that helped you choose your answers in exercise 3A.

**4** Complete the sentences with the correct form of the verbs in parentheses. Scan the text and check.
1 If you really listen, you _____ (find) it makes a big difference.
2 If you _____ (want) to get along with people, remember that …
3 If I were you, I _____ (offer) help whenever I can.
4 If you both like similar music, _____ (share) playlists.
5 If people _____ (want) to hear a good joke, they'd go to a comedy club.

### Text builder  conditionals for advice and suggestions

**Zero conditional:**
If you're both sports fans, this is a great way to connect.

**First conditional:**
People will recall a conversation as being more interesting if you ask questions.

**Second conditional:**
If you wanted to ruin a friendship, an ill-advised comment would be the perfect way to go about it.

**5** Read the Text builder. Which types of conditional are the sentences in exercise 4?

**6** Discuss the questions in pairs.
1 Which writers in the text do you have a similar attitude to?
2 In your opinion, which writer makes the most important point?
3 Do you disagree with anything that the writers say? Why?

identifying attitude ■ conditionals for advice and suggestions    READING    SKILLS    4B

# Friends and colleagues:
## essential tips for getting along

**1 Martin**

Sometimes we come up against problems that we can't work out on our own. Well, "A problem shared is a problem halved," as some of my British friends like to say. So whether I'm with a new acquaintance or an old friend, I always take the opportunity to give the person a hand if I can. The best kind of help is a favor you do for someone with no expectation of a favor in return. Doing people favors not only gives you a warm feeling inside, but it also sends the message that you can be trusted because you have that person's welfare in mind. If I were you, I'd offer help whenever I can because, as we say, "One good turn deserves another." You never know, your generosity may be repaid one day when you most need help from someone else. After all, "No man is an island."

The other day, I was in a face-to-face meeting with a colleague, and she'd sent three texts before I could even finish what I was saying. It drives me crazy when people don't listen, especially when they don't even look you in the eye. I was brought up to listen to people in order to understand them, not just in order to reply to them. If you really listen, you'll find it makes a big difference in understanding what motivates them, what worries them, and what they're enthusiastic about. You just have to ignore everyone around you, ignore your phone, and ignore that voice in your head that's thinking about how to respond. In no time, you'll find yourself connecting with people significantly better than before.

**2 Magda**

**3 Nandeep**

Are you familiar with the expression "six degrees of separation"? It's the theory that every person on the planet is connected to everyone else by a chain of no more than five personal connections. I'm not sure it's completely true, but there's definitely an element of truth in it. So when you meet someone new, find out about the person: ask where he/she is from, where he/she went to school, and where he/she works. You may well find that you have a mutual friend. Try comparing interests, too – if you're both sports fans, this is a great way to connect. I'm into bike riding, and I often connect with others using a cycling app called Strava. Similarly, if you both like similar music, share playlists via Spotify. For business contacts, why not send a message or share an article on LinkedIn? We live in a connected world, and you just have to find the connections.

Do you ever find yourself having a conversation, hearing someone say something pretty shocking, and wondering why on earth the person just said that? I do, and when it happens, I try to keep in mind where he or she is coming from. I'll ask myself something like, "Why does the person feel that way? Why is he or she saying that?" Obviously, you're allowed your own opinion, and you're not obliged to agree with everything someone says, but don't argue for the sake of it – that just causes friction. Try not to criticize or prove the other person wrong. Everyone is different, and if you want to get along with people, remember that someone else's experience isn't necessarily the same as yours. Try putting yourself in the other person's shoes.

**4 Pascale**

**5 Kazuo**

Having a laugh is essential, and I find humor is a great way to break the ice, ease tension, and get along with people. You can't force humor, though – in other words, you can't just switch on your funny side. Otherwise it might come out as awkward, and you could risk upsetting people, which you have to be very careful about. Humor is best when it comes from a laid-back and spontaneous place. I'd also be careful about what or who you make fun of because so much humor is based on being unkind to others. If you wanted to ruin a friendship, an ill-considered comment (humorous or not!) would be the perfect way to go about it. The safest way to enjoy humor is to make fun of yourself. And I don't recommend telling jokes: jokes are not the same as a sense of humor, and it's very hard to tell them well. If people wanted to hear a good joke, they'd go to a comedy club.

**Personal Best**  Write another piece of advice about how you can connect better with friends and colleagues.

33

# 4 LANGUAGE  perfect and past forms ■ word families

## 4C I see you've been busy!

**1** In pairs, choose the correct option to complete the sentences. Then discuss the questions.

1 Do you consider yourself a *create / creative / creativity* person?
2 Describe three jobs that require a lot of *create / creative / creativity*. Would you like to do any of these jobs?
3 What would you prefer to *create / creative / creativity*: a painting or a hit song? Why?

**Go to Vocabulary practice:** word families, page 142

**2 A** Read the text. What is *procrastination*, and why can it sometimes be a good thing?

### Procrastination and Creativity – the new link

Friends who know me well can always tell when I'm working to a deadline on an article or essay. Is it because I don't answer my phone, or because they never see me out and about? No. It's because my house is always impeccably neat, my nails beautifully painted, and my desk perfectly organized. "I see you've been doing the housework. When's the article due?" they say, or, "Wow, you've put all your books in alphabetical order. When do you have to hand the essay in?"

Yes, I'm a procrastinator, and I'm not alone. Many of us feel extremely guilty for putting off important tasks, but recent research has shown that procrastination is, in fact, fantastic for creativity.

Psychologist Adam Grant became interested in this area a few years ago when he found out that one of his most creative students, Jihae Shin, was a chronic procrastinator. Grant and Shin have been studying the link between procrastination and creativity ever since, and they've conducted a great deal of research. In one study, they asked a group of people to submit new business ideas. The people who played games like Minesweeper or Solitaire for five minutes before thinking about the task had the most creative ideas.

Professor Grant explains that procrastination lets the mind wander, and the ideas we have after procrastinating are more creative and innovative than the more conventional ideas we have when we start a task right away. He also claims that some of the greatest achievements of human history are examples of procrastination. For example, it took Leonardo Da Vinci 16 years to complete the Mona Lisa because he kept getting distracted by other things.

So, the next time you have an essay due or a deadline at work, spend five minutes doing something completely unrelated. The creative ideas you have afterwards may change the world!

**B** Read the text again. Answer the questions in pairs.
1 Which important tasks does the writer always leave to the last minute?
2 What activities does she do to put off completing these tasks?
3 How do the researchers explain the link between procrastination and creativity?
4 How long does the writer suggest we procrastinate for?

**3 A** Look at the pictures and sentences a and b below. Then answer the questions.

a  I see you**'ve been doing** the housework.
b  I see you**'ve done** the housework. It's so neat!

1 Which sentence emphasizes the result of a completed action?
2 Which sentence emphasizes the action (which may or may not be completed)?

**B** Read the text again and find four more present perfect or present perfect continuous sentences. What does each sentence emphasize, the action or the result? Then read the Grammar box.

perfect and past forms ■ word families          LANGUAGE   **4C**

### Grammar    perfect and past forms

**Present perfect:**
I'**ve finished** my homework. Let's have dinner.
She'**s** always **been** extremely creative.

**Present perfect vs. simple past:**
I'**ve bought** a new laptop.
I **bought** a new laptop yesterday.

**Present perfect continuous:**
I'**ve been studying** all morning.
How long **have** you **been waiting**?

**Present perfect vs. present perfect continuous:**
He'**s** already **cleaned** the house, and it looks great!
He'**s been cleaning** the house, so he's tired now.

Go to Grammar practice: perfect and past forms, page 119

**4 A** ▶ 4.10 **Pronunciation:** sentence stress in perfect forms Listen to sentences 1–4. Which of the words in the underlined phrases are stressed?
1 They have been doing an important research project.
2 Has he finished his psychology essay yet?
3 How long have you been working at the university?
4 The doctor has gone to the hospital. He's had an emergency.

**B** ▶ 4.10   Listen again and repeat.

**5** ▶ 4.11   Choose the correct options to complete the texts. Listen and check.

**SALLY**

To be honest, I've always ¹*preferred / been preferring* to complete tasks as soon as I'm given them. I've never ²*liked / been liking* to wait until the last minute to do important things, especially at work. This morning, I've already ³*had / been having* a meeting with my boss, and he has ⁴*asked / been asking* me to prepare a sales presentation for next Monday. I've ⁵*prepared / been preparing* the presentation non-stop since the meeting. I would hate to wait until Sunday evening to start working on it. That would completely ruin my weekend!

**RYAN**

Personally, I've always ⁶*put off / been putting off* writing my college essays until just before the deadline. ⁷*I've done / I did* the same thing when I was in high school, and I still ⁸*managed / have managed* to get good grades every time. I think I'm one of those people who are most creative when they're under pressure. My final term paper's due next Wednesday, but I still haven't ⁹*been writing / written* anything. ¹⁰*I'm planning / I've been planning* it for the last two months, and I'm going to spend the next five days writing it, probably 24/7!

Go to Communication practice: Student A page 159, Student B page 165

**6** Discuss the questions in pairs.
1 Which important tasks have you had to do this month? Have you finished them?
2 Which life changes have you been considering recently? Have you made a decision about them? Or have you put them off?
3 What's the most creative thing you've done in the last year? Does procrastination make you more creative?
4 What have you been worrying about recently? Have you found ways to deal with stressful situations?

**Personal Best**   Write a paragraph about an experience when you procrastinated. Did it end well?

# 4 SKILLS  SPEAKING  responding to arguments ■ describing memorable experiences

## 4D Road rage

**1** Look at the pictures. Discuss the questions in pairs.

1 What do you think the expression "road rage" means?
2 Is this a problem where you live?

**2 A** Look at the sentences below from the video. Predict what you think will happen.

1 I was waiting at a traffic light. ... I didn't move immediately when the light turned green.
2 But then the woman behind me gets out of the car and ...

**B** ▶ 4.12 Watch or listen to the first part of *Talking Zone*. How did Abigail react to the woman's behavior?

a She got out of her car and started yelling.
b She didn't get out of her car and kept driving.

**3** ▶ 4.12 Watch or listen again. Fill in the blanks. Do Ben and Abigail seem to agree with each other?

| | |
|---|---|
| **Abigail** | When you're ¹_____ , you're constantly under pressure. |
| **Ben** | It's true. I think there's ²_____ to it than ³_____ , though. ... If you think of your car as an ⁴_____ of your personality, you're more likely to lose your ⁵_____ on the road. |
| **Abigail** | I'm not sure I ⁶_____ . |
| **Ben** | If you see your car as part of ⁷_____ , anything that puts your car at ⁸_____ is like a ⁹_____ to you, personally. |
| **Abigail** | That may be ¹⁰_____ to a certain extent, but a lot of people ... can lose ¹¹_____ of their ¹²_____ when they get behind the ¹³_____ . |
| **Ben** | Yeah but why? |
| **Abigail** | Perhaps it's because they try so hard to ¹⁴_____ their ¹⁵_____ in their day-to-day ¹⁶_____ . |
| **Ben** | No, sorry, I don't get that. |

responding to arguments ■ describing memorable experiences    **SPEAKING**    SKILLS    **4D**

### Conversation builder | responding to arguments

**Agreeing:**
*That makes a lot of sense.*
*I hadn't thought of that.*

**Disagreeing politely:**
*I think there's more to it than that, though.*
*That may be true to a certain extent, but …*

**Asking for clarification:**
*Sorry, I don't get that.*
*I'm not sure I follow.*

**4** Read the Conversation builder. In pairs, look at exercise 3 again. What language do Ben and Abigail use to agree or disagree politely? Look at the Conversation builder.

**5 A** Make notes to explain road rage, using arguments from exercise 3 or your own. Then, in pairs, practice a similar conversation to Abigail and Ben's. Start like this:

**A** *Can you believe how many angry drivers there are?*
**B** *Maybe it's because …*

**B** How many expressions from the Conversation builder did you use? Did you reach an agreement?

**6**  4.13 Watch or listen to the second part of the show and answer the questions.

1 Where did Abigail meet the angry driver from Part 1 again?
2 How did Abigail feel when she met her?

### Skill | describing memorable experiences

When we describe a memorable experience, we use various strategies to maintain the listener's interest:
* creating suspense: *You're not going to believe / You'll never guess what happened today!*
* describing your reaction: *I couldn't believe my eyes!*

When we respond, we can show interest by:
* guessing how the story will continue: *Let me guess – …?*
* showing surprise: *No way!*
* showing empathy: *That must have been so awkward./I bet it was really uncomfortable.*

**7 A** Read the Skill box. What information (a–g) is prompted by the comments or questions in 1–7?

1 You're not going to believe what happened today.    _d_
2 You'll never guess who was there!    ____
3 No way! Did she recognize you?    ____
4 That must have been so awkward.    ____
5 Let me guess – road rage?    ____
6 I bet it was really uncomfortable.    ____
7 Are you serious? Was she angry?    ____

a Tell me about it! And what was the first topic of the lesson?
b No, she apologized.
c Exactly. He showed us a video …
d You know I started that short course on safe driving this morning?
e As soon as she saw me. I couldn't believe my eyes!
f Our friend – you know, the angry driver!
g It was. And she came up to me at the end of the lesson.

**B** 4.13 Watch or listen again and check. Then in pairs, answer the questions.
1 Who says each sentence (1–7) in exercise 7A, Abigail or Ben?
2 Did you feel more sympathetic towards the driver in the end?

**8** Practice Abigail and Ben's conversation from memory, using the sentences in exercise 7A to help you.

**Go to Communication practice:** Student A page 160, Student B page 166

**9 A** **PREPARE** Make notes about a real or imagined road-rage incident. Create suspense and describe your emotions. Prepare to tell your partner about it.

**B** **PRACTICE** Take turns practicing your conversations. Be sure to make your experience sound memorable.

**C** **PERSONAL BEST** Practice your conversation again. Did you change any details or use any new expressions?

**Personal Best** | Describe another memorable experience as if you were telling it to someone.

# 3 and 4 REVIEW and PRACTICE

## Grammar

**1** Choose the correct options to complete the sentences.

1 _____ leave now if you want to catch the bus.
   a You're supposed to
   b You're allowed to
   c You'd better

2 Be quiet! You _____ to talk in the library.
   a aren't allowed to
   b don't have to
   c are supposed to

3 Marta takes _____ her mother – they both have blue eyes.
   a up
   b after
   c on

4 I'm not going to put _____ his behavior any longer.
   a on with
   b up with
   c down with

5 One of my sisters _____ tennis really well.
   a play
   b are playing
   c plays

6 A lot of my friends, including Alberto, _____ for work at the moment.
   a is looking
   b are looking
   c look

7 I _____ in this house for 12 years.
   a have been living
   b live
   c am living

8 Sarah _____ her exams yet – she still has two left.
   a has finished
   b hasn't been finishing
   c hasn't finished

**2** Choose the correct options to complete the sentences.

1 People that work *are allowed / have to* pay tax. If not, they *have to / they'd better* pay a fine.

2 All the classrooms, apart from this one, *is / are* already taken this afternoon.

3 Why didn't you answer your phone earlier? *I'm trying / I've been trying* to contact you all morning!

4 There are two groups of 12 students in my class. My group *want / wants* to watch the video now.

5 I think these shoes will look good on you. Why don't you try *them on / on them*?

6 You *should / have to* go to bed early tonight so you're ready for the exam tomorrow. That's my advice.

7 Oh no! I think we're going to *run out / run out of* gas!

8 I *have been looking / looked* for a job since I graduated.

**3** Choose the correct options to complete the text.

I've ¹*done / been doing* a lot of traveling in my life and I've ²*learned / been learning* you ³*have to / are supposed to* be careful not to do the wrong thing when you're in a foreign country. My biggest mistake happened when I was teaching English in South Korea and I wrote some of the students' names in red ink. The whole class ⁴*was / were* very shocked because ⁵*you don't have to / you're not supposed to* do that. Years later, I spent a few months in a small village in the Philippines. I was surprised to discover that all the children in the village, including my daughter, ⁶*was / were* expected to bow to older people when they saw them. The funniest mistake I've ⁷*made / been making* in my life is to finish all the food on my plate at dinner parties, thinking I was being polite. For years, I couldn't ⁸*figure out / figure it out* why the host always gave me more food but not other people. Apparently, in many countries you ⁹*can't / shouldn't* finish everything on your plate because it means you're still hungry! But it's impossible to know all these cultural differences if nobody tells you. My advice is that you ¹⁰*ought / ought to* ask a local friend if there are any rules or customs you need to know about.

## Vocabulary

**1** Circle the word or expression that is different. Explain why.

1 harbor   traffic congestion   taxi stand   city hall
2 mean   stubborn   charming   unreasonable
3 persuasion   reliability   achievement   critical
4 business district   high-rise building   city hall   courthouse
5 creative   persuade   reliable   risky
6 drive someone crazy   get on someone's nerves   praise someone   upset someone

38

REVIEW and PRACTICE 3 and 4

**2** Match the words in the box with definitions 1–10.

> poverty  pretend  persuasive  achievement
> vandalism  claim  sensitive  sensible
> considerate  stubborn

1  having good judgment _____
2  a result gained by effort _____
3  the state of being very poor _____
4  say that something is true _____
5  not being prepared to change your mind _____
6  easily upset by things _____
7  causing damage to something on purpose _____
8  act as if something is true when it isn't _____
9  careful not to harm others _____
10  able to make other people do what you want _____

**3** Choose the correct options to complete the sentences.

1  I couldn't go to the party, but I really didn't *mind / matter*. I was tired anyway.
2  The main problem in my town is *overcrowding / smog*. There just aren't enough houses!
3  Did you break that glass? You're so *silly / clumsy*!
4  We work as a team, but he always takes *credit for / advantage of* the final piece of work.
5  I know she gets on your nerves, but you have to take into *consideration / considerate* that she's had a really difficult year.
6  It isn't *sure / safe* to ride a motorbike without a helmet.
7  Remember you shouldn't drive too fast in *a residential / an industrial* area because there are often children around.
8  If you want to *success / succeed*, you need to start working harder.

**4** Complete the text with the words in the box.

> bad-tempered  nerves  drive  stand  realize
> silly  matter  argue  annoyed  thoughtful

It's taken me a long time to ¹_____ it, but my best friend is my younger brother! When we were younger I couldn't ²_____ spending time with him. I would get so ³_____ because he was always doing stupid things and getting on my ⁴_____ . I suppose I was a pretty ⁵_____ child. We still ⁶_____ , but it doesn't ⁷_____ so much these days. Yes, he can be ⁸_____ , like when he dances around the kitchen, but he is also very ⁹_____ . He bought me flowers yesterday because I was upset about my job. So that's why, even though we ¹⁰_____ each other crazy sometimes, my brother is my best friend. Just don't tell him!

# Personal Best

**Lesson 3A** Give two rules and two pieces of advice for a new student in your class.

**Lesson 4A** Write three sentences that begin with a countable noun, an uncountable noun, and a collective noun.

**Lesson 3A** Write about four personal obligations you have for the next month.

**Lesson 4A** Describe one person you like and one person you don't like.

**Lesson 3A** Describe the three biggest problems that affect a city you know well.

**Lesson 4B** Make three suggestions to someone new to your town using zero, first and second conditionals.

**Lesson 3B** Name three pairs of words that are easily confused and explain their different meanings.

**Lesson 4C** Describe one thing you have done this year and one thing you have been doing recently.

**Lesson 3C** Write four things about what you usually do on vacation using phrasal verbs.

**Lesson 4C** Name three adjectives from Lesson 4C and then name their verbs and nouns.

**Lesson 3D** Describe a time when something was different to what you expected.

**Lesson 4D** Write two sentences that create suspense about a memorable event.

# UNIT 5

# Our planet

**LANGUAGE** *so and such; so much/many, so little/few* ■ the environment

## 5A Going green

**1** What can you do to help the environment? Make sentences using the prompts below.

drink cans   plastic bags   energy-efficient light bulbs   computers   eco-products

1 Turn off …   2 Stop using …   3 Switch to …   4 Recycle …   5 Use more …

**2** Read Ida's first blog post. What is the *No Impact Experiment*? Would you like to try it?

**Eco watch**   Home | News | Forum | Contact us

**Site of the month:** noimpactproject.org

Climate change is real, and we must act now. This is why the No Impact Experiment is such a great initiative. Basically, it is a one-month "carbon detox" that will help you become more environmentally friendly and live a greener life. You can make simple changes like switching to energy-efficient light bulbs or turning off your faucet when you brush your teeth. I'm actually going to give the experiment a try. Stay tuned for my next post. [posted by Ida]

**Go to Vocabulary practice:** the environment, page 142

**3** Read Ida's second blog post. How far is she into her *No Impact Experiment*?

a She's just started it.   b She's halfway through it.   c She's completed it.

### As promised, this is a summary of my experience so far:

**1** I haven't switched to solar energy (not yet, anyway), but I've replaced all my light bulbs. I've heard that LED bulbs, for example, can reduce energy consumption by up to 90% and last around 100,000 hours, so you end up saving a lot of money in the long run. [1]_____

**2** I've stopped using plastic bags, which I'd actually thought about doing even before the experiment. They litter our cities, pollute our waterways, and kill wildlife. Sea turtles have been confusing jellyfish with plastic bags and choking as a result. [2]_____ There's only one problem: I keep forgetting to take my reusable bag to the supermarket!

**3** I've been walking to work these past two weeks. I know I'm saving money on gas and burning fewer fossil fuels, but, honestly, I hate leaving my car at home. Before, it only took me ten minutes to get to work, but now it takes me an hour. [3]_____

So far the *No Impact Experiment* has been harder than I thought, but I'm looking forward to the next two weeks. Maybe a greener lifestyle takes a little getting used to!

**4** Fill in blanks 1–3 in the text in exercise 3 with a–e below. There are two extra sentences.

a It feels like such a waste of time!
b These are such important decisions.
c I just wish they weren't so expensive – and so bright!
d It's a shame there's so little time left.
e There have been so many shocking deaths you'll never use one again!

**5** Read sentences a–e in exercise 4 again. Complete the rules with *so* or *such*. Then read the Grammar box.

1 Use _____ before nouns or adjectives followed by nouns.
2 Use _____ before adjectives.
3 Use _____ before quantifiers: *little*, *much*, *few*, and *many*.

40

*so* and *such*; *so much/many*, *so little/few* ■ the environment    **LANGUAGE**   **5A**

 **Grammar**    *so* and *such*; *so much/many*, *so little/few*

*So* is followed by an adjective, *so many/few* by countable nouns, and *so much/little* by uncountable nouns:
Living green was **so** <u>easy</u>!
**So many** <u>resources</u> are being wasted, and there are **so few** <u>people</u> to help.
There's **so much** <u>work</u> to do and **so little** <u>time</u>.
*Such a/an* is followed by singular countable nouns, and *such* by plural countable nouns and uncountable nouns:
My diet was **such a** <u>challenge</u>.
I found **such** useful <u>ideas</u> online.
This is **such** important <u>information</u>!
*So* and *such* are often used in sentences that express cause and effect:
He made **so many** changes to his lifestyle **(that)** people couldn't recognize him.

Go to Grammar practice: *so* and *such*; *so much/many*, *so little/few*, page 120

**6**  **A**  ▶ 5.4   **Pronunciation:** sentence stress with *so* and *such* Listen to the comments on the *No Impact Experiment*. Circle the stressed word in each underlined phrase.

1 This is <u>such a great idea</u>.
2 This is <u>such a waste of time</u>.
3 There's still <u>so much to be done</u>.
4 It's a <u>such a shame</u> that <u>so few people</u> take this seriously.

**B** ▶ 5.4   Listen and repeat. Then, in pairs, choose a sentence each and mention an environmental issue it applies to.

**7**  **A**  Read the text and choose the correct options.

Home | Articles | Blog | Log in

### What I learned from a 30-day social media "detox"
*By John Seymour*

Social media has been a massive part of my life for ¹*so / such* long that I can't remember when I became ²*so / such* a heavy user. Last month, though, I decided it was time to simplify my life, so I implemented a month-long detox, which was good for me and for the planet as well, since I used less electricity. Looking back, it was ³*such / such a* valuable experience. Now I realize that I was spending ⁴*so much / so many* time on social media that I no longer knew what real life was. Here are other insights I've had. …

**B** Read the rest of John's experience. Put *so* or *such* in the correct places and join the sentences together.

1 Social media was a big part of my life. I didn't know what to do with my time.
   *Social media was such a big part of my life (that) I didn't know what to do with my time.*
2 I had very few "offline" hobbies. I had to learn how to have fun again.
3 I have many online connections. I don't know who they all are any longer.
4 I spent many hours online. My electricity bill was huge.
5 I spent a long time online. I stopped working out.
6 Doing a 30-day detox was good advice. I think I might extend it to 60 days.

Go to Communication practice: Both students, page 171

**8** In pairs, predict how your life would change if you took part in the *No Impact Experiment*. Use *so* and *such*.

If I started biking everywhere, …
If I stopped using my washing machine, …
If I turned off my air conditioning/central heating, …
If I grew my own food, …
If I carried my own cup wherever I went, …
If I stopped using household cleaning products, …

*If I started biking everywhere, I'd be in such great shape!*

**Personal Best**   Imagine you did the *No Impact Experiment*. Write a paragraph about your experience.

41

# 5 SKILLS
LISTENING  identifying cause and effect ■ linking consonants and vowels ■ moods

## 5B Weather effects

**1 A** In pairs, imagine you've experienced one of these extreme weather events. Describe what it was like.

*1 The snow was so high we couldn't open our door!*

**B** Complete the sentences with the adjectives in the box. There is one extra. Can you think of other words to describe how you might feel?

> desperate   exhausting   miserable   pessimistic

1 We've never had this much snow before! I'm feeling pretty _____ , stuck at home all day.

2 Third flood this year. I'm getting more and more _____ about climate change.

3 I heard on the news there's a fire coming our way. My family and I are _____ to escape.

Go to Vocabulary practice: moods, page 143

### Skill  identifying cause and effect

**When listening, we often need to understand why something happened (the cause) and what happened as a result (the effect). Pay careful attention to:**
- visual information that can help you understand what the speakers are saying.
- pronouns, so you don't get lost trying to understand what the speakers are referring to: *... it snowed the entire time.* **This** *(the fact that it snowed) resulted in our flights being canceled.*
- verbs that describe a result: *Weather always **impacts** mood.*

**2** ▶ 5.7  Read the Skill box. Then watch or listen to the first part of *Talking Zone*. Number the effects of extreme weather in the order Joel mentions them.

a ☐ People sometimes help one another when a disaster happens.
b ☐ Extreme weather can put people under a lot of stress.
c ☐ The population, as a whole, is feeling more concerned about climate change.

Joel

42

identifying cause and effect ■ linking consonants and vowels ■ moods  **LISTENING**  SKILLS  **5B**

**3** **A** ▶5.7  Watch or listen again. Fill in the blanks with the words the speakers use to describe cause and effect.
1 As these stories become increasingly common, it _____ all of us.
2 Extreme weather can be so devastating that it can _____ every aspect of our lives. This has huge _____ for our emotional well-being.
3 Severe weather events can be very traumatic. They can _____ to feelings of stress and anxiety.
4 In 2012, Hurricane Sandy _____ New York to shut down. It was so severe in some areas that people's homes were badly damaged.

**B** What do the underlined pronouns in sentences 1–4 refer to?

**4** Think about an extreme weather event. Discuss the questions in pairs.
1 Have you ever experienced extreme weather?
2 What caused it?
3 What happened as a result?
4 What can we do to prevent these events?

**5** ▶5.8  Watch or listen to the second part of the show. Are the sentences true (T) or false (F)?
1 In the U.S., some people avoid leaving the house during the winter months. _____
2 S.A.D. affects more people in winter. _____
3 Joel says people should get as much sunlight as possible. _____
4 Tasha agrees with Joel that people in warm climates are more optimistic. _____
5 Joel doesn't see a connection between weather and mental health. _____

**6** In pairs, discuss whether you think the weather can influence the character of the people that live in a particular country or city.

> **Listening builder** | **linking consonants and vowels**
>
> When a word ends in a consonant sound and the next word begins with a vowel sound, we often move the consonant sound to the beginning of the next word. It can be easier to understand the two words if you think of them as a single word.
> *In part one, we looked at how global warming is changing our moods. Weather affects our mood every single day.*

**7** **A** ▶5.9  Read the Listening builder. In pairs, guess the missing words in these sentences from the video. Listen and check.
1 My mood completely _____ the weather – just ask my friends! I get very grumpy _____ 's cold.
2 Study after study shows that people who _____ warm climates tend to be more motivated and optimistic, _____ turn makes them more _____ life.
3 So many scientific studies show that light _____ brain. There must be some _____ !
4 Movement _____ happy and energetic, and the _____ makes us grumpy and lethargic.

**B** ▶5.9  Mark the consonant-vowel links in the words you wrote in exercise 7A. Listen again and check. Then practice saying the sentences.

**8** In pairs, discuss the best kind of weather for these activities.

| play your favorite sport | visit your favorite vacation spot | do the housework |
| have a Netflix binge | go for a walk | do your homework |

**Personal Best**  Describe an experience where the weather has affected your mood.

43

## 5 LANGUAGE — future predictions ■ adjective prefixes

## 5C In the year 2100 …

**1 A** Read the headlines below. Complete the words in **bold** with one of the prefixes in the box.

dis-   in-   mis-   un-

1. COOLER SUMMERS ARE _____**LEADING** – CLIMATE CHANGE IS STILL A THREAT, SAYS EXPERT

2. New study finds that most global climate change policies are _____**effective**

3. Scientists warn there may be _____**expected** effects of climate change in future

4. NEW REPORT ACCUSES ENERGY INDUSTRY OF BEING _____**HONEST** ABOUT ITS ROLE IN CLIMATE CHANGE

**B** In pairs, discuss which headline worries you the most and explain why.

**Go to Vocabulary practice:** adjective prefixes, page 143

**2 A** Read the text. Which of the headlines in exercise 1A is the correct one?

Unless you've been avoiding the news for the past twenty years, you probably know that climate change is upon us and is going to continue to cause droughts and floods. And you know that glaciers are melting, sea levels are rising, and storms are definitely going to get more severe. But, get ready. There are other surprises coming our way by the year 2100.

### More lightning

Some scientists predict that by 2100 lightning strikes will have increased by as much as 50%, which is bad news for areas where wildfires are a threat. And it won't be much fun if you're a frequent flyer: flights are likely to be bumpier, too, with an increase in turbulence. This is because if it's warmer, the atmosphere has more water vapor. And this vapor makes lightning and turbulence more likely.

### Worse allergies

When temperatures are high, plants release more pollen. This means that the amount of pollen will continue to increase as the Earth warms. In fact, according to a recent study, pollen levels might more than double by 2040, so if you're allergic, you'll be experiencing even more severe symptoms. And if you don't normally have pollen allergies, you may develop them.

### Faster-growing trees

You may not be aware of this, but over the past five decades, trees in Europe have been growing faster – by up to 70%, in some cases. A number of researchers believe that higher levels of carbon dioxide and nitrogen in the atmosphere are to blame, so we'll probably be seeing trees that are even taller in the coming decades. Having said that, taller trees absorb more carbon dioxide, which might help slow down climate change.

**B** Which of the three predictions brings good news, too?

**3 A** ▶ 5.11  Listen to two friends who have read the text. Why is the woman worried?

**B** ▶ 5.11  Match the two parts to make complete sentences. Then listen again and check.

1. Thanks to climate change, people
2. This rise in temperature
3. At the present rate, by 2050 the world
4. We can't be really sure. I mean, we
5. But I bet your favorite candy bar

a. is going to make it too hot and dry for cocoa trees.
b. will definitely be more expensive than it is today.
c. will be eating less chocolate in the future.
d. will have run out of all its chocolate.
e. might still have chocolate.

future predictions ■ adjective prefixes    LANGUAGE **5C**

**4 A** Look at the sentences in exercise 3B again. Which sentences show …
a predictions based on evidence? ___ ___ ___
b a personal opinion (low certainty)? ___
c a personal opinion (high certainty)? ___
d a future action in progress? ___
e a completed future action? ___

**B** Find more examples of future forms in the text in exercise 2A. Then read the Grammar box.

### Grammar  future predictions

**Future with *will*, *going to*, *may*, and *might*:**
I think the planet **will** probably **be** very hot in 50 years.
We **won't be** better at preventing climate change unless we act now.
I'm positive we**'re going to be** in big trouble!
Things definitely **won't get** better. In fact, they **may/might** even **get** worse.

**Future perfect:**
By the end of the century, we **will have used up** all our resources.
**Won't we have developed** new ways to save energy by 2100?

**Future continuous:**
We**'ll be living** in a very hot climate.
We **won't be enjoying** life very much.

**Look!** We can use *going to* when we're more certain of our predictions:
I'm positive climate change **is going to be** worse in 50 years. (= very certain)
I think climate change **will be** worse in 50 years. (= not as certain)

Go to Grammar practice: future predictions, page 121

**5 A** ▶ 5.13 **Pronunciation:** *will have* Listen to the predictions. Is the vowel /ə/ or /æ/ in *have*? Which sound don't you hear at all?

By 2030 …
1 climate change will have gotten out of control.
2 robots will have learned how to manipulate us.
3 we will have made contact with aliens.
4 sales of electric vehicles won't have increased.

**B** ▶ 5.13 Listen again and repeat each sentence. Do you agree with each prediction?

**6 A** Read Bill Gates's predictions for the future and choose the most logical option for each one.
1 By 2030, two billion people who don't have a bank account today *won't be making / will be making* payments with their phones.
2 Millions of people have already lost their jobs to robots, and I'm absolutely convinced that more jobs *might be / are going to be* lost to automation.
3 In 2016, the world saw just 37 new cases of polio. Today, there are so few cases worldwide that by 2019, the disease *will have disappeared / will be disappearing* forever.

**B** Look again at the predictions in exercise 6A. How likely is each one? Discuss in groups.

Go to Communication practice: Both students, page 161

**7 A** Write questions based on the prompts. Use the future perfect or future continuous.

## Do you embrace or **resist change?**

A year from today will you …
1 live / same / house?
2 still / study or work / same place?
3 change / hairstyle?
4 switch / phone brands?
5 hang out / same people?
6 listen / same kind of music?
7 change / your diet?
8 take up / new hobby?

**B** Interview two classmates and use future forms in your responses.
A So, a year from today, will you be living in the same house?
B No, I don't think so. My neighborhood is getting too noisy, so maybe I'll start looking at other places.

**Personal Best** Write six predictions for your town/city.

45

## 5 SKILLS  WRITING — writing an opinion essay ■ formal linkers

### 5D Let me persuade you …

**1** Look at the advertisements. Which one do you like best? Why? Which one is more effective?

**2** In pairs, think of two reasons why climate change campaigns are not very effective. Then read the essay. Were your ideas mentioned?

### Are **global-warming** campaigns effective?

*Gloria López*

From 2015 to 2018, there were many climate change campaigns worldwide, and most people accept that global warming is real. However, they often don't change their behavior because they feel that experts may be exaggerating the problem and that rising temperatures are not an immediate threat. In general, environmental campaigns are not as effective as they could be, and we need to understand why.

One reason is the use of campaigns that use fear to motivate a person to change his or her behavior. For example, an environmental group might use images of environmental disasters so that people respond positively and take action. **Nevertheless**, they rarely do take action, since fear is an unpleasant emotion, and, **consequently**, people tend to ignore the things that make them afraid.

**Similarly**, the kinds of changes that people are asked to make are often too difficult. It is fairly easy, for instance, to recycle, take shorter showers, or use energy-efficient lightbulbs **as opposed to** more conventional ones. However, it is hard to give up meat, buy expensive organic food, or, in some cases, even leave your car at home. In other words, some changes are fairly easy, whereas others often require a lot of effort. The question is, how many people are willing to make these changes?

**In sum**, people do not respond well to fear or unrealistic demands. For an environmental campaign to be successful, it should encourage people to think about the issue of climate change in a positive and realistic way. In the words of author Ron Kaufman: "Convince people and you win their minds. Inspire people and you win their hearts." We need to do both.

**3 A** Is the answer to the question in the title *yes* or *no*?

**B** Read the essay again. Does it give reasons:

a for and against the main argument?
b for the main argument, but not against?

writing an opinion essay ■ formal linkers  **WRITING**  SKILLS  **5D**

## Skill: writing an opinion essay

One way to write an opinion essay is <u>only</u> to give reasons that <u>support</u> the main argument.
- In paragraph 1, write a thesis statement (a sentence that states the main point of your essay). A good thesis statement isn't too broad and clearly states the writer's position.
- In paragraphs 2 and 3, give arguments that support your thesis statement. Use examples, facts, figures, etc.
- Start each paragraph with a clear topic sentence (a sentence that introduces the main point of the paragraph).
- Summarize the key points in the concluding paragraph. Don't add any new arguments.

**4** Read the Skill box. Then read Gloria's essay again and <u>underline</u>:
1  the thesis statement (paragraph 1).
2  the topic sentences (paragraphs 2 and 3).
3  an argument to support the thesis statement.
4  the summary sentence in the concluding paragraph.

**5 A** Choose the best thesis statement for each essay question.
1  Should pop artists take environmental issues more seriously?
   a  Environmental issues are very important, and we should all take care of the environment.
   b  Influential pop artists should use their fame to encourage people to protect the planet.
2  Is a college degree really necessary?
   a  If Steve Jobs, one of the most influential people in history, did not graduate from college, it could be argued that a college education is not essential.
   b  In my country, more and more people are dropping out of college because of the high tuition fees.
3  Do violent video games cause behavior problems?
   a  I have loved video games ever since I can remember.
   b  Violent games can have a negative impact on children.

**B** In pairs, how would you answer each question? Think of two arguments to support your opinion.

## Text builder: formal linkers

**Two similar arguments:** *Climate change can be difficult for some people to understand.* **Similarly**, *a lot of people feel confused when scientists disagree with each other.*
**A comparison:** *People should be encouraged to buy electric cars,* **as opposed to** *gas or diesel ones.*
**A result:** *Fear about the future of the planet is a negative emotion.* **Consequently**, *we tend to reject it.*
**A contrast:** *People should respond positively to climate change campaigns.* **Nevertheless**, *they rarely do.*
**A conclusion:** **In sum**, *people do not usually respond well to environmental campaigns.*

**6 A** Read the Text builder. Find the **bold** formal linkers in the essay in exercise 2.

**B** Complete the sentences below with the linkers in **bold** from the Text builder.
1  Many families are less well off these days. _____ , a lot of students are dropping out of college because they cannot afford the tuition fees.
2  Many people say that children are not easily influenced by violent video games. _____ , a lot of research suggests that this is not true.
3  Some pop stars have millions of followers on social media. _____ , millions of people watch their favorite stars on TV.
4  To be successful, you need to be smart, creative, and have good interpersonal skills. _____ , these three critical traits are necessary for success.
5  Video games should encourage creativity and cooperation, _____ violence.

**7 A** **PREPARE** Choose an essay question from exercise 5A. Write a thesis statement and make notes of the supporting arguments.

**B** **PRACTICE** Use the Skill box to help you write your essay. Use topic sentences at the start of each paragraph and connect your ideas using formal linkers.

**C** **PERSONAL BEST** Exchange essays with a partner. Choose the best argument(s) supporting the thesis statement, and think of one additional one.

**Personal Best** Think about the essay question, "Are advertising campaigns successful?". Write two different thesis statements.

# UNIT 6 Habits and change

**LANGUAGE**  the habitual past ▪ expressions with *time*

## 6A My best decade

**1** In pairs, ask and answer questions about your interests when you were younger. Use the ideas in the box.

> Music   Food   TV shows   Clothes   Gadgets

**2 A** Read the text about people's past habits. Which of the interests in exercise 1 are mentioned?

### A sign of the times

We all look back fondly on what was in fashion when we were younger. You know that old song you still sing along to in the car **from time to time** when no one is looking? Or that comfortable pair of sweatpants you're ashamed to admit you still love to wear? Looking back on previous decades, what do we think of them now? Mary, Bob, and Raul share their memories from three very different decades.

#### 2000s: *Glee*

**For some time** in my teens, I watched it in bed till late at night. My mom was always coming into my room, though, so I would quickly change channels and pretend I was watching National Geographic. As the "intellectual" in the family, I had a reputation to maintain, and *Glee*, with all its strange dance moves and questionable song choices, was a no-no. It still influences so many of the "teen shows" we watch today.
*(Mary, Chicago)*

#### 1990s: Cooking shows

In the 1990s, I couldn't afford to eat out very often, so I had to learn how to cook. Cooking shows were big then, so when I was making dinner, I used to pretend I was hosting my own show! I often invited a friend to "co-host" and we would use a camcorder to video our "cooking show." It's only **a matter of time** before one of those videos appears on YouTube. *(Bob, Boston)*

#### 1980s: Abba

My dad used to be a huge Abba fan at one time, so I grew up listening to their songs, and eventually got hooked, too. My friends were always teasing me, of course, but I bet some of them secretly sang along to *Dancing Queen* in the shower! I still have a Spotify playlist with all their hits, which I'd memorized **at the time.**
*(Raul, São Paulo)*

**B** Look at the expressions with *time* in **bold** in the text. Match 1–4 with meanings a–d.

1  from time to time  _____      a  then
2  for some time  _____           b  sometimes
3  (only) a matter of time (before)  _____   c  for a period of time
4  at the time  _____              d  certain that something will happen

Go to Vocabulary practice: expressions with *time*, page 144

**3 A** Complete the sentences about the text in exercise 2. Use past forms and include adverbs if necessary.

1  Mary _____ *Glee* in bed till late at night.
2  She _____ channels when her mom entered her room.
3  Bob _____ he was the host of a cooking show.
4  Raul's dad _____ a huge Abba fan.
5  Raul's friends _____ him.

**B** Look at the sentences in exercise 3A and complete the rules below. Then read the Grammar box.

1  *Used to / Would* is used to talk about past states.
2  The simple past *can / can't* be used to talk about past habits.
3  The past continuous with *always* is used to talk about *annoying / positive* past habits.

48

the habitual past ■ expressions with *time*    **LANGUAGE**    **6A**

### Grammar: the habitual past

*used to* and *would*:
I **used to play** video games all the time. I **would spend** hours in front of the computer.
**Did** you **use to be** a good student? I **didn't use to like** studying at all.

Simple past:
I **didn't play** any sports when I was younger. I **hated** sports.

Past continuous with *always*:
My little sister **was always interrupting** us. And she **was always making** noise, too.

*would* vs. *had*:
I**'d** (I **would**) **eat** chocolate every day.
That Thursday, I**'d** (I **had**) **eaten** a whole bar by the time my mother came home.

**Look!** You cannot use *would* to talk about past states:
When I was younger, I **was**/**used to be** a huge fan of horror movies. NOT ~~I would be~~

Go to Grammar practice: the habitual past, page 122

**4  A** ▶ 6.3  **Pronunciation:** *use* and *used* Listen to the conversation. Notice how *use* and *used* are pronounced.

**A** Can I **use** your phone? My battery is dead, and I need to call my sister in Spain.
**B** Yeah, sure. But didn't you **use** to Skype her? That way you can **use** the camera, too.
**A** Well, I **used** to have a Skype account, but I haven't **used** it in years, and I've forgotten my password!
**B** Here, **use** my phone, instead.

**B** ▶ 6.3  Listen again and repeat. Practice the conversation in pairs.

**5** Read the opinion poll. Decide if <u>one</u> or <u>both</u> options are possible.

---

### What was the worst decade for music? Click on a decade and tell us why.

**2010s** 6 votes                                                                                    Vote
"The early 2000s [1]*were / would be* amazing, but I can't stand the stuff they're playing on the radio these days. In the 2000s, I [2]*was always spending / used to spend* hours listening to the radio, and at least 7 out of 10 songs were good. But now …" (Linda, San Francisco)

**2000s** 10 votes                                                                                   Vote
"I was a teenager in the 2000s, and I remember how I [3]*was always complaining / would complain* about bands like Coldplay and Keane. At least the 2000s gave us Lady Gaga, who [4]*had / used to have* her first hit in 2009." (Juan, Mexico)

**1990s** 15 votes                                                                                   Vote
"I grew up in the 1990s, and I [5]*liked / used to like* rock and heavy metal. But my parents [6]*used to listen / would listen* to people like Celine Dion and Mariah Carey – every single day. What a nightmare the 1990s were for me!" (Cynthia, New York)

---

Go to Communication practice: Student A page 160, Student B page 166

**6** In pairs, ask each other at least three questions. Use the simple past, *used to*, *would*, and the past continuous with *always* in your answers.

| Do you think the | 1980s 1990s 2000s | were good for | music? movies? TV? video games? soccer? fashion? |

*I think the 1980s were terrible for fashion. People used to wear some really weird clothes!*

**Personal Best**  Write a paragraph about when you were a child. Use a variety of past forms.

# 6 SKILLS READING understanding non-literal meaning ■ contradicting

## 6B Healthy living: myths and facts

**1** What is your healthiest eating habit? Do you have any bad eating habits? Discuss in pairs.

**2** Look at the four myth headings about food in the text on page 51. Why do you think these may be myths?

**3** Read the text and look carefully at "the facts" for each myth. Choose the correct summary of each fact.

Myth 1    a   Not all types of fiber are equally beneficial.
            b   Certain types of fiber are dangerous.
Myth 2    a   Organic food is safer to eat, but not necessarily more nutritious.
            b   Organic food isn't necessarily more nutritious or safer to eat.
Myth 3    a   What you eat is more important than when you eat.
            b   Eating at night can actually help you lose weight.
Myth 4    a   Water is not your only source of hydration.
            b   Drinking too much water can be dangerous.

### Skill   understanding non-literal meaning

Writers use words with abstract, non-literal meanings to give the text more impact. When you are reading, pay attention to:
- **exaggeration**: *My doctor gave me a **never-ending** list of foods to avoid.* (= huge)
- **comparisons**: *I lost weight and now this dress looks **like a balloon**.* (= round)
- **personification**: *Four food myths that just won't **die**.* (= cease to exist)
- **idioms**: *I hate dieting, but you know what they say, **no pain, no gain**.* (= no hard work, no success)

**4 A** Read the Skill box. Look at this sentence from the introduction. What kind of non-literal language is used?

*We are faced with a flood of information.*

**B** Look at the underlined phrases 1–8 in the text. What kind of non-literal language in the Skill box is used in each one?

**5 A** In Myth 1, find the question "Does this mean you can stop eating broccoli … ?". Read the next sentence. What expression tells you the answer is "no"?

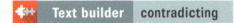

### Text builder   contradicting

We use the expressions in **bold** to contradict something that was said.
*Does this mean you can stop eating broccoli like a health freak? **On the contrary**, most experts are skeptical.*
*If you buy organic food because it's "free from pesticides," keep in mind that **the opposite is true**.*
***The truth of the matter** is that it's the extra calories that lead to weight gain.*
***Contrary to popular belief**, you don't need to drink eight glasses of water a day.*

**B** Read the Text builder and find the expressions in **bold** in the text. Complete sentences 1–4 with two words.

1 Contrary to _____ , not everybody needs eight hours of sleep every night.
2 Some people say you should work out every day, but _____ is true. It's better to work out every other day so your body can recover.
3 We don't only use 10% of our brain. On _____ , we use most of it most of the time.
4 Spending too much time in the cold air doesn't make you sick. The _____ the matter is that you're more likely to get sick indoors, where germs are easily passed around.

**6** Discuss the questions in pairs.
1 Were you aware of the myths in exercise 5B? Which one surprised you the most?
2 Do you know any other popular health myths? Why do people continue to believe in them?

understanding non-literal meaning ■ contradicting   READING   SKILLS   6B

# Four food myths that just won't die

**W**hether at the grocery store, at a restaurant, or in our own kitchens, we are faced with a flood of information about what we should eat. Social media makes it easier than ever to spread myths and half-truths, so how much do we *really* know about the choices we are making when we eat? Our specialists have their say.

### Myth 1: The more fiber you eat, the better.

**The facts:** Your grandparents probably used to tell you about the importance of fiber, but they had no idea just how popular "fiber-rich" foods would become. These days, it seems that food manufacturers are adding specific types of fiber to just about everything – from cereal bars to yogurt and even water! So does this mean you can stop eating broccoli [1]like a health freak? **On the contrary**, most experts are skeptical that processed fiber offers the same benefits as whole grains, fruits, and vegetables, which contain natural fiber. So when it comes to fiber, it's quality not quantity that matters.

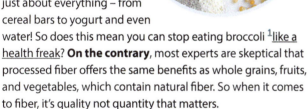

### Myth 2: Organic food is better for you.

**The facts:** [2]Organic foods have shot up in popularity over the last decade. It seems that wherever you shop, every other food item you see also comes in an organic, health-conscious version. So, is it worth spending your hard-earned cash on the apples with the "organic" sticker on them? Recent research suggests the answer is no, since there is no significant nutritional difference between organic and conventional foods. And if you buy organic foods because they're "free from pesticides," keep in mind that **the opposite is true** – organic farms do use pesticides. And while organic foods may taste a little better, the only difference is that it's produced using natural, rather than synthetic, pesticides.

### Myth 3: Eating at night makes you gain weight.

**The facts:** My mother was always telling me not to eat anything after 10 p.m. because evening meals would "make me fat." In certain countries, some people take this idea so seriously that they think twice before eating late in the evening [3]even if they're starving. It may be easy to believe our bodies have an internal clock set to store anything we eat at night as fat, but it's not as simple as that. **The truth of the matter** is that it's the extra calories – not when we consume them – that lead to weight gain. So if you tend to eat late in the evening, you don't have to [4]eat like a horse – just be selective. Stick with vegetables, lean proteins, and complex carbohydrates if you can.

### Myth 4: You should drink eight glasses of water a day.

**The facts:** [5]This is another stubborn myth that has been around for decades, and [6]it just won't go away. Every summer we are flooded with media reports warning us about the dangers of dehydration and urging us to drink lots of water, even if we're not thirsty. But these fears are exaggerated. **Contrary to popular belief**, you don't need to drink eight glasses of water a day, since water is also present in tea, coffee, ice cream, and fruits and vegetables – you name it. In other words, while it's very important to drink water when the weather is hot, we may be less likely to dehydrate than pseudo-science would have us believe.

On a subject where a lot of people [7]talk as if they were experts, there is no shortage of bad health advice out there, so please remember, whatever you read, [8]to take it with a grain of salt.

**Personal Best** — Write a paragraph about some food myths that you believe. Use linkers for contradicting.

## 6 LANGUAGE
*be used to* and *get used to* ■ expressions with prepositions

## 6C My generation and me

**1** Think about your own family, and then discuss the questions below in pairs.
1. How many generations are there in your family? Do you all share the same values?
2. Who do you talk to and what about? Are there any subjects you avoid?
3. Complete the sentences:
   a Unlike my parents, I (don't) care about …
   b Unlike my parents, I (don't) approve of …
   c Unlike my parents, I'm (not) fed up with …
   d Unlike my parents, I (don't) feel I am entitled to …
   e Unlike my parents, I'm (not) comfortable with …
   f Unlike my parents, I'm (not) anxious about …

Go to Vocabulary practice: expressions with prepositions, page 145

**2** Read the text about "Generation Y." How does the writer answer questions 1–3: *yes* or *no*?

### MILLENNIALS: more to them than meets the eye?

When older people think of millennials, also known as "Generation Y," a few images often come to mind: lazy, living in their parents' basement, and addicted to social media. It's easy to get things wrong about those born from 1980 to 1995. Here are three common stereotypes.

**1 Is it true that they need constant encouragement?**

Research shows most millennials feel they are entitled to regular, immediate feedback from their managers, as opposed to formal reviews. This comes as no surprise. As they were growing up, millennials were constantly evaluated in school and taught how to improve their skills – perhaps more than their parents ever were. So, if millennials are constantly seeking regular feedback, _____ .

**2 Do they care about owning a home?**

Some of my friends in their 20s say, "_____ and all the work that comes with it. I'd rather spend my time – and money – doing something I actually enjoy." Fair enough. I'm not sure that's representative of most millennials, though. According to a recent survey, nearly 70% of those aged 18–34 want to own a home and still haven't bought one simply because they can't afford it.

**3 Have they given up on marriage?**

It seems that in some countries, at least, people are waiting longer to get married. At one time, young people in the U.S., for example, used to get married in their early 20s. Last year, the average age was 28. But just because millennials are putting off getting married doesn't mean they have no interest in marriage. Some are waiting to marry until they're more financially secure. Or maybe _____ of being married. That can take a while!

**3 A** Fill in the blanks in the text with a–d below. There is one extra item.
a I'd never <u>get used to</u> a big house
b they're still <u>getting used to</u> the idea
c they <u>were not used to</u> long-term relationships
d that's because <u>they're used to</u> it

**B** Which <u>underlined</u> expressions in exercise 3A mean:
1 be accustomed to?
2 become accustomed to?

**4 A** ▶ 6.6  Listen to two friends discussing the text. Do the man and the woman feel the same way about marriage?

**B** ▶ 6.6  Listen again and complete the sentences. What verb form follows *be used to* and *get used to*? Then read the Grammar box.
1 I'm used to _____ time alone and to _____ my own decisions.
2 I guess I'm used to _____ .
3 He'd never get used to _____ his life with another person.
4 Presumably, some people feel they can get used to _____ !

*be used to* and *get used to* ■ expressions with prepositions  LANGUAGE  **6C**

**Grammar** *be used to* and *get used to*

**be used to:**
Many young people **are used to** living alone.
My first year in Canada was tough because I **wasn't used to** long winters.

**get used to:**
I **haven't gotten used to** living with a roommate.
I don't think I'**ll** ever **get used to** college, no matter how hard I try.

**Look!** *be/get used to* are followed by the *-ing* form or a noun.

**Go to Grammar practice:** *be used to* and *get used to*, page 123

**5** ▶ 6.8 **Pronunciation:** sentence stress with *be used to* and *get used to* Listen and repeat. Notice the /ə/ sound in *to*.

1 My cousin got used to living in a big city.
2 We're used to short summers now.
3 I'm not used to dealing with badly behaved children!
4 My parents are getting used to retired life.

**6 A** Choose the correct options to complete the text.

**GENERATION Z**, the term often used to describe those born after 1995, is essentially a global, social, visual, and technological generation. Here are some common stereotypes often associated with today's teens and young adults.

1 Generation Z was born into a world filled with technology, so they *used / are used* to the technology that millennials had to learn how to use.
2 Generation Z processes information faster than other generations because they are used to *communicate / communicating* with apps like Snapchat.
3 Multitasking is not a problem. They *used to do / are used to doing* it with great skill.
4 The downside is that they can be easily distracted because, over the years, they *get / have gotten* used to *focus / focusing* on too many things at the same time.

**B** In pairs, discuss which ideas from exercise 6A you think are true for people of your age.

**7 A** Complete the sentences with the correct form of *be* and *get*. There may be more than one answer.

1 The best age to learn how to drive is in your early 20s. In your late teens, your reflexes are still developing, so *you probably _____ used to fast responses in traffic*.
2 The best age to find a roommate is from your mid- to late 20s. It's not always easy to share your space with someone else, especially if *you _____ used to your independence*.
3 The best age to become a manager is in your mid-30s. I got promoted at 24, and it was a disaster, partly because *I _____ used to so much pressure*.
4 The best age to live abroad is in your late teens. Young people tend to *_____ used to new experiences* more easily.
5 When you're older, it's harder to *_____ used to another country*.

**B** Rewrite the words in *italics* in exercise 7A with *used to* and verbs 1–5.

1 make   2 have   3 work under   4 have   5 live

*1 You're not used to/You haven't gotten used to making fast responses in traffic.*

**Go to Communication practice:** Student A page 160, Student B page 166

**8** In pairs, answer the questions.

1 Do you agree with the suggested ages in exercise 7A? Why/Why not?
2 What is the best age to do the things below?

 leave home have your first boyfriend/girlfriend have children
 get your first job get married retire

*The best age to leave home is 18. We should get used to living alone as soon as possible!*

**Personal Best** Describe something you never thought you'd get used to, but are used to now.

53

# 6 SKILLS  SPEAKING   challenging assumptions ■ solving problems

## 6D  A suitable roommate

**1** In pairs, choose the three most important characteristics of a roommate. Use the ideas in the box.

| fun   honest   organized   quiet   responsible   the same age   the same values |

**2** ▶ 6.9  Watch or listen to the first part of *Talking Zone*. Write *Ben* or *Abigail*.

1 _____ suggests finding a roommate.
2 _____ thinks the age gap might be a problem.
3 _____ begins to change his/her mind a little towards the end.

**3 A** Match the two parts to make complete sentences from Ben and Abigail's conversation.

1 Just because he's older doesn't mean
2 But hanging out is one thing, sharing an apartment
3 True, but it might be nice
4 Responsibility has nothing
5 But what if he doesn't
6 People can get along no matter
7 But how do you know he won't mind

a to do with age!
b we can't get along.
c watch the same TV shows we do?
d to have someone older and more responsible around.
e sharing an apartment with people half his age?
f quite another.
g how different their tastes are.

**B** ▶ 6.9  Watch or listen again and check. What does Ben say to change Abigail's mind?

### Conversation builder   challenging assumptions

*Just because you like her doesn't mean you should be roommates.*
*Being friends is one thing, living together (quite) another.*
*True, but it's still important to get along.*
*Honesty has nothing to do with age.*
*But what if we have different tastes?*
*People can get along no matter/regardless of how different their tastes are.*
*But how do you know he won't mind helping with the chores?*

**4** Read the Conversation builder. Imagine you and your partner are looking for a roommate. Take turns challenging the assumptions below.
1 "She's only 20. She's probably too immature."
2 "He has two cats. We've never had a pet around here."
3 "She's a vegetarian. Planning our meals will be a nightmare."
4 "He works from home. He'll never leave the house."
5 "He's into classical music. He'll listen to Mozart all day long."

challenging assumptions ■ solving problems **SPEAKING** **SKILLS** **6D**

**5** ▶ 6.10 Watch or listen to the second part of the show. What do Ben and Abigail agree on?

1 The potential roommate who came to their apartment will probably say "No."
2 Spending less on the Internet will help solve their financial problems.
3 Spending less on electricity is a solution, too.
4 Since the rent is going up, they'll probably need a third roommate.

**Skill** solving problems

When you try to solve a problem, you can use some of the following conversation strategies:
- Make a point: *If you ask me, we should hire a nanny.*
- Suggest alternatives: *We could either sell the car or move to a cheaper place./We could always sell the car./Why not see if we can sell the car?/We could sell the car instead of moving.*
- Ask for or offer clarification: *Like what? You mean sell the car? The point I'm making is …*
- Challenge someone to keep thinking: *Is it worth it, though? But is it really a good idea? What difference would it make?*

**6** ▶ 6.10 Read the Skill box. Guess the missing words in Ben and Abigail's sentences below. Then watch or listen again and check.

1 We'll _____ have to look for another roommate _____ find a way to save some money.
2 _____ ? We're pretty economical when it comes to food and stuff.
3 _____ switch to a cheaper Internet provider.
4 But even if we save 10 or 20 dollars, _____ would it _____ ?
5 Like, _____ use LED lights _____ normal bulbs?
6 _____ the ones that are cool to touch?
7 Is it _____ ? They're so expensive to buy.
8 _____ is that if we're serious about saving money, every little bit counts.

**7** Which problem-solving strategy does each sentence in exercise 6 use?

1 *suggest alternatives*
2 _____
3 _____
4 _____
5 _____
6 _____
7 _____
8 _____

**Go to Communication practice:** Student A page 161, Student B page 167

**8 A PREPARE** In pairs, imagine you belong to the same family. You need to solve a problem together. Prepare a conversation, using one of the ideas below.

( an overdue bill )  ( noisy neighbors )  ( sharing the family car )

( apartment cleaning schedule )  ( walking the dog )  ( doing the weekly food shopping )

**B PRACTICE** Practice the conversation. Make sure you make suggestions and offer/ask for clarification. Were you able to solve your problem?

**C PERSONAL BEST** Choose a new problem and practice the conversation again. Did you suggest practical solutions? What improvements can you make?

**Personal Best** Write a paragraph describing a problem you or someone you know has had, including how it was solved.

55

# 5 and 6 REVIEW and PRACTICE

## Grammar

**1** Cross (**X**) the sentence that is NOT correct.

1. a I ate so much food I'm not hungry.
   b I ate such a big lunch I'm not hungry.
   c I ate so big lunch I'm not hungry.
2. a I lived in Norway when I was a child, but I never got used to the cold weather.
   b I lived in Norway when I was a child, but I couldn't be used to the cold weather.
   c I lived in Norway when I was a child, but I didn't use to like the cold weather.
3. a There are so much different phones on sale.
   b There are so many different phones on sale.
   c There are such a lot of different phones on sale.
4. a There will be so few guests at the wedding.
   b There will be so little guests at the wedding.
   c There won't be many guests at the wedding.
5. a By the time I'm 30, I will have saved enough money to buy a car.
   b By the time I'm 30, I'm going to be saved enough money to buy a car.
   c By the time I'm 30, I might have saved enough money to buy a car.
6. a Our teacher had yelled at us all the time.
   b Our teacher would yell at us all the time.
   c Our teacher used to yell at us all the time.
7. a I may never get used to waking up at such an early time.
   b I may never get used to waking up so early.
   c I may never get used to wake up so early.
8. a My children never slept on vacation.
   b My children wouldn't sleep on vacation.
   c My children didn't used to sleep on vacation.

**2** Use the words in parentheses to complete the sentences so they mean the same as the first sentence.

1. The kitchen was a complete mess, so I ordered a pizza, instead.
   The kitchen _____ a pizza instead. (such)
2. My mother would make us sweet tea when we were sick.
   _____ sweet tea when we were sick. (used)
3. She doesn't think she's going to be able to go to work tomorrow.
   _____ able to go to work tomorrow. (might)
4. I never became accustomed to working during the night.
   I never _____ during the night. (used)
5. Will robots be doing all of our jobs by 2050?
   _____ doing all of our jobs by 2050? (going)
6. There were hardly any cars on the road because of the snow.
   _____ because of the snow. (so)
7. My brother and his friends used to wear the same clothes every day.
   My brother _____ the same clothes every day. (would)
8. We will have four meetings between now and next Friday.
   _____ by next Friday. (had)

**3** Choose the correct options to complete the text.

### ▶ INTERVIEW    Thursday, January 4

My name is Marie and I'm 75 years old. I ¹*used to live / have lived* my whole life in the outskirts of Lyon in the south of France. I have ²*so many / so much* wonderful childhood memories. My friends and I ³*used to / were used to* walk to and from school every day, and when it was warm, we ⁴*were playing / would play* outside all evening. In the summer, we ⁵*used to / got used to* swim in the lake near my house. The water was ⁶*so / such* a cold at first, but you ⁷*got used / are used* to it after a few minutes. I had ⁸*so / such* a happy childhood, but I'm rather worried about children today. They seem to spend ⁹*much / so much* time in front of their computers and so ¹⁰*few / little* children today walk to school these days. And there are so many problems in the world! I ¹¹*wouldn't / won't* be here in 50 years, but my grandchildren ¹²*will have been / will be*. But with all this climate change, what ¹³*will be / is going to* happen to the environment? And employment will be very different, too. In 50 years, a lot of people ¹⁴*are going to / may have* lost their jobs because robots ¹⁵*will be / may* doing all the work!

## Vocabulary

**1** Circle the word or expression that is different. Explain why.

1. inaccurate   irregular   improbable   impatient
2. waste time   in time for   on time   for some time
3. passionate   lethargic   motivated   eager
4. grumpy   energetic   positive   enthusiastic
5. wildfires   drought   heatwave   wildlife
6. impolite   illegal   immature   irregular
7. motivated   down   miserable   pessimistic
8. climate change   solar energy   endangered species   toxic waste

# REVIEW and PRACTICE 5 and 6

**2** Match the words and expressions in the box with definitions 1–10.

> fed up with   illogical   dynamic   misleading
> obsessed with   entitled to   insist on sth
> distressing   accuse sb of sth   informal

1 say that somebody did something wrong _____
2 full of energy and new ideas _____
3 unhappy or annoyed about a situation that has been happening for a long time _____
4 thinking about something, all the time _____
5 have the right to do or have something _____
6 causing anxiety or sadness _____
7 not making sense _____
8 having a relaxed nature or style _____
9 giving the wrong idea _____
10 demand something and not accept refusal _____

**3** Choose the correct words from the box to complete the sentences.

> improbable   advised   eager   energy consumption
> optimistic   grumpy   suspicious   irrelevant

1 When my father is hungry, he gets really _____ and starts yelling at everybody.
2 My friend Elena is a very _____ student, and she always asks questions in lectures.
3 I'd love to get the job, but I'm not _____ because the interview went very badly.
4 My teacher said my essay contained a lot of _____ information that wasn't connected to the title.
5 Karina tells some great stories, but I find a lot of them pretty _____ . I think she exaggerates.
6 My roommates and I are trying to reduce our _____ , so we always turn off the lights when we leave a room.
7 I wanted to apply for the manager's position, but my friends _____ me against it.
8 I'm always _____ of news stories because I think journalists often invent things.

**4** Choose the correct options to complete the text.

> Many people are rightly [1]*distressing / concerned* about [2]*climate change / solar power* as it is only a [3]*matter / waste* of time until it becomes the most important issue on the planet. In fact, it is [4]*irrelevant / irresponsible* not to discuss the issue. However, while it is encouraging to hear politicians being sympathetic [5]*of / to* the environmental cause, we should all be suspicious [6]*of / with* government policies which seem too perfect. Although some of these ideas can be beneficial, most of them are [7]*immature / ineffective*. Instead of [8]*wasting / taking* time on short-term solutions, governments need to look at the bigger picture.

## Personal Best

**Lesson 5A**
Write four sentences about your life using *so / such*, *so much / so many* and *so little / so few*.

**Lesson 5A**
Name four environmental issues that affect our planet.

**Lesson 5B**
Name four "mood" adjectives and for each one, say when you last felt this way.

**Lesson 5C**
Make four predictions using *will*, *going to*, *may/might*, the future perfect, or the future continuous.

**Lesson 5C**
Write four sentences using words with these prefixes: *dis-*, *ir-*, *im-*, *mis-*.

**Lesson 5D**
Write three pairs of sentences. Begin the second one with *similarly*, *consequently*, and *nevertheless*.

**Lesson 6A**
Describe four habits or routines from your childhood using *would* and *used to*.

**Lesson 6A**
Write four sentences about yourself and people you know using different expressions with *time*.

**Lesson 6B**
Describe an experience using exaggeration, comparison, and an idiom.

**Lesson 6C**
Describe two things you are used to and two things you can't get used to.

**Lesson 6C**
Use four different adjectives followed by prepositions to describe your generation.

**Lesson 6D**
Write four sentences in which you challenge assumptions about an important topic.

57

# GRAMMAR PRACTICE

## 1A Present forms; *like*, *as if*, and *as though*

 1.2

The Earth **goes** around the sun.
He **looks** great with a beard.
It **sounds as though** you're happy.
It's **as if** you**'re not listening**.
You**'re always making** quick decisions.
I **don't want** to talk to anyone.
I**'m feeling** more relaxed now.

### Simple present with action or state verbs

We use the simple present with action or state verbs to talk about things that are always true and to talk about regular routines.

*Every evening, I listen to music to relax.*
*I like to spend my free time with a good book.*

State verbs include:
- Feelings: *like, love, hate, want, prefer, need*
- Thoughts and opinions: *know, believe, remember, forget, understand, think, feel, consider, realize, expect, agree, suppose, doubt, mean*
- States: *be, have* (possess), *exist, seem, appear, belong, own, matter*
- Senses: *taste, sound, look, feel, hear, smell*

### Present continuous with action verbs

We use the present continuous to talk about things that are happening now and things that are temporary.

*I'm coming! I'm on my way.* NOT *I come! I'm on my way.*
*You're working such long hours this week.*

We can use the present continuous with *always* to talk about things that happen frequently, especially things that are annoying.

*My parents are always criticizing me!  Why are you always interrupting her?*

Some verbs, such as *think*, *have*, and *feel*, can be both action and state verbs, with different meanings. When they are action verbs, we use the present continuous, but when they are state verbs, we use the simple present.

*I'm thinking about taking a course in communication skills.* (the action of thinking = action verb)
*I think everyone has a unique personal style.* (an opinion = state verb)

### Sense verbs with adjectives, nouns, and clauses

When we use sense verbs (*taste, sound, look, feel,* and *smell*), we usually use *like* before a noun, but *as if* or *as though* before a clause.

*Those flowers smell wonderful!* (adjective)
*It looks like gold.* (noun)
*It feels as if you want us to break up.* (clause)

In informal spoken English, we sometimes use *like* before a clause. We do not use *like* in more formal speech and writing. *As though* is a little more formal than *as if*.

*It sounds like she's really mad at you.* (informal)
*If looks as if/as though we don't have the budget.*

> **Look!** Adjectives, not adverbs, follow sense verbs.
> *That sounds wonderful.* NOT *That sounds wonderfully.*
> *You look really good in green.* NOT *You look really well in green.*

112

---

1 Complete the conversation with the correct form of the verbs in parentheses.

A ¹_____ you _____ (think) it's true that people ²_____ (have) different communication styles?
B Maybe. Some people ³_____ (speak) more slowly than others. And my mom ⁴_____ (use) her hands a lot.
A My mom ⁵_____ (be) a very good listener. But she ⁶_____ (like) talking to people too!
C Hey! We're in a library! I ⁷_____ (try) to concentrate!
A Sorry! We ⁸_____ (talk) about communication.
C It ⁹_____ (sound) interesting, but I ¹⁰_____ (hurry) to finish this essay!

2 Complete the sentences with *always* and the simple present or present continuous form of the verbs in parentheses.
   1 You _____ (tell) me what to do! Let me decide for myself!
   2 My mother _____ (give) me good advice when I have a problem.
   3 Why _____ you _____ (copy) my homework? Don't you know that's called cheating?
   4 My neighbor _____ (water) my plants when I'm away.
   5 My boss _____ (arrive) at work on time.
   6 Nancy's kids _____ (take) food out of our refrigerator without asking!

3 Choose the correct options to complete the sentences.
   1 What a mess! It *looks as if / looks* a tornado has hit!
   2 It *seems / is seeming* like a good idea to include Roberto on our team.
   3 This sweater *feels / is feeling* so soft.
   4 Dinner smells really *good / well*. What is it?
   5 They *think / 're thinking* about getting a dog.
   6 Please call an ambulance! I think this man *has / is having* a heart attack!
   7 Your vacation sounds *as / like* an adventure!
   8 I *live / 'm living* with my aunt and uncle this year.

◀ Go back to page 5

# 1C Narrative tenses

1.10

I **rode** my bike every day last summer, and one day I **fell** and **hurt** myself.
When I **arrived**, people **were** already **having** lunch.
I**'d been** to Jim's house a few times before yesterday.
By the time I **got** to the party, Lori **had** already **left**.
I**'d been thinking** of breaking up, but Amy **decided** to do it first.

## Simple past
We use the simple past to describe the main events in a narrative. These are completed actions in the past.

*I opened the door to my house and found a cat inside! I didn't know what to do.*

## Past continuous
We use the past continuous to describe the background events in a narrative. We also use the past continuous to describe an action that was in progress when a completed action happened.

*Lots of people were dancing at the party.* (background event)
*I was drinking my coffee when Amy came up and said hello.* (action in progress)

We usually use the simple past with state verbs, but we can use the past continuous with verbs that can be both action and state verbs.

*We liked our apartment, but we were thinking of selling it.*

We often use *when* and *while* to connect past events.

*When/While I was waiting for my brother, I got a phone call.*

**Look!** *When* may mean "in the moment when" or "during the time when."
*I was just finishing dinner when the bell rang.* = in the moment when the bell rang.
*When/While I was eating dinner, the bell rang.* = during the time when I was eating dinner.

## Past perfect
We use the past perfect to describe an action or state that happened before another action in the past.

*I had just woken up when I started to feel sick.*

We often connect past events with *by the time* or *before* where one verb is in the past perfect.

*By the time I got to school, everyone had finished the exam.*
*Before the flight took off, we'd already been on the runway for two hours.*

In conversation, when the sequence of events is clear, we can often use the past perfect or the simple past.

*I had written/wrote to Bill, and soon after, I got an answer.* (First, I wrote. Then I got an answer.)

## Past perfect continuous
We use the past perfect continuous to describe the background events in a narrative.

*It had been raining heavily for several hours.*

We also use the past perfect continuous to describe an action that was in progress before another action happened.

*My sister had been sleeping for only a few minutes when she heard a loud noise.*
*By the time I graduated, I'd been studying English for six years.*

# GRAMMAR PRACTICE

1 Choose the correct options to complete the sentences.

1 Jim *had waited / was waiting* for us when we arrived at the station.
2 We *'d been dying / 'd died* to see the new movie for weeks by the time we finally *had seen / saw* it.
3 Henry *had been feeling / felt* a little depressed, so he *decided / was deciding* to take a vacation.
4 I *was owning / owned* a great apartment in Italy, right by the sea.
5 *Had your brother not realized / Had your brother not been realizing* that it was an expensive restaurant?
6 While I *had talked / was talking* to some friends, someone *tapped / was tapping* me on the shoulder.
7 By the time Anna *joined / was joining* us for dinner, we *had eaten / ate* most of the food.
8 When I *met / was meeting* Mike in person, it *felt / was feeling* as if I *was knowing / had known* him my whole life!

2 Complete the conversation with past narrative tenses. Use the verbs in parentheses.

A You're not going to believe what ¹_____ (happen) to me a few days ago!
B What? ²_____ (win) the lottery?
A No, but while I ³_____ (wait) for the bus, I ⁴_____ (meet) someone amazing. He ⁵_____ (take) the same bus as me many times before, but I ⁶_____ (not notice) him until then.
B So ... ? Don't stop there!
A Well, I ⁷_____ (stand) at the bus stop, and I ⁸_____ (think) about my day at work. Then when I ⁹_____ (turn) around, I ¹⁰_____ (see) this really good-looking guy. He ¹¹_____ (try) to make eye contact and kept looking in my direction. He ¹²_____ (seem) to want to talk to me.
B And now you're engaged!
A Well, not exactly! But yesterday, while I ¹³_____ (walk) to the bus stop, he ¹⁴_____ (come) up to me, and ¹⁵_____ (ask) me out. He ¹⁶_____ (wait) for ten minutes for me to walk by! And this time, I think it's going to be the real thing!

◀ Go back to page 9

## GRAMMAR PRACTICE

## 2A Question patterns

> ▶ 2.4
>
> **Who took** this great photo?
> **Which** movie **did** you **see**?
> **Haven't** we **been** here before?
> You **like** museums, **don't** you?
> **Do** you **know why** he **didn't go**?
> **Could** you **tell** me **if** they**'re** here?

### wh- subject and object questions

In subject questions, the question word or phrase (*who, what, how many, how much, which, what type of*, etc.) is the subject of the verb. We use the positive form of the verb, so in simple present and simple past tenses, we don't use *do/does/did*.

*Who usually teaches this class?   What happened last week?*

In many *wh-* questions, the question word or phrase is the object of the verb. In object questions, we use an auxiliary verb before the subject.

*Who have you invited to your party?   What are you doing?*

### Negative questions

To form a negative question, we put a contracted negative form of the verb *be*, auxiliary, or modal verb before the subject.

*Wasn't she the woman we met last week?   Don't you want to go out tonight?*

We use a negative question when we think we know something, but we want to check.

*Didn't he write several novels?* = I think he wrote several novels. Is that right?

We also use negative questions to express surprise or to make a suggestion.

*Haven't you been to this museum before?* (surprise)
*Shouldn't you start thinking about graduate school?* (suggestion)

### Tag questions

We can use a statement with a tag question when we think we know something, but we want to check. The intonation rises on the tag question.

*You're from Spain, aren't you?* ↗ = I think you're from Spain. Is that right?
*He doesn't like art, does he?* ↗ = I don't think he likes art. Is that right?

When we use a tag question as a conversation opener or to make a comment, the intonation falls on the tag question.

*It's a hot day, isn't it?* ↘ (conversation opener)
*He's not very organized, is he?* ↘ (comment)

With positive statements, we use a negative tag question. With negative statements, we use a positive tag question. The negative tag for *I am* is *aren't I*.

*I'm usually right, aren't I?*

### Indirect questions

We ask an indirect *Yes/No* question with the following structure:

*Yes/No* question + *if* + subject + verb form + rest of sentence

*Did they play yesterday?* ⇨ *Could you tell me if they played yesterday?*

When we ask an indirect *wh-* question, we use the question word(s) instead of *if*.

*How much will it cost?* ⇨ *Could you tell me how much it will cost?*

> **Look!** In an indirect question, we cannot use the usual question word order.
> *Do you know where the box office is?* NOT *Do you know where is the box office?*

1 Write *wh-* subject or object questions for the underlined answers.

  1 <u>Bordalo</u> painted *Raccoon*.
    _____
  2 I like <u>modern</u> art.
    _____
  3 <u>About a hundred people</u> came to the concert.
    _____
  4 The title of the painting is <u>The Kiss</u>.
    _____
  5 <u>The Belvedere Museum in Vienna</u> has *The Kiss*.
    _____
  6 <u>I was listening to music</u> when the phone rang.
    _____
  7 Oh no! <u>Someone was hit by a car</u>.
    _____
  8 I visited <u>my grandparents</u> on the weekend.
    _____

2 Complete the blanks to make a negative question or a tag question.

  1 Graffiti is really good sometimes, _____ ?
  2 _____ we been to this museum before?
  3 You didn't notice the title of that painting, _____ ?
  4 Modern art can be a real disappointment, _____ ?
  5 _____ that the famous sculpture the *Fearless Girl*?
  6 _____ Klimt have some problems before his gold phase?
  7 I'm a pretty bad photographer, _____ ?
  8 _____ you start studying? Your exam is tomorrow.

3 Complete the indirect questions for the statements.

  1 Could you please tell me where _____ ?
    Yes, the Klimt exhibit is downstairs.
  2 Do you know if _____ ?
    No, Kristan Visbal didn't make this sculpture. It's too traditional.
  3 Could I ask you why _____ ?
    There's a lot of graffiti here because the city is encouraging street art.
  4 Do you know how _____ ?
    Yes, you can get to the Guggenheim by taking the number 4 bus.
  5 Could you explain how _____ ?
    I think Bordalo made this piece of art using garbage.

◀ Go back to page 13

# 2C Using linkers (1)

 2.9

**Although** I love music, I don't listen to it very often.
I don't like to cook. I love to eat, **though**!
I like movies a lot. **However**, I rarely go to see them.
**Despite** a lot of effort, I've never learned to speak French.
**In spite of the fact that** I play tennis regularly, I haven't improved.
**In order to** appreciate classical music, I bought a good set of headphones.
I threw out all my old books **so that** I could have more room at home.

## Expressing contrast

We use *although*, *even though*, and *though* to link two contrasting thoughts. *Although* and *Even though* are a little more formal than *though*.

*Even though/Although I hate to study, I have to do it every evening.*
*I hated my apartment. I loved the neighborhood, though.*

**Look!** Be careful not to confuse *though* and *as though*.
*It looks as though he's not here.* NOT *It looks though he's not here.*

We also use *however* to express contrast. *However* is a slightly more formal way to say *but*. We do not use a comma before *however*; instead we start a new sentence.

*I'm not too crazy about Thai food. However, I had it last night.*
NOT *I'm not too crazy about Thai food, however, I had it last night.*

*In spite of* and *despite* have the same meaning as *although*, *even though*, and *though*. After *in spite of/despite*, we use a noun or the *-ing* form of a verb.

*In spite of her success, she's very modest.* (noun)
*Despite having many problems, he finally finished college.* (*-ing* form)

We put *not* before the *-ing* form of the verb to make it negative.

*In spite of not having very good grades, I managed to get a job.*

Use *the fact that* after *despite/in spite of* when a clause follows.

*Despite the fact that I hate large crowds, I went out on New Year's Eve.*
NOT *Despite I hate large concerts, I went out on New Year's Eve.*

## Expressing purpose

(*In order*) *to* and *so* (*that*) both express a purpose. A clause beginning with *in order to* or *so that* is more formal than one beginning with *to* or *so*.

*We've started a new program so that students can get extra training.* (more formal)
*I downloaded the song to see what everyone was talking about.* (more informal)

We do not use *for* in a purpose clause with (*in order*) *to*.

*I go to the gym every day to get some exercise.* NOT *I go to the gym every day for to get some exercise.*

(*In order*) *to* is followed by the base form of a verb. *So* (*that*) is followed by a clause.

*She works part-time to earn some money for her training.*
*I took a course so (that) I could learn more about history.*

To make most purpose clauses negative, we use *not*, a negative auxiliary, or a negative modal verb. The negative form of *in order to* is *in order not to*.

*I always play my music softly at home so I don't annoy my parents/in order not to annoy my parents.*

# GRAMMAR PRACTICE

1 Choose the correct options to complete the sentences.
　1 I almost never listen to music at home *in spite of / even though* I have a lot of good albums.
　2 The program was really difficult. *However, / Despite,* she never gave up.
　3 Swift talked her family into moving to Nashville *so / in order to* she could pursue her music.
　4 I like jazz. I really don't like folk music *although / though*.
　5 We set out early *in order not to / so that* miss the start of the concert.
　6 *In spite of / Although* having really musical parents, I didn't inherit their talent.

2 Rewrite the sentences. Correct the mistakes.
　1 Despite I don't know much about classical music, I love Beethoven.
　　_____
　2 You need to be really determined for to be successful as a performer.
　　_____
　3 My brother talked me into going to a rock concert however I didn't enjoy it.
　　_____
　4 In spite of I take a course in the history of music, I still feel I don't know a lot about it.
　　_____
　5 I love Adele. I never went to one of her concerts, even though.
　　_____
　6 I gave up studying engineering that I could devote my time to music.
　　_____

3 Write sentences that have the same meaning. Use the words in parentheses.
　1 I love going to concerts. I can't afford to go to many, though. (although)
　　_____
　2 Even though she's very young, she's a very confident performer. (despite the fact that)
　　_____
　3 I practiced swimming for three hours a day so I'd get on the team. (in order to)
　　_____
　4 I really looked up to my older sister, but I didn't share her taste in clothes. (however)
　　_____
　5 In spite of the fact that I'm home a lot, I never read. (even though)
　　_____
　6 He waited in line for hours in order to buy a new cell phone. (so)
　　_____

◀ Go back to page 17

115

# GRAMMAR PRACTICE

## 3A Advice, expectation, and obligation

 3.2

They **should** charge people to park downtown.
I really **ought to** call my parents.
I **wouldn't** pay that price (if I were you).
We**'d better** hurry. The trains stop at midnight.
The train **is supposed to** arrive soon.
You **can't** use that entrance. You **have to** go around the block.
You**'re not allowed to** park there. You'll get a ticket!

### Advice

We use *should* or *ought to* to give advice or make a suggestion.

*Maybe you should/ought to try to do things differently.*
*You shouldn't expect to succeed instantly. It will take a lot of effort.*

We also use *would* and *wouldn't* to give advice. The words "if I were you" are often implied.

*I would stay somewhere else (if I were you). The service at this hotel is pretty bad.*

### Strong advice/warning

We use *had better* (*not*) to express strong advice or a warning. *Had better* is followed by the base form of the verb.

*You'd better drive slowly tonight. The roads are very icy.*
*They'd better not play their music again tonight. I'll call the police!*

In the first person, we can use *had better* to express a strong obligation.

*I'd better renew my passport, or I won't be able to travel.*

### Expectation

We use *be supposed to* to express something that we're expected to do, but don't always do. In a negative sentence *not* goes after a form of *be*.

*You're supposed to wait.    You're not supposed to be here.*

### Personal obligation

We use *should* or *ought to* to express a personal obligation.

*I really should/ought to tell Dan I'm taking the trip with you.*

### External obligation/rules

We use *can* to express permission or talk about rules. We use the negative *can't* to express that permission hasn't been granted.

*You can go to the front of the line, but you can't use your cell phone in here.*

We can also use *be allowed to* to express permission. The negative expresses that permission hasn't been granted and is a little more formal than *can't*.

*You're not allowed to/can't drive on the right in the UK!*

We use *have to* to express external obligation and *don't have to* where no obligation is present. In American English, we use *must* only for very strong obligation or rules.

*You have to pay by tomorrow, but you don't have to pay the full amount.*
*All passengers have to/must board through the door on the right.*

> **Look!** We can use *prohibited* or *forbidden* to talk about rules in more formal or written English. *Taking photos in this exhibit is strictly prohibited/forbidden.*

1 Choose the correct options to complete the sentences.

1 We *'d better / 're supposed to* take a taxi, or we'll be late.
2 You *wouldn't / You're supposed to* take a basket or a shopping cart around the grocery store.
3 Perhaps we *ought to / have to* use the crosswalk, as it's a lot safer.
4 You *'d better not / don't have to* forget my books. They're due at the library today!
5 Are we *supposed to / allowed to* line up at the taxi stand?
6 You *can't / must* have insurance! It's strictly prohibited to drive without it.
7 You *can't / shouldn't* ride a motorcycle without a helmet. It's not allowed.
8 *We're not allowed to / We'd better not* play music now. We might wake up the baby.

2 Complete the sentences with the words in the box. Use the correct form. Add any words you need.

> allowed to    (not) have to    better not    ought to
> can't    supposed to    forbidden    have to

1 You _____ late or your father will be very angry.
2 You _____ put your password in to get into your account. You can't access it without it.
3 The use of barbecue grills inside the apartment is _____ .
4 I totally forgot I _____ be in a meeting later this afternoon. Maybe someone else can go.
5 Good news! They've changed the rules on calculators. Now we _____ use them on the economics exam.
6 You _____ play ball near the windows. You might break one!
7 We really _____ introduce Sam to our group. He's new here.
8 We _____ get up early tomorrow. It's a holiday!

◂ Go back to page 23

116

# 3C Phrasal verbs

 3.13

We **broke up** last week after the party.
I **threw out** my homework by mistake!
Katie **showed** her parents **around** her new apartment.
You dropped a fork. Please **pick** it **up** and put it in the sink.
You **take after** your mother. You're just like her!
If you had to **put up with** my boss, you'd quit, too.

This section gives you an overview of phrasal verbs and how they operate. See page 174 for a list of common phrasal verbs.

## What are phrasal verbs?

A phrasal verb is a verb followed by words like *up*, *down*, *through*, *on*, and *off*. You may be able to guess the meaning from the main verb.

She <u>turned off</u> the light and went to sleep.
I <u>took</u> my girlfriend <u>out</u> for dinner last night.

However, most phrasal verbs have an idiomatic meaning, and the combination of the two words does not make the meaning clear.

I <u>came across</u> a really interesting article. (= found)

The best way to remember phrasal verbs is to learn them in context.

## Without an object

These phrasal verbs are not followed by an object. The two parts of these verbs are never separated.

My daughter wants to be a doctor when she <u>grows up</u>.
What time should we <u>go back</u> tomorrow?

## With an object (separable)

These phrasal verbs are followed by an object. In many cases, the object can go *after* or *between* the two parts of the phrasal verb. (Because the two parts can be separated, these verbs are called "separable.")

I wanted to <u>try</u> my new shoes <u>on</u>/<u>try on</u> my new shoes.

In some cases, the object can *only* be placed *between* the two parts of the phrasal verb.

This afternoon I'm going to <u>show</u> the tourists <u>around</u> the old town.

When the object of these verbs is a pronoun, it always goes *between* the two parts.

I bought you a new jacket. <u>Try</u> it <u>on</u>. NOT ~~Try on it.~~

## With an object (non-separable)

These phrasal verbs are followed by an object. The object can *only* be placed *after* the two parts of the phrasal verb.

You'd better <u>get on</u> the bus now! It's about to leave!

When the object of these verbs is a pronoun, it always goes after the two parts.

The questions aren't hard. I'll <u>go over</u> them with you later. NOT ~~I'll go them over.~~

## With three words (non-separable)

These phrasal verbs are followed by an object. The three parts of these phrasal verbs are never separated. When the object is a pronoun, it goes after the verb.

Do you <u>get along with</u> your sister?
He tried to cheat on the exam, but he didn't <u>get away with</u> it.

---

**GRAMMAR PRACTICE**

**1** Complete the sentences with the correct form of the phrasal verbs in the box. You do not need one of them. Add any pronouns you need.

| eat out | look for | look forward to |
|---------|----------|-----------------|
| look up | put up with | take after |
| take off | talk into | turn down |

1 I really don't know how much longer I can _____ my boss!
2 If you don't know a word, you can _____ .
3 I think my daughter really _____ her father.
4 I've been _____ the party all week.
5 Paul _____ going away last weekend, so I didn't finish my assignment.
6 I can't find my glasses! I _____ all day yesterday!
7 Our plane _____ on time and landed early.
8 Let's _____ tonight! I'm too tired to cook.

**2** Rewrite the sentences. Correct the mistakes. Check (✓) the two sentences that are correct.

1 I love coffee. I could never do it without!
   _____
2 I thought I'd lost my wallet, but then it turned it up.
   _____
3 I came something really weird across. I don't know what it is.
   _____
4 Hey, there's no soap. I hope you didn't use up it!
   _____
5 Why isn't Joe with you? Did you break up with him?
   _____
6 I tried, but I couldn't come up any good ideas.
   _____
7 The course was so much work, but, in the end, it really paid it off.
   _____
8 John was offered a good job, but he turned it down.
   _____
9 I know you don't want to go, but we can't get it out of.
   _____
10 These math problems are hard. I can't figure out them!
   _____

◀ Go back to page 27

# GRAMMAR PRACTICE

## 4A Subject-verb agreement

 4.5

Some of the **things** she said **were** very funny.
The **information** he gave me **was** very surprising.
**One** of you **is** lying!
**Everyone finds** it hard to meet new people.
**A few** of my friends **want** to go traveling together next year.
**My family is** very understanding.
**My friends**, as well as my mother, all **think** I should look for a new job.

### Countable and uncountable nouns

Countable nouns can be singular or plural. When they are plural, they are followed by the plural form of a verb. Uncountable nouns are always singular and are followed by the singular form of a verb.

*Your colleagues think you made the right decision.* NOT *Your colleagues thinks you made the right decision.*
*Your advice was very helpful.* NOT *Your advices were very helpful.*

### Indefinite pronouns

The indefinite pronouns *one*, *everyone*, *no one*, *someone*, and *anyone* are followed by a singular verb.

*Everyone has been trying to help me find an apartment.*
*Does anyone want to go to the beach this weekend?*

*Each* and *each of* are followed by a singular verb. However, *many* (*of*), *some* (*of*), *both* (*of*), *several* (*of*), and *a few* (*of*) are all followed by a plural verb.

*Each neighborhood has its own play area for children.*
*Several of my friends have bought their own apartments recently.*

In informal conversation, singular words like *everyone* and *everybody* are sometimes followed by the word *their* + a noun. However, in American English, this is not considered correct in writing.

*Everyone disagrees with their parents at times.* (spoken, informal)
*Everybody asks his or her parents for money on occasion.* (usually written)

### Collective nouns

In American English, collective nouns are generally singular. (In British English, many collective nouns are frequently plural.)

*My team is playing very well at the moment.*
*The government wants to employ more elementary school teachers.*

Collective nouns referring to a group of individuals, however, are plural.

*The police are stopping cars along the highway.*
*The Japanese are usually very polite.*

### Asides

When a sentence has a comment in the middle as an "aside," the verb always agrees with the subject of the sentence, not the noun in the aside. Asides often begin with inclusive phrases, like *as well as* or *in addition to*, or exclusive phrases, like *aside from* or *apart from*.

*My sister, in addition to a lot of my friends, loves dancing.* NOT *My sister, in addition to a lot of my friends, love dancing.*
*All of my teachers, apart from just one, are planning to come to my wedding.*
NOT *All of my teachers, apart from just one, is planning to come to my wedding.*

1 Choose the correct options to complete the sentences.
  1 Some of the information *was / were* very helpful.
  2 Everyone always *stands / stand* near the door when I try to get on the train.
  3 My boyfriend, as well as my friends, *thinks / think* people don't have any manners.
  4 Only one of us *doesn't / don't* have any pet peeves.
  5 In American English, we say "My family *gets / get* together every weekend."
  6 Some of my decisions *has / have* turned out OK.
  7 The police *believes / believe* that two people were involved in the robbery.
  8 The stores here, apart from one, *is / are* very expensive.

2 Read the text. Choose the correct options.

> **Life in the city – a pet peeve**
>
> Many pedestrians in Barcelona ¹*has / have* experienced nearly being knocked over by a bicyclist riding on the sidewalk. One of my friends ²*was / were* hit by a bike last year. Only a few of these riders ³*is / are* ever fined for this dangerous behavior. Even when bike riders use the street, some of them ⁴*don't / doesn't* stop at red lights, so a pedestrian ⁵*risks / risk* his or her life crossing the street. Of course, pedestrians also ⁶*needs / need* to follow the rules and not walk in bike lanes. Each of us ⁷*has / have* to do our part to make Barcelona a safer city. My advice ⁸*is / are* to look behind you frequently as you walk!

3 Read the text. Correct the eight mistakes.

> One of my pet peeves are tattoos. Almost everyone I know think tattoos are really beautiful, but I think they're ugly. Untattooed skin are much nicer. Some of my friends, as well as my sister, has wanted to have their tattoos removed, but the process are expensive and not always successful. No one think about this, though, in advance. One of my friends really don't want his tattoo with his ex-girlfriend's name anymore! Everyone need to think carefully before getting a tattoo!

◀ Go back to page 31

118

# 4C Perfect and past forms

▶ 4.9

**Have** you **been** here before? I**'ve wanted** to go for months.
We **haven't had** dinner yet. There **has been** a bad accident on the highway.
I**'ve been looking** for a new job since the summer.
The kitchen's a mess because we**'ve been cooking**.

## Present perfect
We form the present perfect with *have/has* + past participle. We use it:
- to talk about past experiences in your life without saying when they happened.
  *I've been to Mexico several times, but I've never been to Brazil.*
- to talk about complete or incomplete past actions. We use *already*, *yet*, and *still*.
  *They've already bought their mother a birthday present.*
  *I haven't spoken to Mike yet./I still haven't spoken to Mike.*
- to talk about actions or states that start in the past and continue in the present, especially with *for* and *since*.
  *Adam's worked here for 20 years/since 1998.*
- to talk about past actions that have an effect on the present.
  *I've left my job. Now I'm working as a freelance journalist.*

## Present perfect vs. simple past
We use the simple past:
- to talk about finished actions or states in the past.
  Simple past: *I lived in London for three years.* (But now I live in Paris.)
  Present perfect: *I've lived in London for three years.* (I still live there.)
- to talk about recent past actions:
  *I bought a car recently.   I just handed in my essay.*
- to talk about finished actions when we know when they happened.
  Simple past: *They saw the new Star Wars movie on Saturday.* (We know when.)
  Present perfect: *They've seen the new Star Wars movie.* (We don't know when.)

## Present perfect continuous
We form the present perfect continuous with *have* + *been* + the *-ing* form of the verb. We use the present perfect continuous:
- to talk about longer or repeated actions that started in the past and continue in the present.
  *We've been waiting for the bus for 45 minutes/since 1 p.m.*
- to talk about a longer action in the past that has an effect on the present.
  *I'm out of breath because I've been running.*

## Present perfect vs. present perfect continuous
We use the present perfect when the action is complete. We use the present perfect continuous when the action is still taking place.
*I've written an essay.* (The essay is finished.)
*I've been writing an essay.* (I'm still writing the essay.)
We can use both forms to talk about the duration of an action that starts in the past and continues in the present with verbs like *live*, *work* and *study*.
*I've lived/been living here for ten years/since 2010.*
We don't use the present perfect continuous with state verbs.
*I've known Melanie for a long time.* NOT ~~I've been knowing Melanie for a long time.~~

# GRAMMAR PRACTICE

1 Choose the correct options to complete the sentences.
  1 I've *preferred / been preferring* to bike to work for a couple of years.
  2 How long *did you live / have you lived* in New York before you *moved / have moved*?
  3 *We've been / We went* to the museum earlier today.
  4 It's the best movie *I've ever seen / I've ever been seeing*.
  5 *I've been sitting / I've sat* in this cold waiting room for three hours, and I'm still waiting!
  6 *They've been deciding / They've decided* to get married, so they're very excited and happy.

2 Complete the sentences with the correct form of the verbs in parentheses. There may be more than one answer.
  1 Tom _____ (have) a motorbike since he was 18.
  2 We _____ (think) of getting a dog since we moved here, but we're not sure if it's a good idea.
  3 _____ (you/take) this type of test before?
  4 I _____ (get up) early this morning, but I _____ (not finish) my paper yet.
  5 We _____ (live) here for the last two years.
  6 My sister _____ (work) hard in the garden, and now I think she should stop.

3 Choose the correct options to complete the conversations.
  1 A How long have you *known / been knowing* Jenny?
    B About four years, I guess.
  2 A When are you going to do your homework?
    B *I already did / I've already done* it.
  3 A Are you OK?
    B Yes, we're just a bit tired. *We've been helping / We help* a friend move.
  4 A *My dad never went / My dad's never been* to a Japanese restaurant, and he'd love to go to one.
    B Let's take him next week!
  5 A You look happy!
    B I am! *I just got / I've just been getting* some good news!

◀ Go back to page 35

GRAMMAR PRACTICE

# 5A  so and such; so much/many, so little/few

 5.3

It's **so difficult** to change the way you eat.
There are **so many** different **ways** to protect our natural resources.
There are **so few** good **shows** on TV at the moment.
I have **so much homework** to do this week.
There is **so little money** to spend on recycling.
It was **such a relief** to go off my diet.
You have **such strange ideas**!
I found **such good information** online.

## so

We use *so* before an adjective for emphasis.

*It's so hard to have a conversation with my sister!*

We use *so many* and *so few* before plural countable nouns.

*There are so many good books on the environment.*
*There are so few days when I have time to cook.*

We use *so much* and *so little* before uncountable nouns.

*There's so much false information on the Internet these days.*
*I have so little time to do the things I want.*

## such

We use *such a/an* before singular countable nouns for emphasis.

*Global warming is such a serious problem.* NOT *Global warming is such serious problem.*
*It makes such an enormous difference if you recycle.*

We use *such* before plural countable nouns for emphasis.

*They sell such nice products here!* NOT *They sell such a nice products here.*
*We've had such interesting discussions on so many issues.*

We also use *such* before uncountable nouns.

*My friends gave me such good advice.* NOT *My friends gave me such a good advice.*
*If you ever need a painter, Joe does such nice work.*

> **Look!** *So* and *such* are often used in sentences that express cause and effect.
> *We've had such a dry summer (that) we may start to get forest fires.*
> *There's so much pollution (that) I can't breathe!*

1  Complete the conversation with *so*, *such*, *so much*, *so many*, *so little*, or *so few*.

A My neighbors are a problem again! They've been making [1]_____ noise that I haven't been able to sleep properly for days!
B There are [2]_____ people these days who are rude. Why do they have [3]_____ respect for others?
A I don't know, but it's [4]_____ a problem that I'm thinking of calling the manager. It makes me [5]_____ angry! I've already talked to my neighbors [6]_____ times, but they just ignore me.
B It must be [7]_____ frustrating.
A It sure is! And tiring. There are [8]_____ nights when I sleep well now.

2  Complete the sentences using the prompts and *so*, *such*, *so much*, *so many*, *so little* or *so few*.

1 almost no clean water
  There's _____ that we have to buy bottled water.
2 lots of benefits to a zero-impact month
  There are _____ that we're going to try it next month.
3 lots of friends on social media
  I keep in touch with _____ that I don't want to stop using it.
4 big problem with recycling
  We have _____ that we don't even try to do it.
5 enjoyable to bike to work
  It's _____ that I do it every morning.
6 a large amount of trash outside my door
  There's _____ that I've complained about it to the city.
7 easy ways to help the environment
  These are _____ that everyone can do them.
8 almost no paper bags in stores
  There are _____ that I bring my own from home.
9 good advice on energy-saving
  This is _____ that I'm going to follow it.
10 expensive to have a car
  It's _____ that I've decided not to get one.

◀ Go back to page 41

## 5C Future predictions

 5.12

In my opinion, public transportation **will improve** in the next ten years.
**Won't** many people **suffer** from the effects of climate change in the future?
We**'re going to have** much more extreme weather.
By 2050, we **will have invented** many new ways to save energy.
When the year ends, we **might not have made** much progress.
We**'ll** definitely **be living** in a different world twenty years from now!
**Will** we still **be working** when we're 100?

### Future with *will, going to, may,* and *might*

We use *will* and *won't* to make predictions about the future, based on our personal opinions.

*In my opinion, the planet will be very hot in 50 years.*

We often use *Do you think ... ?* to ask someone to make a prediction.

*Do you think we'll be better at controlling our resources?*

We use *be going to* to make predictions that we are sure about, based on something we can see or something that we know.

*Look at all this trash. I'm positive we're going to have mice in our apartment!*

We use the adverbs *probably* and *definitely* to make a prediction less or more certain. We use them after *will* but before *won't*.

*They'll probably collect the trash later. It definitely won't be here tomorrow.*
*They're definitely not going to let this continue!*

We use *may* and *might* to make predictions that we're less certain about.

*It hasn't rained at all this month. I think we may/might not have enough water.*

**Look!** To make a negative prediction with *will*, we normally use the negative form of *think*, followed by *will*.
*I don't think we'll be much more aware.* NOT *I think we won't be much more aware.*

### Future perfect

We form the future perfect with *will/won't + have +* the past participle of the main verb. We use the future perfect to predict events that will be completed before a certain point in the future.

*By the year 2020, we will have given up non-electric cars.*
*In 50 years, pollution will have disappeared.*
*How long will you have lived here by 2020?* NOT *How long will you live here by 2020?*

We can also form the future perfect with *may* or *might* to express a possibility that we are less sure of. We sometimes use phrases like *I think* or *It seems that*.

*I think by 2100 some of our lakes may have disappeared.*
*We might not have found other energy sources by then.*

### Future continuous

We form the future continuous with *will/won't + be +* the *-ing* form of the main verb. We use the future continuous to predict events that will be in progress at a certain point in the future.

*In 50 years, we'll be living on a very hot planet!*
*We won't be getting a lot of help from the government.*
*Will people still be wasting so much water?*

◀ Go back to page 45

---

## GRAMMAR PRACTICE

**1** Choose the best options to complete the conversations.
1. A I feel terrible!
   B I'm sure that you *will feel / may feel* better tomorrow.
2. A I'm so worried about Molly.
   B I'm not. I think she *will have solved / might be solving* her problem at work by the time we see her again.
3. A What are you doing this weekend?
   B I'm not sure. I *will go / may go* for a hike with some friends, but nothing's planned yet.
4. A Do you know about this great app that monitors your energy use at home?
   B Yes! I'm already using it. In a year, I *will cut / will have cut* my energy use in half.
5. A I hope they do something soon about people who throw gum in the street!
   B Me too. I read that they *will be getting / might have gotten* fines in the future.
6. A Can I read your report?
   B It's not done yet. But I *might be finishing / might have finished* it by tomorrow.
7. A The traffic's awful this morning! We're not moving at all!
   B I know! *I'm going to miss / I'll miss* my train!
8. A Should we go shopping now?
   B Yes, good idea. The stores *probably won't / won't probably* be too crowded now.

**2** Complete the sentences with *will* + a future perfect or future continuous form of the verbs in the box.

| work | not fly | rain | improve |
|---|---|---|---|
| get | increase | live | use |

1. By the end of the century, forest fires _____ by 50 percent!
2. It's raining again! By tomorrow, it _____ every day this week.
3. If I don't start saving money now, I _____ even when I'm 70!
4. I think many more people _____ solar energy in a few years.
5. I hope that in the future, we _____ in more energy-efficient homes.
6. With all this evidence, it's safe to say that climate change _____ a lot worse by 2050.
7. I think healthcare _____ a lot by the time we're in our fifties.
8. In my view, people _____ so much in the future.

121

# GRAMMAR PRACTICE

## 6A The habitual past

 6.2

I **used to love** rock music, but now I like reggae.
**Did** you **use to play** an instrument when you were young?
I **didn't use to play** soccer, but I **would go** to games.
I **used to spend** a lot of time at home. I **would watch** TV every afternoon.
My teachers **were always yelling** at me because I was late.
She'**d** often **go** running after school. She'**d** also **gone** running that evening.

### used to and would

We use *used to* + infinitive to talk about states or habits that were true in the past but are not true now. Habits are repeated actions.

*I used to hate classical music, but now I love it.    She used to go swimming every day.*

In affirmative statements, *used* in *used to* ends with a *d*, just like other regular verbs in the simple past. *Use to* is incorrect.

*We used to spend every evening outside in the summer.* NOT *We use to spend every evening outside in the summer.*

We form negative statements and questions without a *d*, like other simple past verbs. We may also use *never used to* instead of *didn't use to*.

*I didn't use to like classical music.* NOT *I didn't used to like classical music.*
*Did you use to live around here?* NOT *Did you used to live around here?*
*I never used to watch YouTube videos, but now I like them.*

We often use a mixture of *used to* and *would* when we describe past habits. We start with *used to* and continue with *would*.

*I used to do a lot of exercise when I was in high school. I would play tennis every weekend and go swimming three or four times a week.*

We do not use *would* to describe states. Instead we use *used to* or the simple past.

*I hated/used to hate vegetables when I was a kid.* NOT *I would hate vegetables when I was a kid.*

### Simple past

We may use either *used to* or the simple past when the habitual meaning is clear. We often use a mixture of *used to* and the simple past to describe past situations.

*I didn't use to play any sports when I was younger. I hated sports.*

We use the simple past, not *used to*, when we talk about single actions or say how many times something happened.

*We went to Rio three times when I was young.* NOT *We used to go to Rio three times when I was young.*

### Past continuous with *always*

We can use the past continuous with *always* to show that something happened repeatedly, or to talk about things that were annoying.

*I remember her well. She was always sitting outside when I went by.*
*I never had any privacy. My brother was always listening to my conversations.*

### would vs. had

When we talk about the past, the contraction '*d* may mean the habitual past *would* or the past perfect *had*. Be careful not to confuse them.

*Every evening, we'd go for a swim in the lake.* (= we would)
*We'd just gotten out of the water when we saw my sister.* (= we had)

---

1 Choose the correct options to complete the sentences.
  1 I *used to / would* love visiting my grandparents. They were such wonderful people.
  2 You're such a good tennis player. Did you *used / use* to play when you were younger?
  3 I *used to go / went* to Europe twice when I was in college, but I haven't been since.
  4 I *used to / would* know all my neighbors, but I don't now.
  5 My brother and I *were always arguing / were arguing* when we were younger.
  6 We *didn't used / didn't use* to go on vacation very often.
  7 My sister *used to / would* have a bike that she *rode / was riding* everywhere.
  8 My friends and I never *used / use* to play baseball after school because we had nowhere to play.

2 Rewrite the underlined words. Use a pronoun + *had* or *would*.
  1 Every day I'd _____ come home from school and play video games.
  2 I'd _____ forgotten how much fun it was to go fishing. We'd _____ go fishing all the time when I was a kid.
  3 I used to really enjoy reading, and I'd _____ read at least one book a week.
  4 My sister used to buy really weird clothes, and she'd _____ wear them to parties.
  5 We had no money for the bus home because we'd _____ spent all our money on ice cream.
  6 That summer my brother was going out with Teresa. He'd _____ met her in college and was crazy about her.

3 Complete the text with a form of *used to*, *would*, the simple past, or the past continuous with *always*, and the verbs in the box. There may be more than one answer.

| complain  go (x2)  not listen |
| love  make  stay  take |

When I was a child, my family [1]_____ a trip every summer to the Shenandoah National Park in the state of Virginia. We [2]_____ at a little cabin in the woods, and every day we [3]_____ on long nature walks. My younger sister didn't enjoy them much, and she [4]_____ that she was tired. However, my older sister and I [5]_____ being outdoors all day. We [6]_____ to the reports of bears because we didn't really think there were any! When we went to bed, we [7]_____ sure we hadn't left any food around, though. We loved it so much that we [8]_____ back there at least ten times.

◀ Go back to page 49

# GRAMMAR PRACTICE

## 6C  be used to and get used to

 6.7

I **wasn't used to making** my own decisions.
Now I**'m used to living** on my own.
I've slowly **gotten used to working** in an office.
**Getting used to college life** hasn't been easy.
**Are** you **getting used to not having** a car?

### be used to

*Be used to* means "be accustomed to." We use *be used to* to express a state. *Be used to* is usually followed by the *-ing* form of a verb or a noun.

*When I first started this job, I wasn't used to working on weekends.*
*Are you used to your new home?*

When *be used to* is followed by a clause, use *the fact that*.

*I'm just not used to the fact that I'm now responsible for my own rent.*

> **Look!** Be careful not to confuse *be used to* with the habitual past *used to*.
> *Are you used to getting up early?* (= accustomed to)
> *No, I never used to get up before 10 a.m. until I got this job.* (= habitual past)

The word *used* always has a *d* in *be used to*.

*Is your sister used to driving around here?* NOT *Is your sister use to driving around here?*

### get used to

We use *get used to* to express a process. It means "become accustomed to." *Get used to* is usually followed by the *-ing* form or a noun.

*I can't get used to being away from home.*
*I hope I'll get used to college.*
*You've always gotten used to everything before.*

*Get used to* can also be followed by *the fact that* + a clause.

*I'll never get used to the fact that I didn't get accepted to Harvard.*

The subject of a sentence can also contain the *-ing* form of *get used to*.

*Getting used to a big move has never been easy.*

> **Look!** Be careful not to confuse *get used to* with the habitual past *used to*.
> *I can't get used to living here.*
> NOT *I can't used to live here.*
> *Did you get used to things by the end of the year?*
> NOT *Did you use to things by the end of the year?*

1 Choose the correct options to complete the sentences.

1. I just can't *be used to / get used to* living alone. I don't know what I'm going to do.
2. I *used to / 'm used to* be nervous about flying, but slowly I *got used to / was used to* it.
3. *Are you use to / Are you used to* your new dorm? I hope you have nice roommates.
4. *Getting used to / Being used to* life in the U.S. was hard at first, but it's now easier.
5. My new job is an incredible amount of work, but *I'm being used / I'm getting used* to it slowly.
6. We *weren't used to / didn't use to* living in a city, so we found the move to Chicago hard.
7. I think my new dog *is finally used to / finally used to* me. I'm so happy I have him.
8. My parents couldn't get used to *that / the fact that* I was looking for my own apartment.

2 Complete the conversations with a form of *be used to* or *get used to*. There may be more than one answer.

1. **A** I'm a little worried. My daughter [1]_____ going to school by bus, and she doesn't want to leave home in the morning.
   **B** Oh, don't worry. She [2]_____ it soon, I'm sure. My son didn't like it at first, either, but he [3]_____ to it quite quickly.
2. **A** You know what? I [4]_____ being an adult yet.
   **B** Why do you say that?
   **A** I just can't [5]_____ having so much responsibility.
3. **A** So, [6]_____ living on your own at school now?
   **B** Well, I guess I could say I [7]_____ it little by little. I [8]_____ the food yet, though. It's awful!
4. **A** Your parents [9]_____ their new home, haven't they?
   **B** Yes, I think so. But they [10]_____ the new neighbors yet, who play music at all hours!

◀ Go back to page 53

123

# VOCABULARY PRACTICE

## 1A Body language and communication

1 ▶ 1.1 Match sentences 1–12 with pictures a–l. Listen and check.

1 Come here! **Give** me **a hug**! _____
2 When I asked him the way to the restaurant, he just **shrugged** his **shoulders**. _____
3 No one can hear me unless I **raise** my **voice**! _____
4 When we saw Mike **waving** at us, he **winked**, so we knew he had a secret. _____
5 She **tapped** me **on the shoulder** to get my attention. _____
6 When he asked her if she wanted coffee she **nodded** and said, "Yes, please." _____
7 I'm **shaking** my **head** because I don't know the answer. _____
8 We just **shook hands** because we don't know each other very well. _____
9 When I visit my mother, I always **kiss** her **on the cheek**. _____
10 That man is **staring** at me from across the room. He's trying to **make eye contact**. _____
11 I was **gazing** at the stars last night. They were beautiful. _____
12 I could tell she was annoyed with me because she was **frowning**. _____

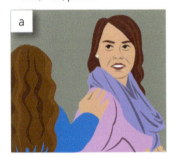

2 Complete the sentences with the expressions in the box. Use the correct verb tenses and make any other necessary changes.

> shake hands   raise your voice   shrug your shoulders   tap someone on the shoulder
> nod   shake your head   wave   give someone a hug

1 I asked Ann where her dad was, but she just _____ – it was obvious she didn't know.
2 As a little boy, I always used to kiss my parents good night and _____ before I went to bed.
3 When she asked Keith if he agreed, he didn't say anything. He just _____ his head up and down.
4 In the business world, you can tell a lot about someone's character simply by how the person _____ with you.
5 When my mother told me the news, I said, "No way!" and _____ from side to side.
6 He was standing with his back to me, so I _____ .
7 "_____ good-bye to Grandpa, Lucy," my mother said.
8 There's no microphone, so the audience won't be able to hear you unless you _____ .

◀ Go back to page 4

136

**VOCABULARY PRACTICE**

## 1B Compound adjectives

1 ▶ 1.4 Put the words in the box in the correct categories. Listen and check.

| far-reaching | forward-thinking | highly respected | life-changing | middle-aged |
| open-minded | record-breaking | slow-moving | time-consuming | well-educated |

| adjective/adverb + present participle | adjective/adverb/noun + past/participle | noun + adjective/present participle |
|---|---|---|
| good-looking | old-fashioned | world-famous |
|  | self-centered |  |

2 Complete the sentences with the correct options.

1 That dress is very *old-fashioned / middle-aged*. It's totally out of style compared to your other clothes!
2 It's really *slow-moving / time-consuming* to do my homework. I'm not good at math.
3 When I meet new people, I always try to be *open-minded / well educated*, even when I don't think I like them.
4 My manager is very *forward-thinking / record-breaking* – he has some very innovative ideas.
5 People who are *highly respected / self-centered* only consider what is important for them.
6 A *world-famous / far-reaching* novelist spoke at our school yesterday, but I'd never heard of him.
7 When Emily was over 50, she made a *life-changing / middle-aged* decision and moved to China.
8 His decision to leave his job had *far-reaching / forward-thinking* consequences for his family.

◀ Go back to page 6

## 1C Expectations

1 ▶ 1.8 What do sentences 1–10 mean? Choose the correct option, a or b. Listen and check.

1 I **can't wait** to meet her. I won't **get a second chance**.
   a I'm really looking forward to meeting her.
   b I might meet her one day, but not now.
2 I was **hoping for** something better.
   a I was pleased.
   b I wasn't pleased.
3 His performance really **impressed** me.
   a I thought it was very good.
   b I didn't think it was very good.
4 She **made a good** first **impression on** me.
   a Before I got to know her well, I liked her.
   b After I got to know her well, I liked her.
5 My brother says he can't **live without** his cell phone.
   a He doesn't mind not having it with him.
   b He hates not having it with him.
6 The experiment was a **failure** because we **failed to** follow instructions.
   a It worked.
   b It didn't work.
7 I **expected** the food to be better, but had to **lower my expectations**.
   a It was as good as I'd hoped.
   b It wasn't as good as I'd hoped.
8 The service **met my expectations**.
   a It was what I expected.
   b It wasn't what I expected.
9 The play **was a success**.
   a People liked it.
   b People didn't like it.
10 The movie **was such a disappointment** to my mother.
   a She expected it to be better.
   b She expected it to be worse.

2 ▶ 1.9 Notice the forms of the nouns and verbs. Complete the chart with words from exercise 1. Listen and check.

| verb | noun |
|---|---|
| disappoint |  |
|  | failure |
| succeed |  |
|  | expectation |
| impress |  |

3 Complete the review with the correct form of the words in the box.

| impress | expect | wait | succeed | hope | disappoint | fail |

Commercially speaking, the band's last album was a big ¹_____, as it sold millions of copies. But, to me, it was a huge ²_____ and ³_____ to meet my ⁴_____. This time, though, I'm ⁵_____ for something much better, and I think the new album will be great. I just heard the first single from the album on the radio, and it made a good first ⁶_____ on me. I can't ⁷_____ to hear the whole album, which comes out next month.

◀ Go back to page 8

137

# VOCABULARY PRACTICE

## 2A Adjective suffixes

1 ▶ 2.1 Put the adjective forms of the words in the box in the correct column. Listen and check.

ambition (n)   end (n)   attract (v)   memory (n)   home (n)   adventure (n)
option (n)   break (n)   power (n)   faith (n)   impress (v)   accident (n)

| -able | -al | -ful | -ive | -ous | -less |
|---|---|---|---|---|---|
| desirable | controversial | colorful | aggressive | cautious | harmless |
| reasonable | conventional | cheerful | decisive | ridiculous | painless |
| washable | _____ | dreadful | effective | _____ | useless |
| _____ | _____ | painful | _____ | _____ | _____ |
|  |  | useful |  |  |  |
|  |  | _____ |  |  |  |
|  |  | _____ |  |  |  |

2 Complete the discussion-forum messages with adjectives from exercise 1.

## WHAT'S YOUR IDEAL PARTNER LIKE?

**Amy27** My ideal partner is ¹a_____ and likes to try new things, visit exotic places, do extreme sports – that sort of thing. I tend to be a ²c_____ person, who plans everything carefully and avoids taking risks, so I need someone who's the opposite of me. Perhaps I should date a skydiving instructor – that way I'd have some ³m_____ experiences I'd never forget!

**LauraZ** Tough question, but, above all, he should be ⁴c_____ and positive. You know, someone who makes me laugh and who's fun to be around. Oh, and being ⁵f_____ is important, too, of course. I don't want my boyfriend to go out with anyone else! I also like people who are ⁶d_____ and know what they want.

**Adam3X** I want her to surprise me from time to time – I'm tired of people with ⁷c_____ attitudes, values, and tastes. I also like people who can make me think. You know, I enjoy discussing ⁸c_____ topics, and I like it when my partner and I disagree on things. Oh, and I hope we meet by accident. I don't want to find love on a dating app.

**Jas82** I've been married for eleven years, and my husband and I have a great relationship. He has most of the qualities I find ⁹d_____ in a partner: He's fair and ¹⁰r_____, and always makes logical decisions. And he wants to be successful, which is great.

**Micky44** My ideal partner? Easy – my wife, Gloria. I really admire her. She's a very talented artist, with an ¹¹i_____ body of work for a young person. Her paintings are really ¹²c_____. Surprisingly, she's not ¹³a_____, but she's been very successful for someone her age.

◀ Go back to page 12

# VOCABULARY PRACTICE

## 2C Phrasal verbs (1)

1 ▶ 2.7 Read the text and match phrasal verbs 1–10 with definitions a–j. Listen and check.

### FOUR secrets to success

**1 DON'T GIVE UP.** One of the reasons why I really ¹**look up to** people like J.K. Rowling, Michael Jordan, and Madonna is that they never give up. J.K. Rowling, for example, was ²**turned down** by several different publishers before Harry Potter became a worldwide phenomenon.

**2 BE PERSUASIVE.** Change can be scary. If you have a new idea, people will sometimes try to discourage you, and say your idea is "crazy" or "not practical." They're just trying to ³**get out of** accepting that change can actually be good. Don't ⁴**give in** and say, "Yes, you're right." Instead, try to find a way to ⁵**talk** them **into** seeing the benefits of your idea.

**3 PAY ATTENTION TO DETAIL.** Steve Jobs had a reputation for being a tough boss. People say he valued punctuality and used to get upset if people ⁶**showed up** late for work. But, more importantly, Jobs was obsessed with perfection, and he wouldn't accept mistakes or ⁷**put up with** negativity.

**4 LOOK FOR SIMPLE SOLUTIONS.** Bill Gates once said that one of the biggest obstacles to success is too much complexity. Throughout his career, he has always tried to ⁸**figure out** simple ways to solve complicated problems, and his efforts ⁹**paid off**: Microsoft Windows is still popular after all these years, and most computer users can't ¹⁰**do without** it.

a persuade or convince someone ___
b admire and respect someone ___
c bring good results; be worth the effort ___
d accept or tolerate something unpleasant ___
e arrive or appear somewhere ___
f refuse an offer or opportunity ___
g stop arguing; admit defeat ___
h finally understand or solve a problem ___
i manage without something ___
j avoid doing something ___

2 ▶ 2.8 Complete the sentences with the correct particles. Listen and check.

| across  after  off  out  up  with |

1 The game was **called** _____ because of the rain.

2 Bernie really **takes** _____ his father.

3 Lucy **came** _____ a briefcase full of money.

4 The tickets **sold** _____ within hours.

5 Helen **came up** _____ a great idea.

6 Someone **used** _____ all the toothpaste.

3 Choose the correct phrasal verbs from exercises 1 and 2 to complete the sentences.

1 Paul wanted to make a cake, but he realized he'd *sold out* / *used up* all the eggs in the fridge.
2 Calvin lost his job, so he had to learn to *do without* / *give in* many of the luxuries he was used to.
3 When I *come across* / *figure out* a word in English I've never seen before, I try to guess what it means.
4 One week before the wedding, Nina realized she didn't love Mike anymore, so the wedding was *paid off* / *called off*.
5 I *do without* / *take after* my mother more than my father.
6 Sandra *came up with* / *put up with* a great suggestion, which everybody liked.
7 The party was a huge success. More than a hundred people *turned down* / *showed up*.
8 I didn't want to get a dog, but my children eventually *talked me into* / *got out of* it.

◀ Go back to page 16

# VOCABULARY PRACTICE

## 3A Urban places and problems

1 ▶ 3.1 Match the words in the boxes with pictures 1–16. Listen and check.

| business district   city hall   courthouse   harbor   high-rise building   industrial area   residential area   taxi stand |
|---|

1 _____

2 _____

3 _____

4 _____

5 _____

6 _____

7 _____

8 _____

| vandalism   lack of parking   waste disposal   poverty   smog   (traffic) congestion   homelessness   overcrowding |
|---|

9 _____

10 _____

11 _____

12 _____

13 _____

14 _____

15 _____

16 _____

2 Complete two news stories with words from exercise 1.

A group of 100 people protested in front of [1]_____ this evening and demanded to speak to the mayor. The city was planning to tear down over 20 houses in one of the city's oldest [2]_____ and build a 70-story [3]_____ instead. The event was peaceful, with no signs of violence or [4]_____ .

A recent survey has shown that workers in the city's downtown [5]_____ think [6]_____ is the number one problem, as they are "shocked" by the number of people living on the streets. [7]_____ came second because of the number of cars, which increase commuting time. And [8]_____ was third as it often takes over half an hour to find a space.

140 ◀ Go back to page 23

**VOCABULARY PRACTICE**

## 3B Easily confused words

**1A** ▶ 3.6 Do you know these pairs of words? Listen and repeat.

1 actual / current _____
2 affect / effect _____
3 annoyed / disgusted _____
4 argue / discuss _____
5 avoid / prevent _____
6 choose / elect _____
7 claim / pretend _____
8 disappoint / deceive _____
9 matter / mind _____
10 notice / realize _____
11 safe / sure _____
12 sensible / sensitive _____

a not dangerous
b keep away from
c be important
d a change that's the result of something
e select something from among different options
f understand clearly or become fully aware
g a little angry or irritated
h state that something is true
i easily able to understand someone's feelings
j talk about something with other people
k fail to fulfill hopes or expectations
l real, existing in fact

**B** ▶ 3.7 Match one of the words in each pair 1–12 with its definition a–l. Listen and check.

**2** Complete the sentences with the correct form of a word from exercise 1.

1 My children _____ with me all the time and never do what I tell them.
2 Sue was very _____ when she wasn't accepted by Harvard.
3 Marty is a very _____ person and always thinks about others.
4 Even though I always _____ eating sweets, I can't seem to lose weight!
5 Wilber Jones was _____ governor although the vote was very close.
6 The robber _____ to be my neighbor, and that's why I opened the door.
7 We were all very _____ by the awful accident.
8 That's not true! The _____ reason I didn't come is that I was sick.

◀ Go back to page 24

## 4A Personality and behavior

**1A** ▶ 4.1 Read the sentences. Then match the adjectives in **bold** in sentences 1–12 with definitions a–l. Listen and check.

1 How **thoughtful** of George to send me a get-well card! _____
2 Britney can be so **bossy**! She's always telling everyone what to do. _____
3 A **clumsy** waiter spilled juice all over Rick's new shirt. _____
4 My boss is extremely **unreasonable** and seems to enjoy saying no to us. _____
5 You've made your brother cry again! Why do you have to be so **mean** to him? _____
6 Julia can be really **stubborn**. It's really hard to get her to change her mind. _____
7 Stella married a **charming**, good-looking man in his mid-thirties. _____
8 I wonder why my father has been so **bad-tempered** recently. He's always yelling at people. _____
9 When I'm stressed out, I like watching **silly** movies on Netflix – nothing too complex or thought-provoking, you know. _____
10 My son is first in his class, but he's not **arrogant**. He says he's just like everyone else, not better than the others. _____
11 Sue seems very **enthusiastic** about her new job. I've never seen her happier. _____
12 Neil is 18, but he's not **responsible** enough to have a car yet. I'm afraid he'll have an accident. _____

a superior
b mature
c unkind
d passionate
e difficult to influence
f friendly and likeable
g unfair
h easily annoyed or made angry
i careless
j controlling
k kind and considerate
l not serious or important; ridiculous

**B** In pairs, discuss which of the adjectives in exercise 1A are usually positive.

**2** ▶ 4.2 Complete the expressions in **bold** with the correct form of the verbs in the box. Listen and check.

| get | stand | upset | forgive | boast | drive | take | praise | encourage | take |

1 Bob wasn't the one who came up with the original idea, but he still _____ **credit for** his colleague's work at last week's meeting.
2 Lucy's teacher said her term paper was fantastic. He really _____ her **for** her achievement, and even _____ her **to** start a Ph.D. next year.
3 Ron really _____ **on** my **nerves**. I can't stand his attitude. Yesterday he embarrassed me, and I'll never _____ him **for** doing that.
4 Gary's new at the company, so his boss makes lots of unreasonable requests and _____ **advantage of** him.
5 Claire and Sophie can't be roommates because Claire loves cats, while Sophie **can't** _____ them. She says cats _____ her **crazy**.
6 Julio sometimes _____ people **by** constantly talking about how rich he is. Nobody likes the way he keeps _____ **about** his wealth.

◀ Go back to page 30

141

## VOCABULARY PRACTICE

## 4C Word families

1 ▶ 4.8 Complete the chart with the words *adjective*, *noun*, and *verb*. Notice the common suffixes. Listen and check.

| 1 _____ | 2 _____ | 3 _____ |
|---|---|---|
| achieve | achieve**ment** | achiev**able** |
| create | creat**ivity** | creat**ive** |
| consider | consider**ation** | consider**ate** |
| criticize | critic**ism** | critic**al** |
| persuade | persua**sion** | persuas**ive** |
| rely | reliabil**ity** | reli**able** |
| risk | risk | risk**y** |
| succeed | success | success**ful** |

2 Complete the text with the adjective or noun form of the verbs in parentheses.

### How to meet deadlines

To be ¹_____ (succeed) at school or at work, you have to be hard-working, smart, and ²_____ (create). But ³_____ (rely) is also important, and so is meeting deadlines. Here are a few things you should take into ⁴_____ (consider):

- First of all, put your deadlines on your calendar. Trusting your memory can be ⁵_____ (risk)!
- Sometimes deadlines may not be ⁶_____ (achieve). If so, consider asking for an extension, even if you have to be a little ⁷_____ (persuade).
- If you find yourself procrastinating, maybe you're afraid of people's ⁸_____ (criticize) of your work. Remember: Nobody's perfect!

◀ Go back to page 34

## 5A The environment

1A ▶ 5.1 Match the highlighted words with pictures 1–6. Listen and check.

Studies have shown that because of ¹**climate change**, ²**heat waves** have become much more common across the globe. When a heat wave occurs during a drought, the situation is even worse, since the lack of rain can contribute to wildfires, too.

We need to reduce ³**energy consumption** because our use of ⁴**fossil fuels**, such as coal and oil, is negatively affecting the planet. These fuels increase the amount of ⁵**carbon dioxide** (CO₂) in the atmosphere, which makes the planet warmer. Governments worldwide have been trying to encourage people to use ⁶**environmentally friendly** sources of power such as solar energy and to buy ⁷**energy-efficient** household appliances.

Life in our oceans is disappearing fast, and the most ⁸**endangered species** include birds, turtles, fish, and dolphins. Plastic bags litter our seas and are extremely dangerous to marine wildlife. Recent estimates suggest that nearly 200 species are at risk because they eat these bags and other kinds of litter. Another problem, of course, is toxic waste, which contains dangerous chemicals and sometimes even radioactive material.

B ▶ 5.2 Match the **bold** words 1–8 in the text with definitions a–h. Listen and check.

a periods of unusually hot weather _____
b a type of animal or plant that might disappear soon _____
c using only a small amount of gas or electricity _____
d the gas formed when people burn carbon _____
e not having a negative effect on the environment _____
f a long-term change in the planet's weather because of human activity _____
g fuels that form in the earth from dead plants or animals _____
h the amount of gas and electricity we use _____

2 Complete the sentences with words from the text in exercise 1.

1 When they're young, kids should be taught not to _____ the streets.
2 _____ , as the name implies, comes from the sun.
3 Although we don't like to admit it, _____ around the world has been caused by our own carelessness.
4 We took a trip to Australia and saw some beautiful _____ on the Great Barrier Reef.
5 Environmental groups help to make sure _____ don't disappear completely.
6 _____ lightbulbs are a little more expensive, but they use less power.
7 Burning _____ releases _____ into the atmosphere, which causes global warming.
8 It hasn't rained since May, and we are experiencing the worst _____ in decades.

1 _____

2 _____

3 _____

4 _____

5 _____

6 _____

◀ Go back to page 40

**VOCABULARY PRACTICE**

## 5B Moods

**1A** ▶ 5.5 Which adjectives in the box describe positive moods (+) and which ones negative moods (−)? Listen and check.

| down   dynamic   energetic   enthusiastic   grumpy   lethargic |
| miserable   motivated   optimistic   pessimistic |

**B** Match the ten adjectives with the pictures below.

_____    _____
_____    _____
_____    _____
_____    _____
_____    _____

**2** ▶ 5.6 Complete the conversations with words from exercise 1 and the box below. Use each word only once. Listen and check.

| desperate   distressing   eager   exhausting   passionate   positive |

1 A It's e_____ to have to shovel snow. I get so tired!
  B I wouldn't be very e_____ to do that, either.
2 A Almost no one around here cares about climate change. I find that so d_____ .
  B We need some new d_____ leaders who can make us feel more m_____ .
3 A I'm not sure what's wrong with me today. I feel g_____ and l_____ – you know, just kind of d_____ in general.
  B That's because it's the shortest day of the year. It's hard to feel e_____ and e_____ when it gets dark at 4:30 p.m.!
4 A Is there anything you're really p_____ about – you know, something that excites you that you really care about?
  B Not really. I feel p_____ about the world these days! Thinking about the future makes me feel m_____ !
5 A Why are you so d_____ to find a new job?
  B I really want to feel p_____ about work again.

◀ Go back to page 42

## 5C Adjective prefixes

**1A** ▶ 5.10 Complete the chart with the prefixes in the box. Listen and check.

| dis-   im-   in-   un-   il-   ir-   mis- |

| 1 _____ | 2 _____ | 3 _____ | 4 _____ | 5 _____ | 6 _____ | 7 _____ |
|---|---|---|---|---|---|---|
| polite | appearing | fortunate | accurate | leading | legal | responsible |
| patient | organized | suitable | effective | pronounced | logical | relevant |
| mature | honest | available | visible | spelled | legible | regular |
| probable | satisfied | expected | formal | | | |

**B** Which prefix is used with adjectives that begin with r? And with l?

**2** Complete the sentences with words from exercise 1A.
1 It's really _____ that Ron failed his final exam. Now he'll have to repeat the course.
2 I'm getting a little _____ with my son. He still hasn't cleaned up his room!
3 In English, a _____ word can sometimes be very hard to understand because there are so many words that sound alike.
4 The bus schedule was completely _____ and had the wrong times. I missed the last bus home!
5 I think it's just so _____ to borrow money from friends and not pay them back.
6 I'm really worried about all the _____ wildlife. We're going to have more endangered species soon.
7 Your call can't be that important. It's really _____ to talk on your cell phone at the dinner table.
8 Plastic bags are _____ for recycling and have to be thrown away, but I don't really understand why.
9 What are you going to wear to the party? I think it's pretty casual and _____ .
10 In my city, littering is _____ . If they catch you, you get a big fine!
11 Some of what we learn in school is just so _____ and will never help us get jobs!
12 My ten-year-old son is still too _____ to understand the value of money.
13 This is the coldest winter ever, so how can the planet be getting warmer? It's completely _____ !
14 I can't find energy-efficient bulbs in any of the hardware stores. They're totally _____ at the moment.

◀ Go back to page 44

143

# VOCABULARY PRACTICE

## 6A Expressions with *time*

1 ▶ 6.1 Match the words in **bold** 1–14 with their definitions a–n. Listen and check.

**WHAT'S YOUR BAD HABIT?**

¹**From time to time**, I get really nervous and bite my nails during tests. What can I do? (Luke, London)

I have cheese twice a day, for both breakfast and dinner. It's ²**only a matter of time** before my cholesterol goes up. (Emily, Manchester)

I ³**waste** a lot of **time** reading readers' comments when I read the newspaper online. I don't know why! (Tomiko, New York)

I never seem to finish my exams because I keep going over my answers. Maybe if I ⁴**time myself** while taking practice exams it will help. (Roberta, Toronto)

I always eat too quickly! My mother was always saying, "⁵**Take your time**. Where's the fire?" (Mike, Boston)

I like to ⁶**pass the time** just looking out the window. I know I should be doing my homework, instead! (Peter, Seattle)

I'm almost never ⁷**on time** in the morning. And so I'm never ⁸**in time for** my first class! (María, Puerto Rico)

I'm always telling my sister to run so we can get to the bus stop ⁹**in no time**. And then, of course, we wait and wait while I tell her the bus is coming ¹⁰**any time now**. (Julie, San Francisco)

¹¹**For some time**, I've been playing computer games every night until two or three in the morning. I always feel exhausted when I'm at work! (Tom, Melbourne)

When I was a teenager I always used to listen to rap music. ¹²**At the time**, it really got on my dad's nerves. (Matt, Oxford)

My husband says I never ¹³**make time** for him. I suppose I should go to the soccer game with him occasionally. (Sara, Madrid)

Our city has been demolishing old movie theaters ¹⁴**one at a time**. It's so sad. (Joe, Sydney)

a don't hurry _____
b occasionally _____
c for quite a long period of time _____
d very soon _____
e early enough for something _____
f certain to happen at some point in the near future _____
g fast _____
h in those days _____
i on schedule _____
j don't use time well _____
k spend time _____
l one by one _____
m measure how long I take to do something _____
n reorganize your time for something/someone _____

2 Complete the sentences with the correct form of an expression with *time* from exercise 1.

1 A Are you ready for the marathon?
  B Yes, I _____ today, and I ran 20 km. in just over two hours!
2 A I'm not ready. I still have to take a shower!
  B _____ . We don't have to be there until 7:30.
3 A Tom's been late to work a lot. He's going to lose his job!
  B I know. It's _____ before his boss fires him.
4 A How's your grandmother?
  B A little better, thanks. She can't go out, but she _____ watching TV.
5 A Hey, Joe. Are you busy? Can I come in?
  B Sure. In fact, you're just _____ some hot chocolate!
6 A My little brother is always _____ playing video games.
  B Well, he's only 12. I'm sure he'll develop other interests.
7 A Where did you and your wife meet?
  B In Paris in 1998. We were both teaching at the university _____ .
8 A So, do you know your neighbors well?
  B Yes, we do. We have them over for dinner _____ .

◀ Go back to page 48

**VOCABULARY PRACTICE**

## 6C Expressions with prepositions

**1** ▶ 6.4 Complete the sentences with the prepositions in the box. Pay attention to the adjectives in **bold**. Listen and check.

> about   of   to   with

1  I'm **addicted** _____ coffee, and I don't think I'll ever be able to give it up.
2  I'm going to work next year instead of starting college, and I'm very **comfortable** _____ my decision.
3  I don't know why people are **suspicious** _____ me. I'm a very nice person!
4  Young people today seem to think they're **entitled** _____ high salaries, even if they have no experience.
5  I'm so **anxious** _____ my exam tomorrow. I really hope I don't fail.
6  We're all very **concerned** _____ the high cost of living here. We might have to move.
7  Most millennials are **obsessed** _____ technology. It's a problem!
8  I'm really **fed up** _____ the term "generation gap." I feel I'm a lot like my parents.
9  Sarah was late for the concert because she was **confused** _____ the time. She thought it started at 8 p.m.
10 I'm **sympathetic** _____ my boyfriend's need for attention, but he's driving me crazy!

**2** ▶ 6.5 Read Marcy's e-mail and her friend Laura's response. Complete them with the prepositions in the box. Listen and check.

> about   against   for   in   of   on   to

Hi Laura,
I was accepted into a theater program this summer, but I'm not sure if I should go! The main ¹**advantage** _____ going is that it will be an incredible experience, but the ²**disadvantage** _____ attending the program is the expense. Maybe there will be the ³**possibility** _____ getting a scholarship.
I don't want to ⁴**insist** _____ any help with the program fees, though. They might not ⁵**approve** _____ that.
Anyway, what's your ⁶**reaction** _____ all of this? Please answer soon!
Love,
Marcy

Hi Marcy,
Wow! We all want to ⁷**congratulate** you _____ your exciting news! I'd really ⁸**advise** you _____ saying no. It's a wonderful opportunity! They can't ⁹**criticize** you _____ being worried about the cost, or ¹⁰**accuse** you _____ not being interested. I think you should explain everything honestly. I'm sure they **believe** ¹¹_____ their work and will ¹²**care** _____ your situation.
Love,
Laura

◀ Go back to page 52

145

COMMUNICATION PRACTICE

## 1C  Student A

1. Think of a hobby or interest that was a disappointment to you. Listen to Student B's questions.

2. Ask Student B questions 1–8 about a disappointing place.
   1. What was the place?
   2. When did you go there?
   3. How did you get there?
   4. Who were you with?
   5. Had you been looking forward to going there?
   6. Had you been saving money so you could go?
   7. Why did it fail to impress you?
   8. Will you give the place a second chance?

## 2A  Student A

1. Look at the chart about the artist David Hockney. Answer Student B's questions.

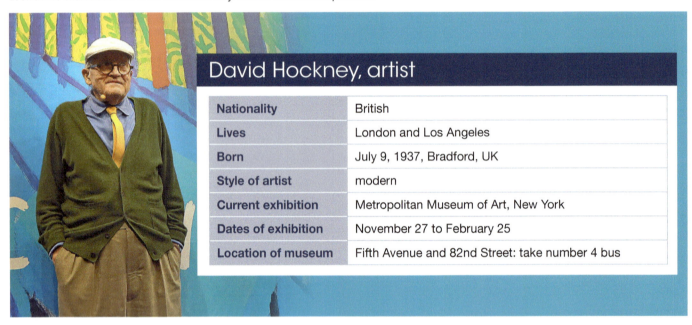

| David Hockney, artist | |
|---|---|
| Nationality | British |
| Lives | London and Los Angeles |
| Born | July 9, 1937, Bradford, UK |
| Style of artist | modern |
| Current exhibition | Metropolitan Museum of Art, New York |
| Dates of exhibition | November 27 to February 25 |
| Location of museum | Fifth Avenue and 82nd Street: take number 4 bus |

2. Ask Student B questions about the singer Adele to complete the chart. Use a variety of question patterns to show how much you already know about her.

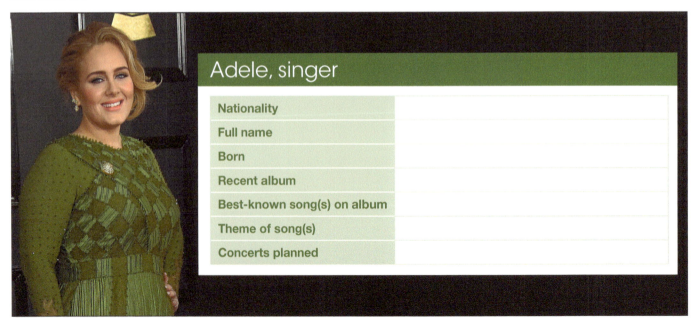

| Adele, singer | |
|---|---|
| Nationality | |
| Full name | |
| Born | |
| Recent album | |
| Best-known song(s) on album | |
| Theme of song(s) | |
| Concerts planned | |

**COMMUNICATION PRACTICE**

## 2D Student A

1 Describe the movie *Jurassic World: Fallen Kingdom* to Student B. Follow the steps below.

> ### Jurassic World: Fallen Kingdom
>
> The movie is set in the future, four years after the Jurassic World amusement park closes. It takes place on the island of Isla Nubar and is about a mission to save the dinosaurs from a volcanic eruption that threatens life on Earth. Directed by J. A. Bayona, the cast includes Chris Pratt, Bryce Dallas Howard, and Jeff Goldblum. If you really enjoyed the original *Jurassic World*, you'll love this movie also.

1 Say when or where the movie takes place.
2 Briefly describe the plot.
3 Mention the cast or director.
4 Give your overall impressions.

2 Listen to Student B describe the movie *The Predator*. Respond by saying whether you'd like to see it.

## 3C Student A

1 Think about how you would answer questions 1–6 about your family. Then ask your partner the questions about his/her family. Take notes on the answers.

### FAMILY QUESTIONNAIRE

1 Who do you take after physically? And in personality?
2 Who do you look up to and admire the most?
3 What do you usually look forward to doing most with your family?
4 Did you ever try to get away with something as a child but you got caught?
5 If someone in your family doesn't want to do something, do you try to talk him/her into it?
6 Is there something your mother/father/brother/sister can't do without?

2 Compare your answers to all 12 questions. Can you find three similarities and three differences between your families?

## 4A Student A

1 Read sentence beginnings 1–6 to Student B. He/She will complete them. Decide together if the sentences are correct.

1 Most of the interesting people I know …
2 Everyone in my class …
3 The advice that my parents have given me …
4 The government these days …
5 A lot of people, including myself, …
6 Only a few young people …

2 Choose two of the sentences to discuss in more detail. Ask follow-up questions.

## 4C Student A

1 Think about these topics and make notes. Then tell Student B about each topic and answer his/her questions.

1 something creative that you enjoyed when you were a child
2 an exotic or unusual food that you've eaten
3 something you've been learning and have been successful at
4 someone you've known for a long time who's very persuasive
5 something you've been saving for and are hoping to buy

2 Listen to Student B. Ask follow-up questions to find out more.

COMMUNICATION PRACTICE

## 4D Student A

1 Choose one of the pictures and describe a memorable experience around it. Follow the steps below.

1 Create suspense and describe your reaction to the experience.
2 Respond to Student B and finish describing the experience.

2 Listen to Student B describe a memorable experience. Be sure to do the following.

1 Guess how the story will continue and show surprise.
2 Show empathy or happiness, as necessary.

## 6A Student A

1 Complete sentences 1–5. Make three statements true and two false. Then read them to Student B, who will try and guess which are true and which are false.

When I was a child ...
1 I lived in a _____ near _____ .
2 I would spend hours watching _____ .
3 I never used to eat _____ , which made my _____ angry.
4 In school, I used to be good at _____ .
5 I would _____ (your own idea) _____ .

2 Student B will read five sentences about himself/herself. Three of the statements are true and two are false. Guess which are true and which are false. How many answers did you guess correctly?

## 6C Student A

1 Look at the photo of Lyall, a young man from Madison, Wisconsin, and read the text. Then answer Student B's questions about Lyall's experience.

So, I've been here in Madrid for a few months now. My Spanish is still pretty basic, but I'm slowly getting used to speaking it. I love the food, and now I'm used to drinking *café con leche* every morning and eating a Spanish tortilla (a kind of potato omelette). It's the best! Some things are harder to get used to – my apartment is tiny! I used to live in a big house, so I don't think I'll ever get used to living in a closet! And they drive so fast – I'm definitely not used to that yet, and I worry when I cross the street. Luckily, I don't drive – I take the subway. I've learned the different train lines, so I'm used to getting around the city. The subway is a great way to travel, but it can take a while to get from one place to another. I'm still getting used to that.

2 Look at Student B's photo of Betty, a young woman from Taiwan. Ask questions about her experience of living in Montreal, using prompts 1–6.

1 how she likes the weather
2 if it's difficult communicating in French
3 how she likes living in a big city
4 if it's hard being away from her family
5 how she finds the Canadian people
6 how she likes the food

COMMUNICATION PRACTICE

## 6D Student A

1 You and Student B are planning a vacation together. Mention problems 1–4 to Student B.

 1 "The direct flights are so expensive!"
 2 "What if it rains? What will we do to pass the time?"
 3 "Should we rent an apartment on Airbnb? Hotels are really expensive there!"
 4 "Maybe we should take a vacation closer to home!"

2 You and Student B are hoping to move. Suggest a neighborhood. He/She will mention different problems. Respond using the skills below.

 1 Make a point.
 2 Suggest alternatives.
 3 Ask for clarification.
 4 Challenge Student B to keep thinking.

## 5C Both students

1 Complete the survey to predict your future. Don't show your partner your answers. On a scale of 1 (low) to 5 (high), how bright does your future look?

 1 What new skill will you have learned to do by this time next year?
 _____

 2 Will you have started a new job or changed jobs a year from now?
 _____

 3 How will you be spending your leisure time six months from now?
 _____

 4 Where will you be living in five years? Who will you be living with?
 _____

 5 Will you be spending more or less money six months from now?
 _____

 6 What important events will have taken place in the world two years from now?
 _____

 7 By this time next year, will you have given anything up?
 _____

 8 How much exercise will you be getting five years from now?
 _____

2 Take turns sharing your predictions. Which of you is more optimistic about the future?

## 2C Answers

1 1 T; 2 F: It took place in 1969; 3 F: They were from Sweden; 4 T; 5 T; 6 T; 7 T; 8 F: It is about New York.

COMMUNICATION PRACTICE

## 1C  Student B

1  Ask Student A questions 1–8 about a disappointing hobby or interest.

1  What was your hobby or interest?
2  When did you start it?
3  Where did you practice it?
4  How did you pay for it?
5  Had you ever tried it before?
6  Had you been saving money to do it?
7  Why didn't it meet your expectations?
8  Will you give the hobby or interest a second chance?

2  Think of a place you've visited that was a disappointment to you. Listen to Student A's questions.

## 2A  Student B

1  Ask Student A questions about the artist David Hockney to complete the chart. Use a variety of question patterns to show how much you already know about him.

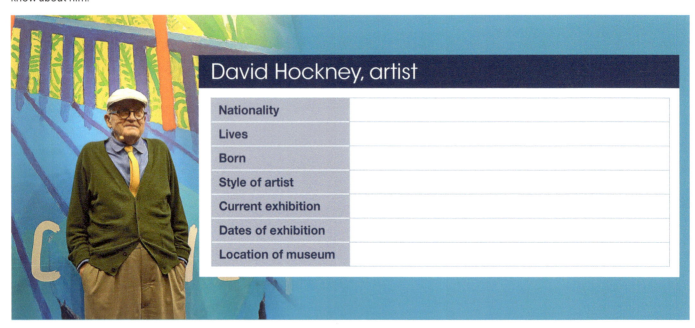

| David Hockney, artist | |
|---|---|
| Nationality | |
| Lives | |
| Born | |
| Style of artist | |
| Current exhibition | |
| Dates of exhibition | |
| Location of museum | |

2  Look at the chart about the singer Adele. Answer Student A's questions.

| Adele, singer | |
|---|---|
| Nationality | British |
| Full name | Adele Laurie Blue Adkins |
| Born | May 5, 1988, London, UK |
| Recent album | 25 |
| Best-known song(s) on album | "Hello" |
| Theme of song(s) | a couple that broke up |
| Concerts planned | none |

**COMMUNICATION PRACTICE**

## 2D  Student B

1  Listen to Student A describe the movie *Jurassic World: Fallen Kingdom*. Respond by saying whether you'd like to see it.
2  Describe the movie *The Predator* to Student A. Follow the steps below.

### The Predator

A long-awaited sequel to the 1987 sci-fi hit *Predator* is set between 1990 and 2010. Directed by Shane Black, the cast includes Jacob Tremblay, Sterling K. Brown, and Yvonne Strahovski. The movie is about a group of men who are stuck in a jungle with a monster that attacks them one by one. You'll be biting your nails from start to finish. It's very suspenseful!

1  Say when or where the movie takes place.
2  Briefly describe the plot.
3  Mention the cast or director.
4  Give your overall impressions.

## 3C  Student B

1  Think about how you would answer questions 1–6 about your family. Then ask your partner the questions about his/her family. Take notes on the answers.

### FAMILY QUESTIONNAIRE

1  Who do you get along best/worst with in your family?
2  When you were little, who looked after you when you came home from school?
3  In your family, do you always use leftover food up, or do you throw it out?
4  Do you keep a lot of mementos from childhood that you really should throw out?
5  Do you have any relatives who have ever called a wedding off? What happened?
6  If you're invited to a family event and you really don't want to go, how do you get out of it?

2  Compare your answers to all 12 questions. Can you find three similarities and three differences between your families?

## 4A  Student B

1  Read sentence beginnings 1–6 to Student A. He/She will complete them. Decide together if the sentences are correct.

   1  One of the most talented people I can think of …
   2  Anyone who doesn't want to go to college …
   3  A lot of information you find on social media …
   4  The police where I live …
   5  All of my friends, except …
   6  Only some of the people I know …

2  Choose two of the sentences to discuss in more detail. Ask follow-up questions.

## 4C  Student B

1  Listen to Student A. Ask follow-up questions to find out more.
2  Think about these topics and make notes. Then tell Student A about each topic and answer his/her questions.

   1  something exciting that you did last year
   2  a personal possession you've lost that you really miss
   3  something you've achieved that you're really proud of
   4  someone you've always admired and who you rely on
   5  an activity you've been doing a lot lately, which may be a little risky

COMMUNICATION PRACTICE

## 4D Student B

1  Listen to Student A describe a memorable experience. Be sure to do the following.
   1  Guess how the story will continue and show surprise.
   2  Show empathy or happiness, as necessary.

2  Choose one of the pictures and describe a memorable experience around it. Follow the steps below.

   1  Create suspense and describe your reaction to the experience.
   2  Respond to Student A and finish describing the experience.

## 6A Student B

1  Student A will read five sentences about himself/herself. Three of the statements are true and two are false. Guess which are true and which are false. How many answers did you guess correctly?

2  Complete sentences 1–5. Make three statements true and two false. Then read them to Student A, who will try and guess which are true and which are false.

When I was a child ...
1  I used to like drinking _____ .
2  I would spend hours playing _____ with my _____ .
3  In school, I didn't use to do well in _____ .
4  I used to be really _____ and _____ .
5  I would _____ (your own idea) _____ .

## 6C Student B

1  Look at Student A's photo of Lyall, a young man from Madison, Wisconsin. Ask questions about his experience of living in Madrid, using prompts 1–6.

   1  if he's having difficulty with the language
   2  how he likes the food
   3  how he likes living in a small apartment
   4  if the traffic is a problem
   5  if it's easy to get around Madrid
   6  what he thinks of the subway

2  Look at the photo of Betty, a young woman from Taiwan, and read the text. Then answer Student A's questions about Betty's experience.

Well, here I am in Montreal, and it's snowing for the first time. It's beautiful, but very cold! I'll never get used to this weather. Everything here is in English and French, but for me that's not a problem. My father is French, and I'm used to speaking the language. I come from a small town in southern Taiwan, and Montreal seems large by comparison, but I guess I'm slowly getting used to living in a big city. It's very hard being away from my family, though, especially my mom. I don't think I'll ever get used to it. But the Canadians are really nice and friendly, and I find them funny, now that I've gotten used to their sense of humor. What else? Oh, the food. It's good, but they eat so much. I'm not used to eating such big portions of everything.

# 6D Student B

1. You and Student A are planning a vacation together. Suggest a place to go. He/She will mention different problems. Respond using the skills below.
   1. Make a point.
   2. Suggest alternatives.
   3. Ask for clarification.
   4. Challenge Student A to keep thinking.

2. You and Student A are hoping to move. Mention problems 1–4 to Student A.
   1. "Some apartments in that area aren't very nice!"
   2. "And the rent may not be any less than we're paying now."
   3. "The neighborhood isn't very close to school, either."
   4. "Maybe we shouldn't move after all!"

# COMMUNICATION PRACTICE

## 1A Both students

Look at pictures a–f and discuss the questions for each one.

1 Where do you think the people are? Is the situation formal or informal?
2 What does it look as if they're doing?
3 Would the behavior be appropriate in your country? Why/Why not?
4 What advice would you give a visitor to your country about gestures and body language?

## 2C Both students

True or false? In teams, take the Oldies' Trivia Quiz. Then check your answers on page 161.

# Oldies' Trivia Quiz

1. Despite the fact that it wasn't a new song, "Candle in the Wind" by Elton John was re-released in 1997 with some new lyrics in memory of Diana, Princess of Wales.
2. In spite of the rain, Woodstock, one of the most famous music festivals ever, took place over three days in 1968.
3. Although they usually sang in English, the 1970s group Abba was from Switzerland.
4. Bruce Springsteen is called "The Boss" because he was in charge of collecting the money so he could distribute it to the other band members.
5. In spite of the fact that he didn't write the song, Barry Manilow had a number 1 hit in 1976 called "I write the songs."
6. The British group The Clash borrowed a World War II phrase so they could name the song "London Calling." The original phrase was "America, this is London calling."
7. The famous nightclub, Copacabana, is in New York City. However, it was named after a neighborhood in Rio de Janeiro.
8. The line "I want to wake up in the city that doesn't sleep" is by Frank Sinatra and is about Los Angeles.

COMMUNICATION PRACTICE

## 3A  Both students

1  Work in pairs. Look at the situations in pictures a–h. Make positive or negative sentences using the prompts in the box.
How many sentences can you make for each picture?

| supposed to   should   be allowed to   'd better   have to   can   ought to |

 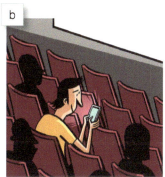  

2  Which pair made the most sentences?

## 5A  Both students

1  Complete the questionnaire with your own opinions. Don't show your partner.

| What do you think? This is what our readers said: | Agree | Disagree |
|---|---|---|
| 1  There's been such an increase in vegetarianism. I might well try it. | | |
| 2  There are so many endangered species. It makes me depressed. | | |
| 3  There are so few electric cars, but they're really fantastic. | | |
| 4  It's such a good idea to save rainwater for household tasks. | | |
| 5  Environmental groups do such vital work. I'm going to join one. | | |
| 6  There's so little organic food available, and it's far too expensive. | | |
| 7  Recycling is such a waste of time. It takes me ages to sort my garbage. | | |
| 8  The planet is in serious danger. There's so little time left to save it. | | |
| 9  Switching to energy-efficient light bulbs is such good advice. | | |
| 10  So many people are living to be 100. It must be due to changes in diet. | | |

2  Share your answers. Do you have similar opinions on health and the environment? How many of the questions did you answer in the same way?

# PHRASAL VERBS

## Phrasal verbs

| Phrasal verb | Meaning |
|---|---|
| back up sb/sth | support sb; save sth |
| break down | stop working |
| break out | start suddenly (war, fire, disease) |
| break up | end a relationship |
| burn out | become exhausted through overwork |
| call off sth | cancel |
| carry out | conduct an experiment (plan) |
| catch on | become popular |
| catch up (on sth) | get information; do sth there wasn't time for |
| cheer up (sb) | make happier |
| come across | find |
| come back (to sth) | return (to sth) |
| come together | join |
| come up | arise (an issue) |
| come up with | invent |
| deal with sth | take action; accept sth |
| do without sth | manage without |
| drift apart | separate without actively trying to |
| figure out sth | understand with careful thought |
| fit in | be socially compatible (in harmony with) |
| get on (along) with | have a good relationship |
| get out of (doing sth) | avoid doing sth |
| give away sth | give something no longer needed |
| give in | surrender |
| go back (a long way) | return; know each other a long time |
| go through sth | experience sth difficult |
| grow up | spend one's childhood |
| hang out | spend time together |
| hang up | end a phone call |
| hang sth up | put sth on a hook (hanger) |
| have sb over | invite sb to your house |
| hit (it) off | get along very well |
| hold sb back | prevent sb from moving ahead (succeeding) |
| let sb down | disappoint |

| Phrasal verb | Meaning |
|---|---|
| live up to | fulfill |
| look after | take care of |
| look down on sb | think one is better or more important |
| look forward to sth | anticipate; be happy about |
| look out for sb | watch (protect) |
| look up to sb | admire (respect) |
| make up | become friendly after an argument |
| mess up sth | spoil (do sth badly) |
| miss out | lose an opportunity |
| note down sth | write sth to not forget it |
| pay sb back | repay a loan |
| pay off | be worthwhile |
| put up with sth | accept without complaining |
| reach out (to sb) | contact; show interest in |
| run out of sth | not have enough |
| sell out | sell the last one and have no more of |
| set up sth | establish; prepare for use |
| settle down | make a home with sb |
| show up | appear |
| stand out | be better; be easy to see |
| talk sb into | convince (persuade) |
| take after sb | be similar to a family member |
| take off | not go to work; succeed |
| tell sb off | reprimand (scold) |
| think over sth | consider |
| think up sth | invent; think of a new idea |
| throw out | discard (get rid of) |
| try out sth | use sth to see if you like it |
| turn up | appear |
| turn up sth | raise (the volume) |
| turn down sth | lower (the volume); refuse |
| turn out | happen (have a certain result) |
| use up sth | finish (use completely) |
| work out | exercise; end successfully |

# Irregular verbs

| Base form | Past simple | Past participle |
|---|---|---|
| arise | arose | arisen |
| awake | awoke | awoken |
| bear | bore | born |
| beat | beat | beaten |
| bend | bent | beaten |
| bet | bet | bet |
| bleed | bled | bled |
| blow | blew | blown |
| broadcast | broadcast | broadcast |
| burn | burned/burnt | burned/burnt |
| burst | burst | burst |
| catch | caught | caught |
| creep | crept | crept |
| cut | cut | cut |
| deal | dealt | dealt |
| dig | dug | dug |
| feed | fed | fed |
| fight | fought | fought |
| flee | fled | fled |
| forbid | forbade | forbidden |
| forecast | forecast | forecast |
| forgive | forgave | forgiven |
| freeze | froze | frozen |
| hang | hung | hung |
| hit | hit | hit |
| hurt | hurt | hurt |
| kneel | knelt/kneeled | knelt/kneeled |
| lead | led | led |
| leap | leaped/leapt | leaped/leapt |
| lend | lent | lent |
| mean | meant | meant |

| Base form | Past simple | Past participle |
|---|---|---|
| mistake | mistook | mistaken |
| overhear | overheard | overheard |
| oversleep | overslept | overslept |
| seek | sought | sought |
| set | set | set |
| shake | shook | shaken |
| shoot | shot | shot |
| show | showed | shown |
| shrink | shrank | shrunk |
| shut | shut | shut |
| sink | sank | sunk |
| sleep | slept | slept |
| slide | slid | slid |
| spin | spun | spun |
| split | split | split |
| spill | spilled/spilt | spilled/spilt |
| spread | spread | spread |
| spring | sprang | sprung |
| stick | stuck | stuck |
| sting | stung | stung |
| strike | struck | struck |
| swear | swore | sworn |
| sweep | swept | swept |
| tread | trod | trodden/trod |
| undertake | undertook | undertaken |
| undo | undid | undone |
| upset | upset | upset |
| weep | wept | wept |
| wind | wound | wound |
| withdraw | withdrew | withdrawn |
| withstand | withstood | withstood |

American
English

# Personal Best

**Workbook**

**B2**
Upper Intermediate

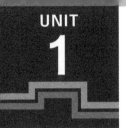

# UNIT 1 Your unique style

## 1A LANGUAGE

**GRAMMAR:** Present forms; *like*, *as if*, and *as though*

1 Complete the sentences with the words in the box. Use each only once. There is one you do not need.

| know | am knowing | thinks | 's thinking |
| play | feels | 's feeling | have | are having |

1 Felipa _____ worried right now because her dad is sick.
2 Gabriel _____ that classical music is boring.
3 We _____ some problems at work right now.
4 It's a difficult question, but I _____ the answer.
5 Renata may come to the movies with us. She _____ about it.
6 It _____ as though it's getting colder.
7 On the weekends, they _____ volleyball on the beach.
8 My grandparents _____ more than thirty grandchildren now.

2 Use the prompts to complete the sentences with the simple present or present continuous.

1 Lucia says that Daniel isn't speaking to Pablo.
_____
(sound / as if / he / be / angry about something)

2 Hi, Julieta. Good to see you!
_____ ?
(where / you / work / right now)

3 Don't touch that laptop. It
_____.
(belong to / Victoria)

4 My grandpa has a smartphone, but
_____.
(he / not understand / how to use it)

5 What is that vegetable? It
_____.
(look / a little like cabbage)

6 My brother plays the piano really well. He
_____.
(practice / for three hours / every day)

7 _____ and it's annoying because she never asks.
(Mia / always / use / my pens)

8 _____ because she has a new job in Chicago.
(Rafaela / learn English)

**VOCABULARY:** Body language and communication

3 Match sentences 1–6 with a–f.

1 Alejandro had to raise his voice. ____
2 Pablo frowned. ____
3 Matias gazed at the painting. ____
4 Diego winked at me. ____
5 Juan Pablo stared at the photo. ____
6 Emmanuel waved at me. ____

a It was absolutely beautiful.
b He knew I would find the situation funny, too.
c He wanted to get my attention.
d It was very noisy in the room.
e He knew the woman in it.
f The letter contained news he did not want to hear.

4 Complete the missing words in the sentences.

1 When I arrived at the party, he k_____ me on the cheek.
2 He introduced me to his friends, and we all s_____ hands.
3 When I asked her if she spoke English, she n_____.
4 When I asked him if he had broken the window, he s_____ his head.
5 She looked very unhappy and refused to make eye c_____ with me.
6 The old man just s_____ his shoulders when she asked him if there was a hotel nearby.
7 As I was getting off the train, someone t_____ me on the shoulder.
8 When he met his daughter at the airport, he gave her a big h_____.

**PRONUNCIATION:** /ə/

5 ▶1.1 Read the sentences aloud. Pay attention to the /ə/ sound in *as*. Listen and repeat.

1 It looks as if we've missed the bus.
2 Tom sounds as though he's disappointed.
3 Do you feel as if we're being unfair?
4 I feel as though I'm in a dream.
5 Those animals look as if they're hungry.
6 It sounds as if you need some help.

2

# SKILLS 1B

## LISTENING: Identifying attitude

**1** ▶1.2 Listen to a conversation between Sophia and her friend Joe. Are the following statements true (T) or false (F)?

1 Sophia reminds Joe that Elon Musk recently sent a sports car into space. _____
2 At first, Joe says that sending a car into space was a good thing to do. _____
3 Sophia says that the car in space was Elon Musk's biggest achievement. _____
4 Sophia says that Elon Musk's company will help the human race. _____
5 Joe suggests that exploring space is bad for the environment. _____
6 Sophia believes that people will not always be able to live on the Earth. _____
7 Sophia says that environmental scientists don't have a good opinion of Elon Musk. _____
8 In the end, Joe still doesn't agree with Sophia that Elon Musk is cool. _____

**2** ▶1.2 Listen again. Focus on the way Sophia and Joe use words and phrases to say how certain their opinions are or how much they agree with each other. Complete the sentences.

1 These are products that will have far-reaching benefits for all of humankind! I _____ that.
2 Joe: That's not very green, is it?
   Sophia: Well, it _____ can be!
3 ... if the Earth is destroyed, people can go and live there. I _____ that this will happen one way or another.
4 I _____ that anyone with *that* much money who does *good* things with it is cool.
5 It's better than hanging out on yachts. That's _____!

**3** ▶1.3 Look at the sentences. Use the mark ‿ to show where consonant sounds between two words have merged. The first one is done for you. Listen, check, and repeat.

1 I just‿can't imagine living like that.
2 Nick calmly handed her the papers.
3 He's the fattest dog I've ever seen.
4 I don't expect to see him there.
5 She said that she was leaving.
6 Tom was sitting at the next table.

**4** Complete the compound adjectives in the sentences with the words in the box.

| thinking moving famous minded changing |
| aged respected looking |

1 Her parents were both good-_____, so it's no surprise that she's attractive.
2 It's only forward-_____ businesses like these that will survive going into the future.
3 She was one of the most highly-_____ lawyers of her generation.
4 He was middle-_____ – I'm guessing about fifty.
5 The article featured the diets of ten world-_____ athletes.
6 In such a large organization, changes are slow-_____, and that can be frustrating.
7 Winning a sum of money as large as that would be completely life-_____.
8 I like to think that I'm open-_____ and willing to change my opinions about things.

3

# 1C LANGUAGE

## GRAMMAR: Narrative tenses

**1** Choose the correct options to complete the sentences.

1 I wanted to tell them my news, but I _____ for the right moment.
   a wait    b was waiting    c had waited
2 I knew she was disappointed with her test results, and I could see that she _____.
   a cried    b had cried    c had been crying
3 Luisa was surprised when I _____ her the letter.
   a showed    b was showing    c had showed
4 He went online and _____ a ticket for a trip to Paris.
   a booked    b had booked    c had been booking
5 I had no idea that Jack _____ to China before.
   a was going    b had been    c had been going
6 We realized that she _____ for months to protect her friend.
   a lie    b was lying    c had been lying
7 When I went to get my passport out, I realized that I _____ it.
   a lost    b had lost    c had been losing
8 I _____ a bath when someone rang the doorbell.
   a took    b was taking    c had taken

**2** Complete the story with the correct form of the verbs in parentheses.

> Last Saturday, I ¹_____ (go) with a group of friends to our friend David's apartment. It was his birthday, and we ²_____ (want) to plan a surprise party. He wasn't there because he ³_____ (play) soccer, as he always did on Saturday evenings. However, his mom ⁴_____ (give) us a key to his apartment, so we went in and ⁵_____ (get) everything ready for the party. There was so much food – we ⁶_____ (prepare) it all day! When David came home he was so shocked. He ⁷_____ (not have) any idea about our plans before. There was lots of music and dancing, and we ⁸_____ (have) a great time when we suddenly noticed that David ⁹_____ (fall) asleep. He ¹⁰_____ (run) around so much at his soccer practice, he was exhausted!

## VOCABULARY: Expectations

**3** Complete the sentences with the verbs in the box.

| fail | be | make | get | lower | meet |

1 Unfortunately, the hotel didn't _____ our expectations.
2 This restaurant is just what the area needs. I'm sure it will _____ a success.
3 These flowers are for my new boyfriend's mom. I want to _____ a good first impression!
4 Apartments are really expensive here. You may have to _____ your expectations.
5 With a fantastic performance like that, you can't _____ to win the competition!
6 If you don't take this opportunity, you won't _____ a second chance.

**4** Complete the second sentence to mean the same as the first. Use a noun or a verb from the same family as the underlined word.

1 My parents are very proud of me, so I don't want to disappoint them.
   I don't want to be _____ to my parents because they're very proud of me.
2 I met my brother's new girlfriend, and she made a good impression on me.
   My brother's new girlfriend really _____ me when we met.
3 If the business succeeds, we'll all become rich.
   We'll all become rich if the business is _____.
4 What expectations did you have when you took the job?
   What did you _____ when you took the job?
5 He was very upset when he failed to get on the team.
   He was very upset by _____ get on the team.
6 I wasn't at all impressed by the hotel.
   The hotel _____ bad _____ on me.

## PRONUNCIATION: Stress in narrative tenses

**5** ▶ 1.4 Underline the stressed syllable in the verb in each sentence, and then read the sentence aloud. Listen and check.

1 They'd seen the man somewhere before.
2 The children were jumping up and down.
3 The police had been searching for evidence.
4 She had given him all the relevant documents.
5 We'd been expecting her to call.
6 My mother was planning to quit her job.

# SKILLS 1D

## WRITING: Making a narrative interesting

# An unexpected HOBBY

1 About this time last year, my manager said, "You look exhausted, Alex. Why don't you take a vacation?" It was true that I had been working very hard, and when I looked in the mirror, I could see what she meant. The skin around my eyes was so dark that I looked like a panda. I hadn't slept properly for weeks.

2 I decided to go on a skiing trip with some friends. I thought the exercise and mountain air would be good for me. On the way, I looked out of the window of the plane at the snow sparkling like diamonds on the mountains below. Before long, I was feeling more relaxed than I had in months, and I couldn't wait to get my skis on.

3 However, when we eventually arrived at the resort, we had a huge shock. "I'm sorry," the receptionist at our hotel said, "but the only snow is at the top of the mountain. And I'm afraid the ski lifts are closed because of strong winds." Lying in bed that night, I could feel my disappointment, like a black cloud over my head.

4 At first, I was sure the vacation would be a disaster. However, the following morning I noticed a sign in the hotel advertising salsa classes. I was nervous because I'd never danced before, but when I anxiously opened the door, the teacher called, "Come on in, you'll love it!" In a matter of minutes, I'd learned some basic steps, and the loud rhythm of the music immediately made me feel more cheerful.

5 After that, I went back every day, even after it snowed more, and I was able to go skiing. As time went on, I realized I had found an activity I absolutely loved. When I got home, I found a local class, and I've been dancing salsa twice a week ever since.

**1** Read Alex's blog post about a vacation that didn't turn out as expected. According to the post, are the sentences below true (T) or false (F)?
  1 Alex didn't want to go on vacation, but his boss made him go.
  2 He was excited about going skiing.
  3 He was surprised to discover that he wouldn't be able to ski.
  4 He knew he would enjoy salsa dancing.

**2** Which paragraphs include the following?
  1 a prediction or comment about the future
  2 an interesting comparison
  3 direct speech

**3** Complete the paragraph with the time linkers in the box or in Alex's post. There may be more than one answer, but do not use the same linker twice.

> at first   in a matter of minutes
> after a while   eventually   in no time

We set off up the mountain path, expecting to reach the top by noon. ¹_____, everyone was cheerful, and we made good progress, but we hadn't gotten very far when the weather changed, and it started to get cold and foggy. ²_____, the fog was so thick that we could hardly see anything. We continued going, but ³_____, we became less and less enthusiastic about the climb. There didn't seem to be much point if we couldn't see anything at the top. However, when we ⁴_____ reached the top of the mountain, the fog suddenly disappeared. The view was like a picture postcard, and ⁵_____, everyone was happy again.

**4** Write a blog post about an experience that didn't turn out as you had expected.
  - Include different narrative tenses and time linkers.
  - Use comparisons, predictions, and direct speech to make your story more interesting.

# 1 REVIEW and PRACTICE

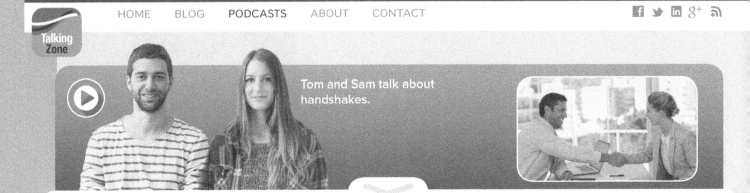

## LISTENING

**1** ▶ 1.5 Listen to the podcast and number a–f in the order that you hear them (1–6).

a smiling when you shake someone's hand ____
b an article Sam read on handshakes ____
c the two-handed handshake ____
d Tom saying that Sam shook his hand ____
e how hard you should squeeze the other person's hand ____
f the peaceful origin of the handshake ____

**2** ▶ 1.5 Listen again and choose the correct options.

1 Sam is thinking about handshakes because
  a she has recently written an article about shaking hands.
  b she has recently read an article about shaking hands.
  c she has just shaken Tom's hand.
2 Originally, shaking someone's hand showed that
  a you did not want to hurt the person.
  b you knew the person.
  c you wanted to work with the person.
3 Sam claims that
  a all handshakes are basically the same.
  b there are many different handshakes.
  c there are two different handshakes.
4 The chief executive clearly thought
  a that people should shake hands more.
  b that the way someone shakes hands isn't important.
  c that the way someone shakes hands is very important.
5 Sam says that when you shake someone's hand, you should
  a look at the person.
  b smile at the person.
  c look at and smile at the person.
6 Tom says he never
  a shakes hands using both hands.
  b presses the other person's hand.
  c shakes hands with anyone.

## READING

**1** Read Daniel's blog on page 7 and choose the best summary.

a He would like to become a better person in general.
b He would like to make more friends and generally be more sociable.
c He would like to be better at telling jokes.

**2** Are the sentences true (T), false (F), or doesn't say (DS)?

1 Daniel blogs regularly on a variety of subjects. ____
2 Daniel shares a home with at least one other person. ____
3 Daniel sometimes goes out with Charlie. ____
4 Charlie is popular because he is good at listening to people. ____
5 Daniel's neighbor was pleased to see him smiling more. ____
6 He tried telling people about his unusual interests. ____
7 He succeeded in listening more than talking at the party the previous night. ____
8 Using people's names more had been a great success. ____
9 He isn't looking forward to the pirate party. ____
10 He hasn't prepared for the pirate party. ____

# REVIEW and PRACTICE 1

HOME   BLOG   PODCASTS   ABOUT   CONTACT

## Being a little more like Charlie

My roommate, Charlie, is the most sociable person I've ever met. He has – I'm not joking – more friends than he can count. Walk down a street with him, and people wave and call his name. Sit down in a coffee shop with him, and an old friend will tap him on the shoulder. I've always been – I'm not going to lie – a *little* jealous of Charlie and his army of friends.

**As some of you know, my new year's resolution was to try and widen my circle of friends. Determined to be a little more like Charlie, I found a website about self-improvement last week and came up with the following five-point action plan for myself:**

1 Smile and make eye contact to establish that you're both friendly and confident.
2 Be yourself. Tell people about your unusual interests and experiences! Apparently, what makes you different makes you interesting!
3 Listen. Forgotten all your funny stories? Can't think of anything to contribute to the conversation? Relax! Listen and let the other person do the talking.
4 Use people's names (even though it feels strange). People feel special when you say their names.
5 Accept invitations even though you'd much rather stay at home.

**So how am I doing? Mm ... I'll let you be the judge:**

1 This has been a struggle. It must be said, I'm not by nature a smiler. Two days into my "be a little more like Charlie" project, my neighbor asked me what the joke was. I explained there was no joke and that I was just pleased to see her. She looked a little uncomfortable and cut short the conversation. That said, I've had two very enjoyable, smiley chats with strangers (friends of friends). One of them even resulted in a party invitation – result! (See no. 5 below.)
2 This one's a little disappointing. It turns out *nobody* wants to know about my love of old maps.
3 Interesting ... I went to a party last night feeling tired (I'd been studying all day), but instead of desperately trying to think of entertaining stories, I *listened*. To begin with, it felt strange. Would people think I was shy or, worse, boring? But, as the evening went on, I started to relax and actually *enjoy* the experience.
4 Note to self: people <u>don't</u> feel *special* when you get their names wrong. Enough said.
5 The invitation was to a *pirate-themed* party this Saturday. Not my usual thing – it sounds like a nightmare, to be honest – but I'm going! And, yes, I have the hat and the (toy) parrot.

**So, a mixed experience, all in all, but I feel as if I should continue. Will let you know how Week 2 goes ...**

# UNIT 2 Culture vultures

## 2A LANGUAGE

### GRAMMAR: Question patterns

1 Choose the correct words to complete the sentences. There are two you do not need.

| won't | wasn't | hasn't | didn't | 're not |
| weren't | haven't | doesn't | isn't | don't |

1 _____ your uncle have a sports car?
2 Do you know why Joe _____ go to the party?
3 Your brother's a great cook, _____ he?
4 Why _____ the doors locked last night?
5 Samuel will give us a ride, _____ he?
6 Can you explain why you _____ done your homework?
7 Why are you here? _____ you usually play tennis on Fridays?
8 They _____ expecting us to pay them, are they?

2 Use *wh-* subject or object questions, negative questions, tag questions, or indirect questions to complete the questions in the conversation. For questions that need verbs, use the verbs in parentheses.

**Ava** Hi Brad! I didn't expect to see you today. What ¹_____ (you, do) here?

**Brad** I came to see Alex. Do you have any idea where ²_____ (he, be)?

**Ava** Yes, he's in his office upstairs, but I don't think you should interrupt him. He's very busy. He said he has over 100 e-mails to answer.

**Brad** That's a lot! I guess he gets a lot of letters, too. Who ³_____ (deal) with them?

**Ava** Nobody – he does everything himself.

**Brad** Really? ⁴_____ (he, not have) a secretary?

**Ava** No, it's ridiculous, ⁵_____? Anyway, what ⁶_____ (you, want) to speak to him about? Is it anything I can help with?

**Brad** I was hoping he could help me move some furniture on the weekend. But if he's so busy, I'd better not ask.

**Ava** Oh, well my son Diego's a big strong boy. Why ⁷_____ (you, not ask) him, instead? I'll give you his number.

**Brad** That's great, thanks! ⁸_____ (you, know) if he's free on Saturday morning?

**Ava** Hmm. Well he doesn't usually get up until lunch time. Teenagers are always like that, ⁹_____?

**Brad** I know. What ¹⁰_____ (make) them so tired all the time?

### VOCABULARY: Adjective suffixes

3 Add suffixes from the box to complete the words.

-ful  -al  -able  -ous  -ive  -less

1 These snakes are completely harm_____.
2 Our trip to New York was really memor_____.
3 I had a dread_____ trip. Our train was very late.
4 He's very convention_____. He always wears a tie.
5 She enjoys adventur_____ sports like rock climbing.
6 They have a very aggress_____ dog.

4 Complete the adjectives.

1 C_____ people think carefully before they do anything and don't take risks.
2 A u_____ tool helps you do or make something.
3 A_____ damage is damage that nobody intended to happen.
4 A h_____ person doesn't have a home.
5 An e_____ treatment for an illness is one that works very well.
6 If your feet are p_____, they hurt.
7 If an activity is o_____, you can choose whether to do it or not.
8 Someone who is a_____ wants to have a successful career.
9 If an object is d_____, a lot of people want to have it.
10 If you make decisions fast, you're d_____.

### PRONUNCIATION: Intonation in tag questions

5 ▶ 2.1 Listen to the sentences and decide whether the speaker is asking a real question in order to check something or is making a comment. Then listen again and repeat.

|   | Question | Comment |
|---|---|---|
| 1 Daniel enjoyed the museum, didn't he? |   |   |
| 2 These paintings are beautiful, aren't they? |   |   |
| 3 You don't like opera, do you? |   |   |
| 4 Your brother lives in Lima, doesn't he? |   |   |
| 5 Teresa is very strict with her children, isn't she? |   |   |
| 6 He's on vacation, isn't he? |   |   |

8

# SKILLS 2B

## READING: Skimming and scanning

**A** Have you ever tried to be more like a character in a novel? Perhaps you started using one of the character's phrases or bought clothes to look more like him or her. If this describes you, you are not alone! Research suggests that readers of novels sometimes start behaving – and even thinking – like the fictional characters in their favorite books. Some may even start believing what the characters believe. It seems that what we read can have a huge effect on us.

**B** Other studies on the effects of reading found that many readers could actually "hear" what the characters on the page were saying. Characters had an actual "voice." For some readers, that voice wasn't silenced when the book was put down. A reader might be choosing a dish in a restaurant and find him- or herself wondering what a character from a favorite novel might order. In fact, some readers even reported having regular conversations in their heads with characters as if they had a real-life relationship with them. Others said that once a novel was finished, they found themselves "missing" a character, just as they would miss a departed friend or lover.

**C** Interestingly, it seems that what people experience when reading isn't quite the same as their experience when watching a movie. People watching a movie might react emotionally to what they see, but they remain aware that they are watching someone else. People reading a story lose their sense of "separateness" and personally feel what the character feels. What we read, then, has a powerful effect on the human mind.

**D** So what is it about the written word that makes characters live and breathe for us? Why do we feel this unique connection with people in books? The answer might lie in the brain's reaction. What scientists have recently discovered is that reading causes activity in many more areas of the brain than previously thought. You would expect that the words "lemon," "roses," and "perfume" would cause activity in the language-processing parts of your brain. However, it seems they also excite the areas of the brain related to smells. In other words, reading about an experience is more like actually having that experience than we previously thought.

**1** Skim the text quickly. Match paragraphs A–D with summaries 1–4.

1 How fictional characters can seem real to some readers. _____
2 The part that the brain plays in the reading experience. _____
3 How the characters in books can sometimes influence the behavior of readers. _____
4 The difference between people's reactions to novels and movies. _____

**2** Read the questions and underline the key words. Then choose the correct answers.

1 What did studies show about people who read novels?
  a They are rarely influenced by the behavior of the people in the novels they are reading.
  b They sometimes change their behavior to be more like the people in the novels they are reading.
  c They like reading novels in which the characters have the same beliefs as them.

2 What did some readers report about the "voice" of a fictional character?
  a It was similar to their own.
  b They could hear it sometimes when they weren't reading.
  c They sometimes used it, for example, to order food in a restaurant.

3 When they are watching movies, people …
  a never forget that the action is happening to someone else.
  b do not experience the emotions that the characters feel.
  c feel as if the action is happening to them personally.

4 Which parts of the brain are affected by words like "lemon" and "roses"?
  a the parts that deal with language
  b the parts that are concerned with smell
  c the parts that are concerned with language and smell

**3** Complete the second sentence so that it means the same as the first, using clauses with *what*. The first one is done for you.

1 I liked the dress that she wore for the Oscars ceremony.
  I liked *what she wore* for the Oscars ceremony.
2 The food that we eat can have an enormous effect on our health.
  _____ can have an enormous effect on our health.
3 I still can't believe the things that she told me last night!
  I still can't believe _____!
4 I gave him the money I had in my pocket.
  I gave him _____.
5 The things that I saw that night will stay with me forever.
  _____ will stay with me forever.

9

## 2C LANGUAGE

### GRAMMAR: Using linkers (1)

**1** Choose the correct options to complete the sentences.

1 I went to the bakery _____ buy some bread.
   a to    b so that    c despite

2 He went to work _____ the fact that he had a bad cold.
   a even though    b although    c in spite of

3 She took a bottle of water _____ she wouldn't be thirsty on the trip.
   a in order to    b to    c so that

4 I planned to meet Luciana at the station. _____, she didn't come.
   a Despite    b However    c Though

5 The movie wasn't what I was expecting. I enjoyed it, _____.
   a however    b despite    c though

6 _____ I've lived in Mexico City for years, I've never visited the pyramids.
   a Even though    b Despite    c However

7 We had a pleasant walk _____ the weather wasn't very nice.
   a in spite of    b although    c however

8 _____ our thick coats, we were still cold.
   a Even though    b Despite    c Although

**2** Are these sentences correct or incorrect? Remember to check the punctuation as well as the words. Rewrite the incorrect sentences.

1 There was a lot of work to do however we managed to finish it all.
   _____

2 Despite not going to college, she is very well-educated.
   _____

3 He got a job in order to saving money for his vacation.
   _____

4 I called Samuel for to invite him to dinner.
   _____

5 She always travels first class, despite the fact that it costs a lot.
   _____

6 We took the food with us in order not waste it.
   _____

7 I sat near the stage so that see the play better.
   _____

8 She passed all her exams, despite not study very much.
   _____

### VOCABULARY: Phrasal verbs (1)

**3** Match the two parts of the sentences.

1 We had to do without        a her mother.
2 Amy really takes after      b the meeting.
3 The tickets sold out        c his older brother.
4 I've used up                d hot water for several days.
5 They've had to call off     e anything like this before.
6 He looks up to              f all the credit on my phone.
7 He decided to turn down     g within two hours.
8 I'd never come across       h the job.

**4** Complete the text with the correct form of the phrasal verbs in the box.

> put up with   come up with   give in   show up
> figure out   talk into   get out of   pay off

I have a Saturday job in a bike shop. I love it, but last year my boss's son started working there, too. It didn't take me long to ¹_____ that he wasn't interested in bikes at all – only the money he was earning. He usually ²_____ late at the store and even then, he would try to ³_____ actually doing anything useful. I ⁴_____ it for a few weeks, but I was getting more and more fed up.
In the end, I ⁵_____ an idea. I persuaded his dad to pay us according to how many bikes we sold. He agreed, and my plan soon ⁶_____. I was earning more, and his son was earning much, much less. His friends told him he should leave, and after a few more weeks, he ⁷_____. Then I managed to ⁸_____ my best friend _____ applying for his job, and he got it, so now things at the store are perfect!

### PRONUNCIATION: Sentence stress

**5** ▶ 2.2 Read the sentences aloud and underline the stressed words in the phrases in **bold**. Listen and check.

1 I borrowed some money from my parents **in order to buy a car**.
2 **In spite of my worries**, the exam was fine.
3 I wore gloves **so that my hands wouldn't get cold**.
4 I'm proud of my work **despite his criticism**.
5 **In order not to upset my parents**, I came home early.
6 **Despite having studied French for five years**, she can't speak it very well.

# SKILLS 2D

## SPEAKING: Making and responding to recommendations

**1** ▶2.3 Complete these phrases connected with making and responding to recommendations. Then listen to the conversation between Emma and Alex and check.

1 It's one of the best things I've seen in a _____ time.
2 If you _____ superhero movies, you're going to _____ this one.
3 I'm not _____ on superhero movies.
4 My cousin is _____ about movies with lots of action.
5 It's _____ shocking and fascinating at the same time.
6 I don't really _____ like watching that kind of thing right now.
7 I'm in the _____ for something more cheerful.
8 It's definitely _____ seeing some time.

**2** Look again at the sentences in exercise 1. Which are used for making recommendations (M), and which for responding to recommendations (R)?

1 ___   3 ___   5 ___   7 ___
2 ___   4 ___   6 ___   8 ___

**3** ▶2.3 Listen again. Give a short answer to each question.

1 What's the movie *Black Panther* about? _____
2 When does it take place? _____
3 What did Alex like about it? _____
4 What's the name of the actor who played the king's son? _____
5 What's the name of the writer of *I Tonya*? _____
6 What's *I Tonya* about? _____
7 Does Alex want to watch it? _____

**4** Match questions 1–5 with responses a–e.

1 What's it about? ___
2 Why did you like it so much? ___
3 Who's in it? ___
4 When does the story take place? ___
5 Who wrote it? ___

a I think what I loved was the relationship between the characters.
b Roy Scheider plays the police chief, and Robert Shaw is the shark hunter.
c It was written by Peter Benchley and Carl Gottlieb.
d It tells the story of some men who want to kill a shark.
e In the 1970s.

**5** Complete the dialogue with information about a movie you like.

A I think I'm going to stay in tonight. Can you recommend a movie?
B Yes, how about _____?
A What's it about?
B _____.
  If you like _____, you're going to love it.
A Oh, OK. Who's in it?
B _____.
A And when does it take place?
B _____.
A OK, and what is it that you like about it?
B _____.
A Sounds great, thanks!

11

# 2 REVIEW and PRACTICE

HOME    BLOG    **PODCASTS**    ABOUT    CONTACT

Tom and Sam talk about modern art.

## LISTENING

**1** ▶ 2.4 Listen to the podcast. Check (✓) the things that Tom, Sam, and Lucas discuss.

1 The Tate Modern art gallery in London ____
2 how the Tate Modern chooses its exhibits ____
3 an unusual work of art ____
4 Lucas's favorite museum in Brazil ____
5 how popular modern art is in Brazil ____

**2** ▶ 2.4 Listen again. Choose the correct options to complete the sentences.

1 Lucas ____ the art that is always on display in the gallery.
  a disliked
  b enjoyed
  c didn't see

2 Sam tells listeners about a work of art that consists of ____ made of clay.
  a seeds
  b a clay sculpture
  c a sunflower

3 People ____ about Ai Weiwei's work.
  a often disagree
  b sometimes joke
  c usually agree

4 Lucas ____ Ai Weiwei's work in Brazil.
  a has never seen
  b would like to see
  c has seen

5 Lucas admires Ai Weiwei's ____.
  a artistic talent
  b hard work
  c imagination

6 Lucas talks about an art museum that is ____ a botanical garden.
  a near
  b next to
  c in

7 Lucas says that in South America, you often see modern art ____.
  a in parks
  b in neighborhoods
  c in galleries

## READING

**1** Read the blog on page 13. Complete 1–5 with the adjectives in the box.

attractive   ridiculous   effective
conventional   ambitious

**2** Are the sentences true (T), false (F), or doesn't say (DS)?

1 Eva was still a child when she decided she wanted to become a photographer. ____
2 At first, she had to do a lot of jobs she didn't enjoy. ____
3 The hard work she did at that time was good for her career. ____
4 Nowadays, Eva does not need any help taking great photos. ____
5 Annie Leibovitz knew most of the people she photographed very well. ____
6 Eva admires her photographs of John Lennon and Yoko Ono. ____
7 Eva gets all her information about her subjects by talking to them. ____
8 She has plenty of time to prepare the lighting. ____
9 Eva enjoys photographing her less famous customers more than the very famous ones. ____
10 She gets annoyed with celebrities who want her to make them look better in photos than they do in real life. ____

# REVIEW and PRACTICE 2

HOME  BLOG  PODCASTS  ABOUT  CONTACT

Guest blogger Eva talks about the art of celebrity photography.

## Snapping the stars

Ever imagine spending your working life mixing with the stars? What better way than to become a celebrity photographer? However, it's not as easy as it looks!

I was only 10 when I first saw a book of photographs by Annie Leibovitz, but from then on, I was certain I knew what I wanted to do with my life. I wanted to be a photographer, but not the ¹_____ kind that takes pictures of weddings; I was more ²_____ than that. I wanted to be a celebrity photographer or "shooter," as they're often called in the business.

Being a shooter is hard work, especially in the beginning when nobody knows you. In the first few years, I worked ³_____ hours, and I never turned down a job. At times, I was exhausted, but, eventually, it paid off as I started to get calls from magazine editors, and sometimes even from the stars themselves or their agents.

I've been a professional photographer for over 10 years now, and I've been lucky enough to work for some of the best magazines, but I still look up to Annie Leibovitz, and I still study her work so that I can learn how to be the most ⁴_____ photographer possible. When you look at her pictures, it seems as though she was able to see inside the heads of her subjects. She helped me figure out that a photograph needs to show someone's personality, not just what the person looks like. Look at her pictures of John Lennon and Yoko Ono to see what I mean!

Of course, in order to achieve that, you have to make a connection with the people you're photographing. I always research their lives before I meet them, and I try to keep the conversation going while I'm working, even though that can be difficult when – as is often the case – you only have a few minutes to do your job. Because of that, I always get the lights ready in advance – another thing Annie has taught me is that lighting really is the key to a great photo.

In spite of my best efforts, I know I'll never be as good as her, but I love my job, and I've never regretted choosing it. Most of the celebrities I meet are charming – even the very famous ones. The only problem I've had is with people who want me to make them look more ⁵_____ than they really are, but who can blame them when they work in an industry where looks are so important?

# UNIT 3 A sense of place

## 3A LANGUAGE

### GRAMMAR: Advice, expectation, and obligation

**1** Choose the correct options to complete the sentences.

1 It's going to rain today. You *'re supposed to / should / 're allowed to* take an umbrella with you.
2 You *'re not allowed to / 're not supposed to / wouldn't* go swimming after a big meal. It's unhealthy.
3 If you want to park here, you *have to / 're allowed to / can't* get a ticket from the machine.
4 I need to learn these words because we *shouldn't / 'd better not / can't* use a dictionary on the exam.
5 That dog bites. I *wouldn't / shouldn't / can't* go near it if I were you.
6 My bedroom is such a mess! I *'m allowed to / would / ought to* clean it up.
7 You *'re not allowed to / 'd better not / wouldn't* travel on this train if you don't have the correct ticket.
8 It's almost time to go – you *'d better / can / 're supposed to* hurry up!

**2** Use the prompts to complete the sentences.

1 You'll probably miss your plane if you go by bus. _____ a taxi.
 (better / take)
2 The door is shut. _____?
 (we / allowed / go in)
3 We started the exercise in class, and we _____ it at home.
 (supposed / finish)
4 The area downtown is dangerous at night. _____ there if I were you.
 (wouldn't / go)
5 You look terrible. _____ a doctor.
 (ought / see)
6 He's a little overweight. _____ more exercise.
 (should / do)
7 _____ your seatbelt while the car is moving.
 (have to / wear)
8 Put your camera away. You _____ it in here.
 (not allowed / use)

### VOCABULARY: Urban places and problems

**3** Read the sentences and circle True or False.

1 Places usually look good if there is a lot of vandalism in them. — True / False
2 A harbor is a place where you can park your car. — True / False
3 Smog is a mixture of things like smoke and chemicals that pollute the air. — True / False
4 If there is overcrowding in an area, too many people live there. — True / False
5 It is a good idea to drive your car to places where there is a lack of parking. — True / False
6 Companies often have their offices in the business district of a city. — True / False
7 People who live in poverty are usually quite rich. — True / False
8 In places where there is homelessness, you may see people sleeping on the street. — True / False

**4** Complete the sentences.

1 We were late for our meeting because of _____ congestion.
2 We took all the broken equipment to a _____ disposal center.
3 We had to go to the _____ house to testify at her trial.
4 The mayor held a party at _____ hall.
5 This is the _____ area of the city, where there are lots of factories.
6 Most people here live in _____ buildings with at least 15 floors.
7 There was a huge line at the taxi _____.
8 The _____ area of a city is the place where most people live.

### PRONUNCIATION: /aw/, /ow/, and /ɔ/

**5** ▶ 3.1 Listen to the sentences and check (✓) the correct column for the underlined vowels. Listen again and repeat.

| | /aw/ | /ow/ | /ɔ/ |
|---|---|---|---|
| 1 You're not supp<u>o</u>sed to use a dictionary. | | | |
| 2 Are we all<u>ow</u>ed to take photos? | | | |
| 3 He's supp<u>o</u>sed to come home early today. | | | |
| 4 You really <u>ou</u>ght to eat something. | | | |
| 5 You're not all<u>ow</u>ed to swim in the lake. | | | |
| 6 I <u>ou</u>ght to go to the gym later. | | | |

14

# SKILLS 3B

## LISTENING: Identifying advice

**1** ▶ 3.2 Listen to Isabel and Ben's conversation and choose the correct options.

1 Why is Isabel worried about Ben?
  a He isn't sleeping well.
  b He hasn't seen anyone for a while.
  c He looks depressed.

2 What does Isabel say about people in general?
  a They should be happy on their own for long periods.
  b They should always be with other people.
  c They probably shouldn't be alone for long periods.

3 What does Isabel say she did recently?
  a She watched a show about working from home.
  b She read an article about working from home.
  c She spoke to a friend about working from home.

4 How was the woman who wrote the article affected?
  a She was feeling unhappy.
  b She was sleeping badly.
  c She was feeling unhappy and sleeping badly.

5 What does Isabel suggest that Ben could do?
  a work from her friend's home
  b meet her work colleagues and socialize with them
  c work in a place where there are other people

6 What does Isabel offer to do?
  a put Ben in touch with a friend who might help him
  b give Ben the address of an office where he can work
  c show Ben an office that he can work in

**2** ▶ 3.2 Listen again. Focus on the way Isabel gives Ben advice. Complete the sentences.

1 Oh, Ben, _____ spend so much time alone!
2 Yes, but _____ need company, don't they?
3 _____ supposed to be on our own for days on end.
4 _____ consider renting an office space nearby?
5 You _____ speak to her. I'll give you her number.

**3** ▶ 3.3 Listen again. Focus on these negative questions. Mark (R) where the intonation rises because the speaker is checking information. Mark (F) where the intonation falls because the speaker is giving an opinion.

1 Have you really not seen anyone for three days? _____
2 Yes, but people need company, don't they? _____
3 We're social creatures, aren't we? _____
4 People can still suffer if they're working in an office, can't they? _____
5 Yes, but it happens less, doesn't it? _____
6 I would imagine you miss that, don't you? _____

**4** Underline the correct word in each sentence.

1 He claimed that 200 people came to hear him speak but the *actual / current* number was closer to 100.
2 I try to *prevent / avoid* eating after eight o'clock in the evening.
3 Stress *effects / affects* different people in different ways.
4 Paolo is a very experienced driver. I always feel *safe / sure* when he's at the wheel.
5 We don't need to make a decision now. We can *discuss / argue* it later.
6 It doesn't *mind / matter* how little I eat I never seem to lose weight.
7 As I was speaking to Ali, I *realized / noticed* a man at the back of the room wearing a dark suit.
8 I *elected / chose* a black tie because I was going to a funeral.

15

# 3C LANGUAGE

## GRAMMAR: Phrasal verbs

**1** Use the prompts to complete the sentences.

1. What time does _____? (off / plane / take / the)
2. I don't know if the dress will fit me. I _____. (to / it / need / on / try)
3. How well do you _____? (your / along / sister / with / get)
4. David _____ for Dad's birthday present. (up / a good / with / idea / came)
5. Oh no! Alex has _____! (up / milk / used / the / all)
6. The principal asked me to _____. (visitors / around / school / show / the / some)
7. The lights are too bright. _____, please? (them / off / turn / you / can)
8. María's always late for work. I don't know how _____! (away / she / it / gets / with)

**2** Rewrite the underlined parts of the sentences with the correct form of the phrasal verbs in the box.

| throw away | take up | come across | turn down |
| turn into | take after | look forward to | come back |

1. They offered me the job, but I said no. _____
2. The children are excited about the party. _____
3. If you want a relaxing hobby, you should start doing yoga. _____
4. My mother made our home become a meeting place for artists. _____
5. The doctor can see you at three, so could you return then, please? _____
6. It's a beautiful beach. I was very happy when we found it. _____
7. Luciana is very similar to her aunt. _____
8. These newspapers are really old. You should get rid of them. _____

**3** Complete the text with objects from the box, where they are needed. You will not need all of them, but you will need one twice. Write ^ where the object should go and write it above the line.

| it | them | the house | that behavior | my little sister |
| an adult | her favorite cookies |

Yesterday I had to **¹look after** while my parents were at work. She's only five, and she can be pretty difficult. First, she started screaming because we'd **²run out of**, so I said we could go to the store and buy some. While we were **³looking for**, she noticed an enormous chocolate bar. I told her she couldn't have it, but she **⁴picked up** anyway and started eating it, so I had to pay for it. Then, when we got outside, she dropped it on the sidewalk. The chocolate was so dirty, we had to **⁵throw away**, and she started screaming again. And that's how the day went. I was so pleased when my parents **⁶came back**. I don't know how they **⁷put up with** every single day. I can't wait for her to **⁸grow up** and be more fun to spend time with.

## PRONUNCIATION: Linking in phrasal verbs

**4** ▶ 3.4 Read the sentences aloud. Pay attention to how the words in the phrasal verbs link together. Listen and repeat.

1. I looked after her apartment while she was away.
2. What time did the plane take off?
3. I saw the dress in a store, and I tried it on.
4. She came up with a great idea for a present.
5. They called off their wedding.
6. I threw out all my old high school books.

SKILLS 3D

# WRITING: Writing a persuasive article

**1** Read the article about Naples and complete 1–6 with a–f.

a At first glance
b However, they are so delicious that no one needs more choices
c You might think
d but, in fact, it wasn't particularly cold
e Initially, you get the impression that
f but, actually, it's a wonderful place to go

**2** Find words in the article that are stronger synonyms for the adjectives below.

1 Paragraph 1: nice = _____
2 Paragraph 2: interesting = _____, attractive = _____, good = _____
3 Paragraph 3: tasty = _____
4 Paragraph 4: surprising = _____, big = _____, cold = _____
5 Paragraph 5: good = _____

**3** Use your own ideas to complete the sentences by contrasting expectations with reality.

1 You might think that a place this hot would be very dry. However, _____
_____.

2 Initially, you get the impression that the scenery is rather boring, but, actually, _____
_____.

3 At first glance, the buildings all look the same, but, actually, _____
_____.

4 You might think that a hotel like this would be really expensive, but, in fact, _____
_____.

5 At first glance, the coast looks attractive. However, _____
_____.

6 Initially, you get the impression that nothing happens in this town, but, actually, _____
_____.

**4** Think about a place you have enjoyed visiting or a place you would like to go. Write a text explaining why it is a good place for a vacation.

- State your point of view clearly.
- Give reasons and support them with facts and examples.
- Use persuasive language.
- Include at least two expressions for contrasting expectations with reality.

# Naples
## *City of food and fun!*

*1* I just came back from a week in the Italian city of Naples, and I'd say it's one of the best places in Europe for a vacation. ¹_____ it's a noisy, rather dirty place where no one ever relaxes, ²_____.

*2* There are so many fascinating places to visit, including castles, palaces, and the most spectacular churches you've ever seen. Every corner brings something new, for example, incredible fish markets with fish so fresh that many of them are still alive, or tiny stores selling pasta in all shapes, colors, and sizes.

*3* Of course, Naples is famous for being the home of pizza, and I certainly wasn't disappointed! ³_____, their pizzas may look a little boring – for example at the famous Pizzeria Michele, there are only two types of pizza to choose from, and one of them doesn't even have cheese! ⁴_____.

*4* One of the most amazing things about Naples is what goes on underground! We walked down hundreds of steps into an enormous area of rooms and passages under the city. The Romans used it to store clean water, and during the second world war, the city's citizens hid there to escape from the bombs. ⁵_____ it would be freezing that far down, ⁶_____. You have to be quite thin to squeeze through some of the stone passages, though!

*5* If you ask me, Naples is a fantastic place to visit. Just don't go in August, when it's much too hot, and don't even think about trying to drive – the traffic is the craziest I've ever seen!

17

# 3 REVIEW and PRACTICE

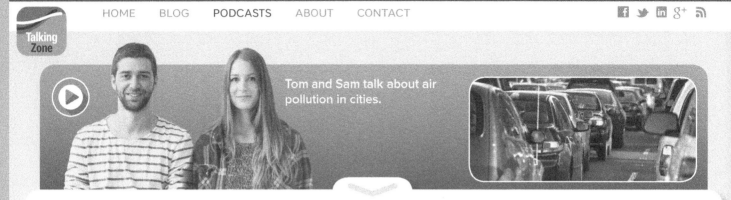

Tom and Sam talk about air pollution in cities.

## LISTENING

**1** ▶ 3.5 Listen to the podcast. Check (✓) the statement which is NOT true.

1 In some cities, you are not allowed to drive in particular areas. ____
2 Tom and Sam rarely use their cars. ____
3 Many cities are trying to provide better public transportation. ____

**2** ▶ 3.5 Listen again and complete the sentences with one or two words.

1 Sam accuses Tom of trying to _____ their guest.
2 Tom tells Sam she'd better _____ her car keys.
3 In Paris on the weekend, cars are not _____ in some areas of the city.
4 In a _____ of the German city of Freiburg, parking near your home is prohibited.
5 In return for not parking near your home, you get a _____ house or apartment.
6 Sam says we all know we _____ to drive less.
7 Many cities are trying to _____ their public transportation systems.
8 In the city where Gabriel comes from, there is now no _____ in the air.

## READING

**1** Read Sylvie's blog on page 19 and choose the best summary.

a Sylvie thinks Singapore is much better than New York.
b Sylvie thinks New York is much better than Singapore.
c Sylvie is very impressed with Singapore although she also admires New York.

**2** Check (✓) the correct sentences.

1 Sylvie knows for sure where she will live in the future. ____
2 New York has a number of bad features that all big cities have. ____
3 Sylvie was annoyed that she couldn't chew gum in Singapore. ____
4 Sylvie stayed downtown the whole time she was in Singapore. ____
5 Sylvie didn't come across any litter while she was in Singapore. ____
6 Sylvie thinks that all writing or pictures on the walls of public places is bad. ____
7 Singapore doesn't feel like a dangerous city because it is so neat and clean. ____
8 Sylvie was surprised by the appearance of the trees in Singapore. ____

**3** Match the definitions below with six words in Sylvie's blog that are associated with living in cities.

1 when garbage, such as paper, bottles, and cans, is left lying on the ground in public places
2 the act of damaging things deliberately, especially public property
3 when rude, humorous, or political words or drawings are illegally written or drawn on walls or other surfaces
4 when there are not enough places to leave your car
5 when damage is caused to the air or water by harmful substances or waste
6 when there are too many cars on a road

REVIEW and PRACTICE   3

HOME   BLOG   PODCASTS   ABOUT   CONTACT

Guest blogger Sylvie writes about her recent trip to Singapore and compares urban living there with New York.

# A TALE OF TWO CITIES

(Well, OK, one of them is a country ... )

First off, let me say that I love New York – I really do. I moved here six years ago to study and if I end up staying in the U.S., it'll definitely be in this huge, fascinating city with more than 8.5 million inhabitants (and 800+ languages!).

That said, as a "New Yorker," I have to put up with all the usual disadvantages of a major city – the pollution, the traffic congestion, and the lack of parking. (Hey, get rid of the car – that way all three problems are solved!) Usually, I'm so used to these things that I don't even notice them but, after a recent trip to Singapore, I'm maybe seeing my adopted city a little differently ... For those of you who haven't yet had the opportunity to visit this *astonishing* city-state and island country in Southeast Asia, these were a few of the differences that struck me.

It's so *incredibly* clean. Like everyone, I knew that you weren't allowed to carry chewing gum with you in Singapore. (Didn't matter to me – I don't chew the stuff.) What I didn't know before I visited was how clean it is *in general*. I can honestly say that in the seven days that I was there – between the residential area where my friend has her apartment and the business district downtown – I didn't see one piece of litter. People are fined or made to clean up if they litter so, naturally, they tend not to do it. (I'm not saying this is a good thing or a bad thing, by the way – just making the point that if people know they won't get away with something, they don't do it.)

There's no graffiti on any of the walls. Call it street art or vandalism, depending on your point of view – it simply doesn't exist. In Singapore, you can't write or paint on any public or private building without permission, and there are *heavy* fines and even prison sentences for those who break this rule. The combined effect of garbage-free streets and clean walls is that it looks very attractive everywhere and also feels very *safe*. Having said that, by the end of my stay, I was kind of missing New York's street art. It adds interest to the urban environment ... to me, it's art!

It's so *green*! I don't know why I wasn't expecting this. Yes, New York has trees on the street, and the parks are beautiful. But the thing about Singapore's tropical trees is that they are just so ... *green*. And the Gardens by the Bay – a huge nature park – is unlike anything I've ever seen. Maybe I'll finish with a picture or two ...

# UNIT 4 Mind and behavior

## 4A LANGUAGE

### GRAMMAR: Subject-verb agreement

**1** Check (✓) the sentences that are correct.

1 Everyone was able to come to the party. _____
2 Some of the sandwiches has been eaten. _____
3 The information were very useful. _____
4 Everyone, including you, has to help. _____
5 Several of the plants have died. _____
6 One of the plates are broken. _____
7 Our teacher is great, and most of the students enjoy her lessons. _____
8 My friends, except for Josh, all has cars. _____

**2** Complete the conversation with the simple present or present continuous form of the verbs in parentheses.

A  Hey, Mia, one of my friends ¹_____ (plan) a picnic this Saturday. Do you want to come?
B  Sounds great, but my sister and I ²_____ (go) to the movies that day. There's a movie that both of us really ³_____ (want) to see.
A  What time ⁴_____ the movie _____ (start)?
B  Not until 7:30.
A  Well the picnic starts at four, so why ⁵_____ you, and your sister _____ (come) for an hour or two? Oh, by the way, everyone ⁶_____ (bring) food and something to drink.
B  OK. I love picnics – food always ⁷_____ (taste) better outside! What should I bring?
A  Anything you'd like. If each person ⁸_____ (bring) something to share, there should be plenty.

### VOCABULARY: Personality and behavior

**3** Choose the correct options to complete the sentences.

1 She's so *unreasonable / bossy / responsible* – she's always telling people what to do.
2 Alvin was very *arrogant / stubborn / bad-tempered* today. He yelled at me several times.
3 Our boss wants us to work the whole weekend. I think he's being totally *bossy / foolish / unreasonable*.
4 I would definitely trust Becky to babysit. I know she's only 15, but she's very *responsible / stubborn / bossy*.
5 Mia's so *bad-tempered / arrogant / unreasonable*. She thinks she's better than everyone else.

6 Leo let his friend use his credit card. It was a very *foolish / clumsy / responsible* thing to do.
7 Pilar is so *foolish / bad-tempered / stubborn*. It's hard to persuade her to change her mind.
8 Luke is really *clumsy / unreasonable / arrogant* – he's always breaking things.

**4** Complete the sentences with the correct form of the verbs in the box. Add prepositions where necessary.

| forgive | get | drive | upset | boast |
| praise | encourage | take (x2) | stand |

1 Yesterday my English teacher _____ me _____ criticizing my accent in front of the whole class. I really don't think that's the best way to _____ students _____ try harder.
2 My brother's always _____ _____ how good he is at soccer. I have to leave the room when he does that because I just can't _____ it.
3 My cousin persuaded my sister to give him a lot of money even though she doesn't have much herself. I can't _____ him _____ doing that. In my opinion, he _____ advantage _____ her because she's so kind.
4 It _____ _____ my nerves when people litter. If I see someone picking it up, I always _____ them _____ it.
5 One of my colleagues is always trying to _____ credit _____ work that I've done. It _____ me crazy!

### Pronunciation: *of*

**5** ▶ 4.1 Check (✓) the correct sound for the word *of* in each sentence. Listen, check, and repeat.

| | /əv/ | /ə/ |
|---|---|---|
| 1 My grandparents keep a lot of animals. | | |
| 2 Some of our customers are very nice. | | |
| 3 Many of my friends still live with their parents. | | |
| 4 You need to turn off both of the lights. | | |
| 5 I think that's one of Aunt María's earrings. | | |
| 6 I've already done most of my homework. | | |

20

# SKILLS 4B

## READING: Identifying attitude

**WED 13:02**

**Zoe:** Hello, dear housemates! Just wondering whether anyone else is starting to get a little ... fed up with Tom's behavior. 🤔

**Max:** Yup!

**Klara:** Tell me about it! He woke me up at three o'clock this morning! Tell me if I'm being unreasonable, but I expect people not to make noise when they come home in the middle of the night. 😠

**Javier:** I didn't hear a thing.

**Max:** Javier, nothing wakes you up! For your information, Tom dropped a pan in the kitchen, and then tripped and fell while he was coming up the stairs.

**Javier:** Yeah, he's a little clumsy sometimes.

**Zoe:** Personally, I could forgive Tom for coming home late now and then. I'm more annoyed by the fact that he "borrows" food and never actually replaces it. Twice this week, he's finished my orange juice and hasn't even mentioned it. To my mind, that's completely unacceptable.

**Max:** Totally agree, Zoe. If you want to upset your housemates, taking food without their permission is a really great way to do it! And he never washes the dishes. I'm always having to wash his dirty plates and mugs. To be honest, I think he takes advantage of us. And, OK, he's very charming and funny, but as far as I'm concerned, that's just not enough.

**Javier:** Yeah, but no one's actually told him, have they? He probably has no idea that he's doing anything wrong. If I were you, I'd talk to him. Generally, people are glad if you tell them how they can improve their behavior.

**Klara:** Javier, I totally get what you're saying, but Tom is pretty sensitive ...

**Max:** Javier, what planet are you on? People hate it when you criticize them!

**Javier:** Well, if you don't say anything, but keep getting mad at him, he'll be more upset. That's for sure! While we're on the topic, if you guys came to our monthly house meetings, you could discuss Tom's behavior with him then. Last time, none of you came. It was just Tom and me. 😕

**Klara:** That's a good point, Javier. Maybe we should try that.

**1** Are the following statements true (T) or false (F)?

1 Javier seems less annoyed by Tom's behavior than his housemates do. _____
2 Javier is easily woken up during the night. _____
3 Klara thinks that people who share a house should be quiet late at night. _____
4 What irritates Zoe about Tom is that he takes other people's food. _____
5 Max refuses to wash Tom's dishes for him. _____
6 Max does not accept that Tom has some good qualities. _____
7 Tom's housemates have already told him that he is behaving badly. _____
8 Javier recommends that his housemates speak to Tom about the problem. _____

**2** Read the text and decide who has the following opinions. Write K for Klara, M for Max, Z for Zoe, and J for Javier.

1 Being noisy at night is not the worst thing Tom does. _____
2 Tom's good qualities do not make his bad behavior less serious. _____
3 We like it when others suggest how we can be better people. _____
4 Tom is easily upset by other people's comments. _____
5 We don't like it when other people say we are doing something bad. _____

**3** Choose the correct options to complete the sentences. Then check your answers in the text.

1 If you want to upset your housemates, taking food without their permission *is / was* a really great way to do it!
2 If I were you, *I'll / I'd* talk to him.
3 In general, people *are / were* glad if you tell them how they can improve their behavior.
4 People *hate / hates* it when you criticize them!
5 Well, if you don't say anything but keep being mad at him, *he'll / he'd* be more upset.
6 If you guys *will come / came* to our monthly house meetings, you could discuss Tom's behavior with him then.

## 4C LANGUAGE

**GRAMMAR: Perfect and past forms**

**1** Choose the correct options to complete the sentences.

1 I ___ Daniel at the bus stop this morning.
  a 've seen   b saw   c 've been seeing
2 How long have you ___ the guitar? You're very good.
  a learned   b learn   c been learning
3 I ___ this movie twice already.
  a 've been seeing   b 've seen   c seen
4 She ___ a new laptop last week.
  a 's been buying   b 's bought   c bought
5 He ___ on his book for more than five years, and it still isn't finished.
  a 's been working   b worked   c is working
6 I have lots of homework, and I ___ started it yet.
  a haven't been   b didn't   c haven't
7 We haven't started our meal yet because we ___ waiting for Felipe to arrive.
  a been   b have been   c had

**2** Find six mistakes in the text. Cross out the mistakes and write the corrections above them.

> I'm going to Australia next summer. I'm very excited because I never went there before. I save up for the trip for over a year now. I want to go to Darwin in the north because I've heard that the scenery is amazing, and I really want to see some crocodiles! I'm also planning to go to Sydney. My dad has lived there for four years when he was younger, and he says it's a great city. I've been doing a lot of research on the Internet, and I find some great places to stay, including a treehouse in the jungle near Cairns. Yesterday, I have received an e-mail from one of my dad's old friends in Sydney, offering me a room there – he knew my dad for over 30 years now, and he's promised to tell me some funny stories about him!

**VOCABULARY: Word families**

**3** Match words 1–8 with definitions a–h.

1 reliable       ___
2 criticism      ___
3 create         ___
4 persuasive     ___
5 achievement    ___
6 risk           ___
7 consider       ___
8 succeed        ___

a able to make people agree with you
b able to be trusted to do something
c something that is dangerous
d something good that you manage to do
e achieve what you want to achieve
f things people say when they think something is bad
g think carefully about something or someone
h make something

**4** Complete the second sentence to mean the same as the first. Use a noun, verb, or adjective from the same family as the underlined word.

1 She often criticized my work.
  She was often _____ of my work.
2 I'm not certain of David's reliability.
  I'm not sure if we can _____ on David.
3 I wish you wouldn't do so many risky things.
  I wish you wouldn't take so many _____.
4 Do you think it's possible to achieve these goals?
  Do you think these goals are _____?
5 His work is very creative.
  His work shows a lot of _____.
6 Their business was extremely successful.
  Their business was a great _____.

**PRONUNCIATION: Sentence stress in perfect forms**

**5** ▶ 4.2 Listen to the sentences. Underline the stressed words in the phrases in **bold**.

1 **Julieta has done** all her work.
2 Why **have you invited** Tom?
3 **She's been annoying** me all morning!
4 I don't think **they have noticed** the mistake.
5 **Have you been waiting** for a long time?
6 Do you know if **she's bought** a ticket?

# SKILLS 4D

## SPEAKING: Responding to arguments

**1** ▶ 4.3 Listen to Anna telling her friend Paul about something that happened to her. Are the sentences true (T) or false (F)?

1 Anna was angry because the people in the car were driving too fast. ____
2 She put their burger boxes in a garbage can. ____
3 The people in the car were angry with her. ____
4 Other people thought that what they had done was wrong. ____
5 Anna knew that the police officer was the driver's father. ____
6 The police officer thought his son and his friend had behaved badly. ____

**2** ▶ 4.3 Choose the correct options to complete the sentences. Complete the phrases they use. Listen again if you need to.

1 When Paul says that people throw out garbage because they don't want their car to smell, Anna *agrees / disagrees / asks for clarification*:
   I think there's more _____ than that, though.
2 When Anna says that littering is a statement about the way people view society, Paul *agrees / disagrees / asks for clarification*:
   I'm not sure I _____.
3 When she explains more about what she means, Paul *agrees / disagrees / asks for clarification*:
   That makes a lot of _____.
4 When Paul says the police officer is responsible for his son's behavior, Anna *agrees / disagrees / asks for clarification*:
   That may be true to a certain _____.

**3** ▶ 4.4 Fill in blanks 1–5 in the conversation with phrases a–e. Listen and check.

a I couldn't believe my eyes!
b Let me guess
c No way!
d You're not going to believe what happened last night!
e That must have been so difficult.

A ¹_____ I went to see a band at a bar in town, but when I saw the singer, ²_____
B Why?
A It was our old math teacher, Mrs. Hoskins. Do you remember her?
B ³_____ What's she doing singing in a band?
A I wondered that, too. So I went to talk to her during the break.
B ⁴_____ – easier than controlling a class full of naughty kids, right?
A Yeah, something like that. And she said that some of the parents were awful to her and said it was her fault if their kids didn't do well on their exams.
B ⁵_____ Teaching's a tough job, isn't it? I think I'd rather be a singer, too!

**4** Look at phrases a–e in exercise 3 again and match them with functions 1–5 below.

1 to describe a reaction ____
2 to show empathy ____
3 to guess how the story will continue ____
4 to create suspense ____
5 to show surprise ____

**5** Use your own ideas and phrases you have learned to complete the conversation.

A You'll never guess what happened yesterday! I was getting off the bus when I tripped and fell on the sidewalk. I cut my leg pretty badly.
B (Show empathy.) _____
A Yes, it really hurt. I blame my friend Irene.
B (Ask for clarification.) _____
A Well, she persuaded me to wear these shoes. I'm not used to such high heels. She said I need to look more attractive for my job. She says that customers expect receptionists to wear high heels.
B (Disagree politely.) _____
A Anyway, I've made one decision.
B (Guess what A will say.) _____
A That's right! Only comfortable shoes for me from now on!

23

# 4 REVIEW and PRACTICE

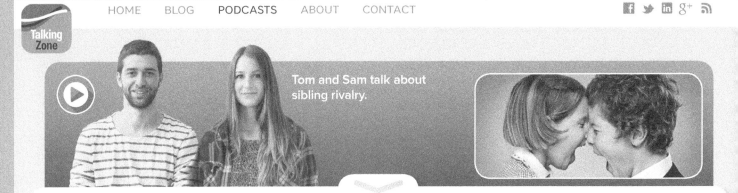

## LISTENING

**1** ▶ 4.5 Listen to the podcast. What do you think the term "sibling rivalry" means?
  a when parents do not treat their children equally
  b when one child is more successful than the others
  c when brothers and sisters argue and fight

**2** ▶ 4.5 Listen again. Check (✓) the words that you hear.
  1 silly ____    5 arrogant ____
  2 stupid ____   6 mean ____
  3 unreasonable ____  7 creative ____
  4 bossy ____   8 critical ____

**3** ▶ 4.5 Listen again. Choose the best options.
  1 Now that they're adults, Tom and his brothers
    a always behave like grown-ups.
    b get along well together.
    c still argue a lot.
  2 Carrie Fletcher has written a book about brothers and sisters who
    a don't change their personalities when they become adults.
    b had a bad relationship with their parents.
    c still argue although they're not children any more.
  3 According to her, if our siblings behaved badly as children, we
    a don't always realize that they're not the same now.
    b often continue to dislike them forever.
    c don't believe they're able to change.
  4 The proportion of people who thought their parents treated all the children equally was
    a 15%.    b 50%.    c 85%.
  5 She says that it's important
    a to be as successful as your siblings.
    b not to criticize your siblings.
    c not to blame your siblings for the way your parents behaved.
  6 According to Carrie Fletcher, it's possible to stop rivalry with your siblings by
    a agreeing to be polite and kind to each other.
    b making an effort to be nice to them.
    c accepting that they've changed.

## READING

**1** Read Tom's blog on page 25. Choose the best summary of what he says.
  a Tom went to a psychologist to learn how to be more positive, and in this blog, he shares what he has learned.
  b Tom has to fight against having negative thoughts, and he writes about some of the effective ways he has found for doing this.
  c Tom writes about different methods that people use to make themselves more positive because in his job, it is important to sound happy.

**2** Does Tom say these things in his blog? Circle Y (Yes) or N (No).
  1 His natural personality is not positive.        Y / N
  2 It took him many years to stop having negative thoughts.   Y / N
  3 It is possible to learn how to have positive thoughts.   Y / N
  4 Bad events are often not as important as we think they are.   Y / N
  5 His cousin is a difficult person to have as a visitor.   Y / N
  6 If you have negative thoughts about an experience, it will be better than you expected.   Y / N
  7 He finds it helpful to write down positive events.   Y / N
  8 You should stay away from people who make you miserable.   Y / N
  9 When he is at work, Sam helps keep him happy.   Y / N
  10 You should only smile when you're feeling happy.   Y / N

HOME    BLOG    PODCASTS    ABOUT    CONTACT

Tom writes about the power of the mind.

# Think yourself positive!

**In my job, it's essential to sound confident and cheerful, and I'm sure that most of our listeners think that this is my natural personality. Well, I'm sorry to disappoint you, but, in fact, I've had to work pretty hard over the years to learn how to deal with the negative thoughts that sometimes come into my head — thoughts that could have destroyed my career if I'd allowed them to.**

The good news, though, is that if I can make myself more positive, anyone can. You just need to learn the right techniques — and, in my opinion, anyway — you really should. After all, many scientific studies have proved that positive thinking has physical, as well as mental, benefits, and that has to be a good thing, right?

Obviously, I'm not a psychologist, but I've been thinking about the things that have worked best for me, and I would say that number one is to try to keep your mind in the present. It's easy to be upset by something that has happened recently and to think about it again and again, like a bad movie playing in your head. But will it really matter in five years? Five months? Five weeks? Even five hours?

On the other hand, one of my personal bad habits was wasting energy on negative thoughts about the *future*. For example, if my cousin was coming to visit me, I'd drive myself crazy worrying that she'd be bored, or that she'd want to go to expensive restaurants that I couldn't afford. So, by the time she actually arrived, I'd be annoyed with her for no reason at all! And that's the thing, isn't it? If you expect an experience to be bad, it probably will be!

Also, I keep a notebook by my bed. If I've been noticing my mood getting low, I make myself record all the good things that have happened that day. It sounds a little silly, but it works for me. I also try to surround myself with positive friends, and, of course, my colleague Sam is like a ray of sunshine every day! I always seem to be in a good mood when she's around.

And, finally, however you're feeling, don't forget to smile! Practice in front of the mirror if you need to. It really does make a difference!

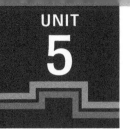

# Our planet

## GRAMMAR: *so* and *such*; *so much/many, so little/few*

**1** Complete the sentences with the words in the box.

> so few   such (x2)   so much
> such a   so   so many   so little

1 That's expensive! I didn't realize the vacation cost _____ money.
2 Mr. Ashton is _____ good teacher!
3 I didn't realize that studying could be _____ enjoyable.
4 The beach is never crowded because _____ people know about it.
5 This coffee shop makes _____ good hot chocolate!
6 He made _____ effort to study, it's not surprising he failed the exam.
7 We had _____ problems, I thought we would never finish the work.
8 I don't think I've ever eaten _____ delicious doughnuts.

**2** Are these sentences correct or incorrect? Cross out any mistakes and write the correct words at the end of the sentences.

1 Traveling by plane is such bad for the environment. _____
2 We had such wonderful teachers at that school. _____
3 I was lonely because I had so few friends there. _____
4 My sister has so beautiful hair. _____
5 I had so great time in Mexico. _____
6 How can I write a good essay when I have so few time to do it? _____
7 There was so much salt in the soup, I couldn't eat it. _____
8 There are so much things to do in Paris. _____

## VOCABULARY: The environment

**3** Choose the correct options to complete the sentences.

1 We all helped pick up _____ from the park.
   a wildfires   b wildlife   c litter
2 Aircraft produce a lot of _____.
   a carbon dioxide   b drought   c endangered species
3 Because of the _____, the farmers had no water for their crops.
   a carbon dioxide   b wildfires   c drought
4 We need to help protect the world's _____.
   a heat wave   b endangered species   c litter
5 Hot, dry weather meant that the _____ spread quickly.
   a heat wave   b wildfires   c endangered species
6 We went to the mountains, where it's cool, to escape the _____.
   a litter   b drought   c heat wave
7 We went to Africa to see the _____.
   a wildlife   b carbon dioxide   c wildfires

**4** Complete the phrases with words that mean the same as the words in parentheses.

1 I'm really worried about c _ _ _ _ _ _ c _ _ _ _ _ (the way the weather is changing).
2 We should rely much less on f _ _ _ _ _ f _ _ _ _ (energy sources such as coal and gas).
3 We should use fuel that is e _ _ _ _ _ _ _ _ _ _ _ _ _ - f _ _ _ _ _ _ _ (not harmful to the planet).
4 We could produce a lot more s _ _ _ _ e _ _ _ _ _ (electricity from the sun).
5 We need to reduce our e _ _ _ _ _ c _ _ _ _ _ _ _ _ _ _ (the amount of fuel we use).
6 We should buy household appliances that are e _ _ _ _ _ - e _ _ _ _ _ _ _ _ (only use small amounts of fuel).
7 Solar power does not produce any t _ _ _ _ w _ _ _ _ (poisonous substances after it has been used).

## PRONUNCIATION: Sentence stress with *so* and *such*

**5** ▶ 5.1  In each sentence, one of the stressed syllables is in **bold**. Read the sentences and underline the other stressed syllable. Listen and check.

1 She's such a good **teach**er.
2 I had such a terrible **head**ache.
3 They cooked so much **food**.
4 It was such a windy **day**.
5 There are so many **peo**ple here.

26

# SKILLS 5B

## LISTENING: Identifying cause and effect

**1** ▶5.2 Listen to James interviewing his guest, Grace, on the radio. Are the following statements true (T) or false (F)?

1 James says that everyone knows that cold weather makes them feel miserable.
2 Grace talks about how the weather affects our moods.
3 Grace gives two examples of how warm, sunny weather makes us treat other people better.
4 According to Grace, cold weather makes us notice the things that are around us more.
5 According to Grace, warm weather only affects us in a good way.
6 James suggests a different explanation for the way that warm weather causes people to become aggressive.
7 Grace says that weather influences people's behavior even when they are outdoors for very short periods.
8 James jokes that people get annoyed on sunny days when they have to stay indoors.

**2** ▶5.2 Listen again. Check (✓) the sentences that you hear in the interview. Pay particular attention to the underlined words.

1 We all know that the weather <u>affects</u> our mood.
2 So how can the heat and the cold <u>impact</u> our behavior?
3 But sunny weather has other – more surprising – <u>consequences</u>.
4 Did you know it <u>makes</u> us notice more about our surroundings?
5 Could this just be an <u>effect</u> of the better light?
6 Warm weather can <u>lead to</u> aggressive – even violent – behavior.

**3** ▶5.3 Listen to these phrases from the interview. Use the mark ‿ to show where a consonant sound ending one word is moved to the next word.

1 the weather affects our mood
2 she's going to talk about
3 let's start with a good example
4 sunny weather has other effects
5 it makes us notice more
6 being stuck indoors on a beautiful day

**4** Choose the correct options to complete the sentences.

1 We had to walk twenty miles in the heat with heavy backpacks on. It was completely *distressing / exhausting*.
2 We need a young, *lethargic / dynamic* leader who can change the whole organization.
3 I feel very *pessimistic / optimistic* about the future of this company. I just know it's going to be a great success.
4 She's very *eager / passionate* about the environment and speaks with great energy on the subject.
5 I think this plant-based diet is really good for me. I feel so much more *grumpy / energetic* on it.
6 Poor Helen's having a few problems at home. She seemed a little *motivated / down* when I saw her.
7 I don't have the energy to do anything in this heat. I feel so *lethargic / enthusiastic*.
8 Carlo was in a terrible mood this morning. He was so *positive / grumpy*.

## 5C LANGUAGE

### GRAMMAR: Future predictions

**1** Choose the correct options to complete the sentences.

1 I can't go to the party with you now because I still have work to do, but I ____ later.
   a might go   b will have gone
   c may have gone

2 I'm sure we ____ glasses in 50 years.
   a may not be wearing   b not going to wear
   c won't be wearing

3 Look at all those dark clouds. I'm sure it ____.
   a might rain   b won't be raining
   c 's going to rain

4 Ask Dad to drive you to the airport. I don't think he ____.
   a is going to mind   b 'll mind
   c might mind

5 She's certain that scientists ____ a way to stop climate change by then.
   a will have invented   b going to invent
   c will inventing

6 Do you think that Pablo ____ disappointed with his test results?
   a will be being   b will
   c will be

7 Victoria says she definitely ____ any more because of the damage aircraft do to the environment.
   a might not fly   b isn't going to fly
   c won't flown

**2** Use the prompts to complete the sentences using *will* or *won't* with the future perfect or future continuous.

1 I hope that _____ by next week.
   (the workers / will / put / the roof on)

2 I plan to go traveling next summer. _____ by then.
   (I / will / finish / college)

3 Do you think we _____ in 2060?
   (will / still / use / gas and coal)

4 It is likely that _____ by a meter by 2100.
   (sea levels / will / rise)

5 Engineers are building a road across the desert, but _____ by next year.
   (they / won't / finish / it)

6 We have planted a large forest. I hope that _____ hundreds of years from now.
   (people / will / enjoy / the trees)

7 Maybe in twenty years, _____ a better way to generate electricity.
   (someone / will / invent)

### VOCABULARY: Adjective prefixes

**3** Match the two parts of the sentences.

1 I think it was rather dis ____
2 We had to learn a list of ir ____
3 We were disappointed by her im ____
4 I didn't know it was il ____
5 He gets annoyed when people mis ____
6 Accidents are un ____
7 It's fine to use these phrases in in ____
8 It was extremely im ____

a legal to take shells from the beach.
b pronounce his name.
c avoidable without the correct safety equipment.
d honest to pretend you didn't see her e-mail.
e polite to ignore her.
f mature behavior.
g formal situations.
h regular verbs.

**4** Complete the words in the text with the prefixes *dis-*, *im-*, *in-*, *un-*, *il-*, *ir-*, or *mis-*.

This morning, I received an ¹____expected piece of good news: my boss has decided to retire. He's a nice man, but he's so ²____organized. His office is really messy, and he gets incredibly ³____patient when he can't find the things he needs, and then wastes my time talking about totally ⁴____relevant things such as soccer. He goes to meetings and comes back with lots of ⁵____spelled and almost ⁶____legible notes that I can't read. I also have to check his sales figures, which are usually ⁷____accurate, as well as deal with ⁸____satisfied customers, who often accuse him of giving them ⁹____leading information about our products. It's a mystery why he's stayed in the job so long when it's obviously so ¹⁰____suitable for him.

### PRONUNCIATION: *will have*

**5** ▶ 5.4 Read the sentences aloud. Remember to pronounce *have* as /əv/. Listen and check.

1 Will we have covered all the topics by June?
2 We'll have found a cure for many more diseases.
3 I won't have finished my degree by then.
4 In fifteen years, the children will have grown up.
5 Won't they have completed the new road by May?
6 I don't think you'll have finished by 3:00 p.m.

# SKILLS 5D

## WRITING: Writing an opinion essay

### Should people take more PERSONAL RESPONSIBILITY for the environment?

**A** Another reason is that some of our actions are more harmful than we probably realize. A flight from Amsterdam to Beijing will put around 740 kg. of $CO_2$ into the atmosphere: recycling everything for a year will not save that amount or anything close to it. ¹_____, over 25 million people travel through New York's JFK airport alone each year. If every one of those people took one less flight a year, it would make a big difference.

**B** ²_____, we should not wait for governments to take action on climate change. We all have a responsibility towards the planet we live on. We should do our best to take care of it and, therefore, make it more likely that other people, including politicians, will take care of it, too.

**C** It is easy to feel hopeless when we think about the huge problem of climate change. Many people think that only governments can make the significant changes we need to prevent it. ³_____, they don't understand why they should take personal responsibility, especially if it makes their own lives harder. Why should they bike to work if everyone else comes by car? However, this attitude is wrong: we all need to play our part in helping save the planet.

**D** One reason is that the more we make changes in our own lives, the more we are likely to influence other people. If your colleagues see you on your bike, they might consider riding a bike, too. ⁴_____, the politicians who represent us can be influenced by knowing what is important to us, and they are more likely to listen to us if we do things that show we want to protect the environment, ⁵_____ just talking about it.

---

**1** Read the opinion essay and number paragraphs A–D in the correct order 1–4.

1 ____
2 ____
3 ____
4 ____

**2** Fill in blanks 1–5 with formal linkers a–e.

a  Nevertheless
b  as opposed to
c  Consequently
d  In sum
e  Similarly

**3** Imagine you are answering the same essay question, but have the opposite view. Write the following:

1  a thesis statement: _____
2  a topic sentence for a paragraph arguing that individual people cannot make a difference: _____
3  a topic sentence for a paragraph arguing that governments control what industries do: _____
4  the first sentence of a concluding paragraph: _____

**4** Write an opinion essay on the following topic:

**Should we be prepared to accept a lower standard of living in order to protect the environment?**

- Provide a clear thesis statement.
- Start each paragraph with a topic statement.
- Support your thesis statement with examples, facts, figures, etc.
- Summarize the key points in the concluding paragraph.
- Use at least three formal linkers to connect your ideas.

# 5 REVIEW and PRACTICE

HOME  BLOG  **PODCASTS**  ABOUT  CONTACT

Tom and Sam talk about protecting the environment.

## LISTENING

**1** ▶ 5.5 Listen to the podcast and choose the best summary of Tom's plan for this week.

a He's going to try to find the best app to help him protect the environment.
b He's going to use some apps that will help him protect the environment.
c He's going to make his home more energy-efficient.

**2** ▶ 5.5 Listen again. Are the sentences true (T), false (F), or doesn't say (DS)?

1 Earth Day started thirty years ago. _____
2 Earth Day started as a result of an accident that happened. _____
3 Tom will be using three apps. _____
4 He will use one of the apps when he's buying food. _____
5 Tom thinks he will do less driving as a result of using one of the apps. _____
6 Tom usually drives a lot. _____
7 Another app will tell Tom how much energy he is using in his home. _____
8 The makers of the litter app want to help solve the problem of littering. _____

## READING

**1** Read Ellie's blog on page 31 and number topics a–f in the order that they appear (1–6).

a a new way of cleaning the seas _____
b the effect of bad news on the author's mood _____
c the increase in global temperatures _____
d the areas of land that are being protected _____
e the people who are trying to help the environment _____
f animals that may soon not exist _____

**2** Choose the best options to complete the sentences.

1 Ellie says that depressing predictions about the environment
   a sometimes make her feel pessimistic.
   b are not true.
   c always make her feel pessimistic.

2 According to Ellie
   a there is no good news about the environment.
   b the news about the environment is mainly good.
   c there is good *and* bad news about the environment.

3 Ellie claims that things are being done to protect the environment, but we
   a never hear about them.
   b sometimes don't hear about them.
   c are not interested in them.

4 In Chile and Papua New Guinea
   a most of the trees are being cut down.
   b no trees are being cut down.
   c some of the trees are now protected.

5 The situation in relation to Uganda's mountain gorillas is
   a extremely hopeful.
   b slightly hopeful.
   c not at all hopeful.

6 To help solve the problem of plastic, some supermarkets
   a are using less plastic in their packaging.
   b have stopped selling some items.
   c are only using paper in their packaging.

# REVIEW and PRACTICE 5

HOME  BLOG  PODCASTS  ABOUT  CONTACT

Guest blogger Ellie gives some reasons for us to be cheerful about the environment.

## Green – and happy!

Scientists say that by the end of the century, increased levels of carbon dioxide in the atmosphere will have caused the average global temperature to rise by two degrees. As a result, heatwaves, droughts, and wildfires will all be happening much more frequently. With so many pessimistic and distressing predictions about the future of the planet, it's not always easy to be positive. Now, I'm cheerful by nature, but even I sometimes struggle to feel optimistic about the future. But being miserable isn't going to help. And there's some good news out there, I promise you. With this blog – the first of many – I intend to tell you about it!

First of all, there are some passionate and dynamic people out there, making a real difference. (It has to be said, it helps when they have money!) Did you know, for example, that the Leonardo DiCaprio Foundation has donated huge sums of money to organizations that protect endangered species and the environment? Or that other charitable foundations are protecting our oceans by preventing illegal fishing and plastic pollution? We don't always hear about the good stuff that's happening.

We're always hearing about the world's disappearing forests, and that is, of course, *extremely bad* news for our planet. But in several parts of the world, for example, in Chile and Papua New Guinea, *new* conservation areas are actually being created, and existing conservation areas are being expanded. In these places, the cutting down of trees will be forbidden, and wildlife, in all its many forms, will find a home for generations to come. This is all very encouraging.

Meanwhile, in Uganda's Bwindi National Park, there's such good news about the mountain gorilla. Their numbers have actually gone up! Admittedly, they're still "critically endangered," but at least there's now hope that these beautiful and amazing creatures will have a future.

We're all *finally* waking up to the fact that plastic is not fantastic. Governments the world over have started banning the sale of certain plastic products. Supermarkets are reducing

the amount of plastic in their packaging, replacing it with paper or other substances that will decay naturally. Major cities in the world will soon get drinking fountains, reducing the need for people to buy mineral water in plastic bottles. Things can change and *are* changing.

In the meantime, new technologies are being developed all the time that can be used for environmental purposes. There are astonishing machines that can suck waste out of the oceans, knives and forks that you can actually eat (rather than throw away), and apps that can help with anything from car-sharing to choosing local food when it's in season.

There is hope, and don't you forget it!

# Habits and change

## GRAMMAR: The habitual past

**1** Complete the sentences with *used*, *use*, *would*, or *was*.

1 Our parents never _____ to let us play near the river.
2 Our grandmother _____ usually be at the station to meet us.
3 Did you _____ to play with dolls when you were little?
4 We didn't _____ to have a TV in our house.
5 I found Irene boring because she _____ always talking about her horses.
6 After dinner, we _____ sit and talk for a while.
7 We had a car, but it _____ always breaking down.
8 We all _____ to help on the farm.

**2** Find six mistakes in the conversation. Cross out the mistakes and write the corrections above them.

A When you were a child, did your parents both used to work?
B Yes. I used to grow up on a farm, so, in fact, everyone was expected to work. Before school, my sister would feed the chickens, and I would collect the eggs. I would hate getting up so early! Mom and Dad both worked on the farm during the day, but Mom was always waiting for us when we got home. She never use to leave us alone when we were young.
A Would you like living on a farm?
B Yes, I loved it!
A My uncle was a farmer, too. I used to stay at his farm a few times during school vacations, and I loved everything about it, except the farm dog because he was always barking at me!

## VOCABULARY: Expressions with *time*

**3** Choose the correct prepositions to complete the sentences.

1 The concert is at 8, but I don't expect it will start *in / on / at* time.
2 I've been learning French *for / from / at* some time now.
3 Do you think we'll be there *in / for / on* time to see María before she leaves?
4 I used to go to a lot of baseball games because we were living in the U.S. *in / from / at* the time.
5 I like my job, but it gets a little stressful *for / from / at* time to time.
6 Make sure you add the eggs one *in / at / on* a time.
7 If everyone helps, we'll get this work done *on / from / in* no time.

**4** Complete the phrases with the missing words.

1 There's no hurry to finish eating, so please _____ your time.
2 While we were waiting, we played cards to _____ the time.
3 I think you work too hard. You need to _____ time to have some fun!
4 Are you ready? Our guests will be arriving _____ time now.
5 I jog on the same path every week, and I time _____ to see if I'm improving.
6 This street is so dangerous – it's only a _____ of time before there's an accident.
7 Why don't you keep your keys in a safe place? We _____ so much time searching for them!

## PRONUNCIATION: /s/ and /z/ in *use(d)*

**5** ▶ 6.1 Read the sentences aloud, being careful to pronounce *use(d)* correctly. Listen and check.

1 My great-grandparents didn't use to have electricity in their house.
2 I used to use my exercise bike every day, but now I don't.
3 Didn't Samuel use to play the drums?
4 Diego didn't want me to use his laptop, but I used it anyway.
5 Have you ever used a personal trainer?
6 We used to live in Panama City.

SKILLS 6B

**READING:** Understanding non-literal meaning

# Can a leopard change its spots?

We all describe each other in terms of character traits. We are "cheerful" or "miserable," "hard-working" or "lazy," etc. Yet personality has been a controversial subject over the years. Some psychologists have even argued that, contrary to popular belief, there is no such thing as a personality trait. Our behavior, they claimed, was just the result of the situations that we found ourselves in.

Generally, however, research has seemed to suggest that the opposite is true, and that character traits do indeed exist. In studies, when people are observed in a variety of situations, they tend to show more or less the same type of behavior in all of those situations. This shouldn't be a great surprise to anyone. After all, when we describe a friend as "polite," we are thinking of the way he or she speaks to other people in class, at the train station, or in a restaurant, and not just in one of these places.

What is less clear, however, is whether those personality traits are fixed or, on the contrary, change over time. It used to be thought that our traits developed throughout childhood and early adulthood, but were then set in stone for life. A recently published study suggests that this may not be the case. A group of people were observed over several decades and their behavior studied. Their characteristics after forty or more years were very different from the traits that they had shown in their youth. After all, everyone knows a person whose character has changed significantly over the years. My husband's father, for example, a strict and controlling parent in his thirties and forties, later became the kindest, sweetest grandfather the world has ever known, as gentle as a lamb.

The truth of the matter seems to be that personality traits are generally fairly fixed, but they can change gradually over the course of a lifetime. Certain experiences tend to cause personality change more than others. Great career success and tragedy are two of these. However, what's encouraging is that the changes are usually positive, most people becoming nicer and calmer as they grow older.

**1** Check (✓) the statements that are true.

1. Some experts have claimed that personality does not exist. \_\_\_
2. Most people agree that our characters are made up of particular qualities. \_\_\_
3. People usually show different characteristics in different situations. \_\_\_
4. Previously, it was believed that our personalities were formed in early childhood. \_\_\_
5. In the past, psychologists thought that our personalities stayed the same for all our adult lives. \_\_\_
6. Most people know someone whose personality is different from how it was when he/she was younger. \_\_\_
7. When people's characters change, this generally happens quite quickly. \_\_\_
8. When very sad things happen to people, it can change the way that they behave. \_\_\_

**2** Identify whether each underlined phrase is an exaggeration (E), a comparison (C), a personification (P), or an idiom (I). There are two of each.

1. ... our traits developed throughout childhood and early adulthood, but were then set in stone for life. \_\_\_
2. My husband's father [...] later became the kindest, sweetest grandfather the world has ever known ... \_\_\_
3. ... became the kindest, sweetest grandfather the world has ever known, as gentle as a lamb. \_\_\_
4. Regarding Helen's remark, I've never heard anything so stupid in all my life! \_\_\_
5. There's a slice of chocolate cake in the kitchen, and it's calling my name! \_\_\_
6. It broke her heart when Jamie left. \_\_\_
7. Once outside, we were viciously attacked by the rain and the wind. \_\_\_
8. Oh, you poor thing! Your hands are as cold as ice! \_\_\_

**3** Complete each phrase with one word.

1. _____ to popular belief, we do not need animal products in our diet in order to be healthy.
2. Most people worry that their kitchens aren't clean enough. In fact, the _____ is true, and they're probably too clean!
3. The truth of the _____ is that most of us spend way too much time sitting down.
4. She certainly wasn't lazy. On the _____, she rarely had a break from work.

33

## 6C LANGUAGE

### GRAMMAR: *be used to* and *get used to*

**1** Choose the correct options to complete the sentences.

1 I've been getting up at 5 a.m. for two years now, so I _____ to it.
  a get used  b 'm used  c used
2 This is my new bike. I haven't _____ to it yet.
  a been used  b used  c gotten used
3 _____ to a new school or college can be hard.
  a Getting used  b Being used  c Using
4 It took Rafaela a long time to _____ to the fact that Daniel had gone.
  a get used  b be used  c used
5 I could tell that Lucia _____ to such hard work.
  a didn't use  b didn't get used  c wasn't used

**2** Complete the sentences with the correct form of (*not*) *be used to* or (*not*) *get used to* and the verbs in parentheses. There may be more than one answer.

1 I _____ (cook) for so many people.
2 Manuel had worked in a coffee shop for years, so he _____ (talk) to lots of different people.
3 Is it hard to _____ (live) on a boat?
4 In the UK, I had to _____ (drive) on the left.
5 These boots can be uncomfortable, especially if you _____ (wear) them.

### VOCABULARY: Expressions with prepositions

**3** Complete the text with the expressions in the box.

> advantage of   fed up with   approve of   cared about
> advised me against   confused about   possibility of
> comfortable with   anxious about   sympathetic to

As a teenager, I was very ¹_____ what I wanted to do for my career. All I really ²_____ was acting, but my parents ³_____ it because acting is such a risky career.
After I finished school, I got a job in a bank. I soon got ⁴_____ it: the work was boring. My roommate was ⁵_____ my situation and asked me if I'd ever considered the ⁶_____ becoming a teacher. At first, I was ⁷_____ dealing with the kids, but I found that I loved teaching and felt very ⁸_____ them. The other ⁹_____ working in a school is that I now spend a lot of time helping out with the drama club, which I love. Luckily, my parents ¹⁰_____ my new career, too!

**4** Complete the crossword puzzle.

**Across**

6 She watches TV every evening. She's absolutely _____ with soap operas! (8)
7 What was his _____ to Martin calling him an idiot? (8)
8 The _____ of living in Chicago is that the weather is terrible. (12)
9 He's _____ to a cheaper ticket because he's under 16. (8)
10 My grandmother is very independent. She _____ on doing all her own housework, and she's still driving. (7)

**Down**

1 I have to remember to _____ Diego on his fantastic test results. (12)
2 I'm _____ to chocolate. I eat it every day. (8)
3 Their story about seeing ghosts was silly. I don't _____ in them at all. (7)
4 You should be very _____ of strange e-mails – don't click on any links in them! (10)
5 She was extremely upset when they _____ her of lying. (7)

### PRONUNCIATION: *be used to* and *get used to*

**5** ▶ 6.2 Read the sentences aloud. Pay attention to the /ə/ sound in *to*. Listen and check.

1 I'll never get used to getting up so early!
2 We're not used to this hot weather.
3 These children aren't used to sitting still for so long.
4 You'll get used to the traffic noise.
5 She's used to telling other people what to do.
6 We're slowly getting used to working together.

# SKILLS 6D

## SPEAKING: Challenging assumptions

**1** ▶ 6.3 Listen to Luís and Eva discussing their plans for a cheap vacation. Check (✓) the phrases you hear that are related to solving problems.

1 If you ask me, … _____
2 We could either … or … _____
3 We could always … _____
4 Why not …? _____
5 We could … , instead of … _____
6 Like what? _____
7 You mean …? _____
8 The point I'm making is … _____
9 I'm just saying … _____
10 Is it worth it, though? _____
11 But is that really a good idea? _____
12 What difference would it make? _____

**2** ▶ 6.3 Listen again and complete the sentences that Luis and Eva use to challenge each other's assumptions.

1 Just because we're _____ doesn't mean we can't _____.
2 True, but it's still _____, isn't it?
3 We can _____ in the daytime, regardless of _____ at night.
4 _____ is one thing, but riding a bike for miles, carrying a tent, is _____.
5 _____ has nothing to do with _____ ourselves.

**3** Use your own ideas to write responses that challenge A's assumptions. Use phrases from exercise 2.

1 A I go jogging most days, so I think I'll be fine running a marathon.
  B _____ is one thing, but _____ is quite another.
2 A You can't walk to work if it's raining.
  B _____
3 A I know he loves me because he gives me lots of expensive presents.
  B _____
4 A It's better to send a birthday card late than not to send one at all.
  B _____
5 A Let's stay in our hotel room. We only have two hours before we need to be at the station.
  B _____

**4** ▶ 6.4 Complete the conversation. Then listen and check.

A If you ¹_____ me, there's no point going to Sara's party. She's invited so many people that we won't get a chance to talk to her.
B True, but I think it will ²_____ be fun. Just ³_____ she'll be busy with her other guests ⁴_____ we can't enjoy the party.
A Is it ⁵_____ it, though? It's a long way to go, isn't it? … and taxis are so expensive.
B We could ⁶_____ take a bus ⁷_____ maybe see if someone will give us a ride. Sara's parties are always great, and she's hired a DJ for this one.
A But ⁸_____ if we can't get one?
B I don't know. The ⁹_____ I'm making is that I think we'll have a good time, no ¹⁰_____ whether Sara has time to talk to us or not, so I really think we should go.
A OK, you've convinced me! We could ¹¹_____ share a taxi with someone else if we can't get a ride.

**5** Imagine your friend needs to pass an English exam, but has a bad teacher. Write a short conversation between you and your friend. Include phrases for making suggestions, and offering or asking for clarification.

# 6 REVIEW and PRACTICE

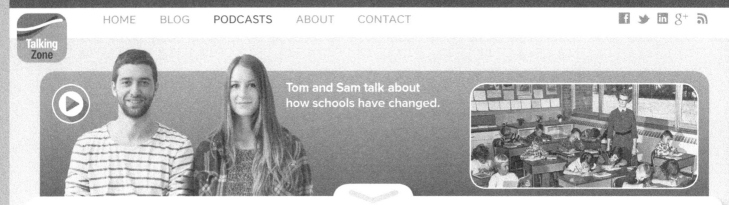

## LISTENING

**1** ▶ 6.5 Listen to Tom and Sam's interview with Tony and check (✓) the correct sentences.

1. School life is different now from how it was when Tony was in school. ____
2. Teachers were less easygoing when he was in school. ____
3. Teachers used the same punishments when Tony was in school as they do today. ____
4. Tony's teachers made sure that he made good progress. ____
5. Tony thinks today's students have too much stress. ____
6. He is pleased that students stay in school longer now. ____

**2** ▶ 6.5 Listen again and complete the sentences with one or two words.

1. When Tony was in school, students had to _____ when the principal came in.
2. Students who talked in class had to do _____.
3. Nobody wanted to be seen outside the classroom by the _____.
4. Tony used to _____ by staring out of the window.
5. Tony thinks that schools are obsessed with _____.
6. He thinks that students nowadays need time to _____ and be kids.
7. Tony was only 16 when he _____.
8. His first job was in a _____.
9. Nowadays, almost everyone goes to high school _____ until they graduate.
10. Tony believes that a _____ means a better life.

## READING

**1** Read Sam's blog on page 37. Put these strange family habits a–f in the order that Sam mentions them (1–6).

a. doing strange things to bring luck ____
b. continuing to pronounce words like a child ____
c. keeping things in strange places ____
d. eating unusual food ____
e. pretending a pet is a real person ____
f. using a toy in a strange way ____

**2** Are the sentences true (T), false (F), or doesn't say (DS)?

1. Silvana likes to have milk with her ice cream. ____
2. Silvana makes sugar sandwiches for her family. ____
3. Sam's family buys her presents and says they are from her cat. ____
4. Sam thinks it is funny that Tom's family puts a doll in the fruit bowl. ____
5. The tradition of taking a potato to exams has existed in Dan's family for a long time. ____
6. Lola's family thinks that folded potato chips are unlucky. ____
7. Sam and her sister have a strange habit related to going up and down their parents' stairs. ____
8. Sam's cousin expected the waiter to know the word "marbies." ____

## REVIEW and PRACTICE 6

HOME   BLOG   PODCASTS   ABOUT   CONTACT

Sam writes about the strange habits some families have.

# It runs in the family!

Have you ever said or done something that your friends think is really weird? It happened to me yesterday when I was at my friend Silvana's house. She offered me some ice cream and, without thinking, I asked for some milk to pour on it. It was only when I noticed the expression on her face that I realized something was wrong. Don't we all put milk on our ice cream? Apparently not!

It can be embarrassing when you realize that some of the things that you're used to doing when you're with your own family aren't shared by most other people. Once Silvana stopped laughing, she admitted that she herself has been addicted to sugar sandwiches ever since her grandmother gave them to her as a child. And that her boyfriend puts mayonnaise on bananas. Now that's weird!

The thing is, all our families do things that we think are normal until we meet other people who tell us that they're not. I'm in my twenties now, and I still get birthday presents "from the cat." Tom thinks that's strange, but his family keeps bread in the microwave oven, and they have a doll they call the "No Fruit Dolly" that they put in the fruit bowl when it's empty!

Some habits go back for generations. My friend Dan's grandfather discovered a potato in his jacket pocket after he'd passed his driving test. After that, his dad would always take a potato with him if he had an exam of any kind, and now Dan and his sisters do the same! It seems that lots of families have strange activities they perform to bring them luck. In my friend Lola's family, if they find a potato chip that's completely folded over, they can make a wish, but only if they press the chip against their forehead and break it first! Of course, I shouldn't criticize them for that because even today, neither my sister nor I will step on the third stair of my parents' staircase in case it brings us bad luck!

And then there are family words that make no sense at all to other people. Often, they're childish mispronunciations that never got replaced with their adult versions. My 30-year-old cousin still insists on calling curtains "turtens" and cookies "tooties." I'm used to it now, but I was with her in a restaurant recently when she accidentally asked the waiter for extra "marbies" on her pizza – her childhood word for "tomatoes." Her face turned bright red when she realized her mistake!

Anyway, I'll stop now because I'm hungry, and my sister is making chocolate omelets for lunch ... oh, wait, are you telling me that it's only my family that eats them?

# WRITING PRACTICE

## WRITING: Making a narrative interesting

**1** Read Irene's blog post about a scary movie. Complete the post with the time linkers in the box. There may be more than one correct answer, but do not use the same linker twice.

> after a while   before long   at first   in a matter of minutes/hours
> in the beginning   eventually   in no time   as time went on

1 Last night my friend Elena and I went to see a movie called *The Other Child* at the Cinema Royale. I knew it was about a ghost, but I didn't expect it to be too scary. "My aunt María saw it on Monday and she loved it," I told Elena, "so it can't be that bad." How wrong I was!

2 ¹_____, it seemed like any other movie. The characters were a little bit weird, but there were several funny moments, and people in the audience were laughing. However, ²_____, the laughter stopped. It's hard to explain exactly why, but a feeling of fear was spreading through my body like ice. "Come on, Irene," I told myself. "You know it's just a story."

3 Suddenly, I realized that as we'd been sitting there, the whole theater had become colder, and ³_____, the lights had been turned down until it was almost completely dark. I could feel my heart beating like a drum in my chest. I didn't say anything to Elena because I thought she'd think I was being silly, but ⁴_____, I noticed that her body was shaking. She was just as scared as me!

4 By this time, the whole audience was silent. We all knew that something awful was about to happen, but when the ghost ⁵_____ appeared on the screen, everyone screamed in shock. Elena turned to me, "Why did you make me come to this?" she demanded.

5 Afterwards, we took a long walk to calm down. We agreed it was the scariest movie we'd ever seen. Elena said she had enjoyed it, but my legs felt like jelly, and I'm not sure I ever want to see a movie like that again!

**2** Answer the questions.

1 How scary did Irene think the movie would be?
2 What did she say about her aunt's experience at the movie?
3 How did Irene describe her feeling of fear?
4 What did Irene say to herself when she felt frightened?
5 How did she describe the way her heart felt?
6 Why didn't she tell Elena how scared she was?
7 What did Elena say when the ghost appeared?
8 What did Irene's legs feel like after the movie?

**3** Look at the third paragraph of Irene's post. Which tenses does she use? Now choose the correct tenses to complete the paragraph below.

Yesterday evening I ¹*had watched / watched* a really interesting show on the Arctic. The show's producers ²*had worked / were working* for over a year with a group of scientists who ³*will research / were researching* wildlife there. They ⁴*had managed / had been managing* to film a family of polar bears, and it was wonderful to watch them. However, one of the scientists ⁵*was working / had been working* in the Arctic for over 30 years, and he ⁶*explained / had explained* how difficult it can be these days for polar bears to find enough food.

**4** Write a blog post about a movie, play, or TV show that turned out to be different from what you had expected.

- Include different narrative tenses and time linkers.
- Use comparisons, predictions, and direct speech to make your story more interesting.

# WRITING PRACTICE

## WRITING: Writing a persuasive article

**1** Read the text. <u>Underline</u> the two sentences in which the author gives her general opinion about the value of neatness very clearly.

### Love the mess you live with!

Marie Kondo has written several books about being organized. In her opinion, you shouldn't have anything in your house that doesn't "spark joy" (in other words, cause great happiness), and she has very strict instructions about things like folding clothes in a way that "respects" them. Well, in *my* opinion, this obsession with being neat is a complete waste of time.

At first glance, her ideas look simple and easy to carry out. However, my friend Jayne tried them, and it took her days and days. Personally, I'd much rather read a book or go out with friends than fold shirts or waste time thinking about whether or not a particular lamp gives me happy feelings.

And as for objects "sparking joy" – initially, that might seem like a great idea, but, actually, there are several problems with it. First, the cost. People can't afford to replace everything they're not totally happy with. Second, the environment. No, I don't feel joy when I look at my toaster, but, hey, it makes great toast, and it would be wasteful to throw it away.

Third – and most important – I don't really approve of spending so much energy on objects. You might think it would be nice to buy that beautiful set of mugs, but, in fact, it's the *people* who will be drinking coffee with you that really matter. A warm and friendly atmosphere is much more important than having a perfect home.

I'm well aware that Marie Kondo's books have been very popular. I guess everyone's different, but in my view, life's too short to spend so much time worrying about how neat and clean your house is.

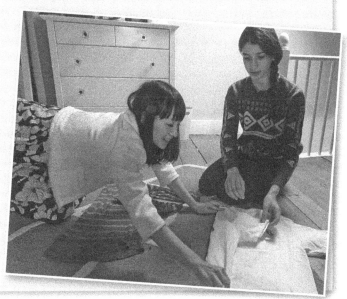

**2** The writer does not agree with the idea that every object in a home should "spark joy." Check (✓) the reasons she gives.

1 It's too expensive. _____
2 It's silly. _____
3 It's not possible for everything to spark joy. _____
4 It's not environmentally-friendly. _____
5 It's not good to think about objects so much. _____
6 She doesn't want her home to be perfect. _____

**3** How important do you think it is to have a neat home? State your opinion clearly and give three reasons.

1 (opinion) _____
_____

2 (reason 1) _____
_____

3 (reason 2) _____
_____

4 (reason 3) _____
_____

**4** Find these phrases for expectations in the text and <u>underline</u> the words that show the reality of the situation.

1 At first glance, …
2 initially, that might seem …
3 You might think …

**5** Write a text about the importance of being neat.

- State your point of view clearly.
- Give reasons, and support them with facts and examples.
- Use persuasive language.
- Include at least two expressions for contrasting expectations with reality.

# WRITING PRACTICE

## WRITING: Writing an opinion essay

**1** Read the essay and add the topic sentences to the correct paragraphs.

a One reason is that, in those days, people didn't use to have as much pressure in their lives.

b **In sum**, despite progress in modern times, life is worse now than it was fifty years ago.

c There is no doubt that life is totally different today from how it was for our grandparents when they were in their twenties.

d In addition, we are less active and, in many ways, less healthy than we were 50 years ago, and that is definitely not a good thing.

---

### Is life better today than it was 50 years ago?

1 ¹_____ Of course, there has been enormous progress in certain areas of our lives, for example, in medical care and communications technology. For example, since 1980, we have been able to prevent measles, a dangerous disease which used to kill around 2.6 million people a year. Inventions such as Skype mean that it is easier than ever to stay in touch with friends and family. **Nevertheless**, I believe that life was better 50 years ago.

2 ²_____ Many families could afford for the woman to stay at home and take care of the house, **as opposed to** now, when women often have to go to work and then do most of the housework as well. **Similarly**, before social media, people didn't have to worry about posting the perfect picture on Instagram or seeing how many "likes" they could get for their latest selfies.

3 ³_____ Everyone is busier, and fast food is available everywhere. **Consequently**, the number of adults in the U.S. who are overweight has continued to rise, and 7% more adults are obese than a decade ago. So, while we may live longer, our health is likely to suffer.

4 ⁴_____ We are more stressed and, in some ways, less healthy, and no recent invention – not even the Internet – is worth more than our physical and mental health.

---

**2** Identify the paragraph or paragraphs in the essay that include the following:

1 dates and figures to support an argument  _____
2 arguments to support the thesis  _____
3 a thesis statement  _____
4 a conclusion  _____

**3** Look at the linkers in **bold** in the text. Now use them to complete the sentences.

1 We have plenty to eat, _____ our grandparents who were often hungry when they were children.

2 Today we all have washing machines and dishwashers, and, _____, life is easier.

3 These days, it is much easier to travel. _____, it is easier to keep in touch with friends and family all over the world, for example, by Skype.

4 It is true that social media can cause problems. _____, I believe it also has many advantages.

5 _____, I believe that life today is definitely better than it was in the past.

**4** Write an opinion essay giving the opposite view to the one in the text.

- Provide a clear thesis statement.
- Start each paragraph with a topic statement.
- Give arguments to support your thesis statement, with examples, facts, figures, etc.
- Summarize the key points in the concluding paragraph.
- Use at least three formal linkers to connect your ideas.

# NOTES

# NOTES

# Richmond

58 St Aldates
Oxford
OX1 1ST
United Kingdom

**ISBN:** 978-84-668-2652-5
© Richmond / Santillana Global S.L. 2019

All rights reserved. No part of this book may be reproduced, stored in a retrieval system or transmitted in any form by any means, electronic, mechanical, photocopying, recording or otherwise, without the prior permission in writing of the Publisher.

**Publishing Director:** Deborah Tricker
**Publisher:** Simone Foster
**Media Publisher:** Sue Ashcroft
**Workbook Publisher:** Luke Baxter
**Content Developer:** Deborah Goldblatt
**Editors:** Peter Anderson, Jamie Bowman, Lauren Cubbage, Debra Emmett, Sarah Foster, Shannon O'Neill, Emma Wilkinson
**Americanization:** Shira Evans, Debbie Goldblatt
**Design Manager:** Lorna Heaslip
**Cover Design:** This Ain't Rock'n'Roll, London
**Design & Layout:** Lorna Heaslip, emc Design Ltd
**Photo Researcher:** Magdalena Mayo
*Talking Zone* **video:** Bagley Wood Productions
**Audio Production:** Tom, Dick and Debbie Productions
**App Development:** The Distance

We would also like to thank the following people for their valuable contribution to writing and developing the material:
James Styring, Jake Hughes, Brigit Viney, Diarmuid Carter (video script writer), Belen Fernandez (App Project Manager), Rob Sved (App Content Creator)

We would like to thank all those who have given their kind permission to reproduce material for this book:

**Illustrators:** Beach-o-matic Ltd; Victor Beuran c/o Astound Inc.; Roger Harris c/o NB Illustration; Guillaume Gennet c/o Lemonade; Julia Scheele

**Photos:**
D. Lezama; V. Atmán; 123RF; AGILEBITS INC.; ALAMY/Moviestore collection Ltd, Photofusion Picture Library, seewhatmitchsee, Everette Collection Inc, RosalreneBetancourt 6, ZUMA Press, Inc., Steve Moss, RosalreneBetancourt 9, Martin Parker, Moviestore Collection Ltd, Jeff Greenberg, Mr Pics, Hemis, RosalreneBetancourt 7, Collection Christophel, Magdalena Mayo, Radharc Images, Game Shots, urbanbuzz, NetPhotos, Image Source, CandyAppleRed Images, Art Directors & TRIP, RosalreneBetancourt 3, Chris Willson, Education & Exploration 2; COLIN BEAVAN; EVERNOTE; FERDI RIZKIYANTO; GETTY IMAGES SALES SPAIN/Flashpop, WALTER ZERLA, BSIP/UIG, hoozone, ImagesBazaar, Dmitry Ageev, Tolimir, By LTCE, Newton Daly, sturti, alxpin, AndreyPopov, Tainar, pinkomelet, jaochainoi, CasarsaGuru, izusek, Paul Morigi, Astarot, chepkoelena, DenBoma, Svtist, YangYin, MachineHeadz, ilbusca, bymuratdeniz, FS-Stock, CarmenMurillo, JGalione, Rouzes, Thinkstock, Tom Merton, RUSS ROHDE, Peter Cade, CoisaX, Maskot, AnaBGD, Adam Berry, thall, mrgao, istock/Thinkstock, Roberto Westbrook, omgimages, kali9, jacoblund, isitsharp, pixdeluxe, roundhill, tommaso79, Jose Luis Pelaez Inc, Chema Alba, Detailfoto, M.M. Sweet, acilo, Placebo365, flashfilm, SensorSpot, Richard l'Anson, Nikada, gradyreese, gregobagel, Westend61, MileA, Stockbyte, AngiePhotos, Jon Hicks, Felix Wirth, Hero Images, Matt Dutile, dszc, JangoBeat, PetrePlesea, Sam Edwards, franckreporter, hanapon1002, mediaphotos, Dan MacMedan, Walter Bibikow, Goodshoot, Jaunty Junto, Kieran Stone, CHBD, PeopleImages, Prasit photo, Ben Gabbe, A330Pilot, ferrantraite, Bernhard Lang, FOX, Caspar Benson, Daniel Ingold, Dougal Waters, ronnybas, Barcroft Media, Anadolu Agency, richiesd, SIphotography, Peathegee Inc, quavondo, Patrick Orton, Michael Blann, funstock, Florin Prunoiu, Jemal Countess, PhonlamaiPhoto, Sigrid Gombert, Thomas Barwick, Thomas Bullock, Mark Mainz/BC, James Devaney, jackscoldsweat, Comstock Images, Emir Memedovski, Gabriela Tulian, LWA/Dann Tardif, Photos.com Plus, cirano83, BahadirTanriover, Deborah Harrison, Dennis Macdonald, TravisPhotoWorks, blackestockphoto, David Paul Morris, Fancy/Veer/Corbis, GraphicaArtis, Fredrik Skold, Fred Stein Archive, Hannelore Foerster, MacFormat Magazine, Oleksiy Maksymenko, BG008/Bauer-Griffin, Fitria Ramli / EyeEm, RichLegg, Kantapat Phutthamkul, Gareth Cattermole/TAS, Maximilian Stock Ltd., Michael Ochs Archives, Photos.com/Thinkstock, Science Photo Library, Patchareeporn Sakoolchai; GREENPEACE; I. PREYSLER; ISTOCKPHOTO/Getty Images Sales Spain, monkeybusinessimages, Joel Carillet, cindygoff; PIRIFORM; SHUTTERSTOCK/Linda Bestwick, Mike Kuhlman, Giovanni G, Dima Moroz, kibri_ho; SOUTHWEST NEWSSWNS; WWF INTERNATIONAL; Chris Griffiths; Iwan Baan; ARCHIVO SANTILLANA; 123RF; ALAMY/Arco Images GmbH, Oliver Knight, Elizabeth Whiting & Associates, Moviestore collection Ltd; GETTY IMAGES SALES SPAIN/Sturti, Bloomberg, Serts, Alex Wong, Filadendron, Yuri_Arcurs, DGLimages, LEON NEAL, PhotoAlto, Erierika, Thinkstock, Ronniechua, Diane39, Piotr Marcinski/ EyeEm, Hero Images, Sam Edwards, Scott Olson, Emir Memedovski, Boston Globe, Ethan Miller, Image Source, bymuratdeniz, Inti St Clair, Martinedoucet, Antnio Guillem, PhotoQuest, ClarkandCompany, Rindoff/Dufour, Photos.com Plus, Dreet Production, TheCrimsonMonkey, valentinrussanov, Caiaimage/Sam Edwards, Sdominick, Tetra Images-Rob Lewine, Highwaystarz-Photography, Future Publishing/Olly Curtis, Alvarez; ISTOCKPHOTO/Getty Images Sales Spain; SPACEX

**Cover Photo:** GETTY IMAGES SALES SPAIN/Martin Dimitrov

**Texts:**
p15 Text adapted from article 'Dear Juliet: the fans who write to Shakespeare's heroine' by John Hooper, 19 May 2010, *The Guardian*, Copyright Guardian News & Media 2017, reprinted by permission.

We would like to thank the following reviewers for their valuable feedback which has made Personal Best possible. We extend our thanks to the many teachers and students not mentioned here.
Brad Bawtinheimer, Manuel Hidalgo, Paulo Dantas, Diana Bermúdez, Laura Gutiérrez, Hardy Griffin, Angi Conti, Christopher Morabito, Hande Kokce, Jorge Lobato, Leonardo Mercato, Mercilinda Ortiz, Wendy López

The Publisher has made every effort to trace the owner of copyright material; however, the Publisher will correct any involuntary omission at the earliest opportunity.

Printed in Brazil by Forma Certa Gráfica Digital
Lote: 796888
Código: 290526525